THE GULF AND INTERNATIONAL SECURITY

Also by M. E. Ahrari

THE DYNAMICS OF OIL DIPLOMACY: Conflict and Consensus
ETHNIC GROUPS AND US FOREIGN POLICY
OPEC: The Failing Giant

The Gulf and International Security

The 1980s and Beyond

Edited by

M. E. Ahrari
Associate Professor
Department of Political Science
Mississippi State University

Foreword by Janos Radvanyi
Professor of History, Director of CISS

St. Martin's Press   New York

First published in the United States of America in 1989

Printed in Hong Kong

ISBN 0–312–02819–9

Library of Congress Cataloging-in-Publication Data
The Gulf and international security: the 1980s and beyond/edited by
M. E. Ahrari.
p.   cm.
Includes index.
ISBN 0–312–02819–9 ✓
1. Gulf Region—Strategic aspects.   2. Gulf
States—National security.   3. United States—Military relations—
Gulf States.   4. Soviet Union—Military relations—
Gulf States.   5. Gulf States—Military relations—United
States.   6. Gulf States—Military relations—Soviet Union.
I. Ahrari, Mohammed E.
UA832.G85   1989
355′.0330536—dc19   88–37947
                                                                          CIP

To my lark who wishes to be my quest

Contents

Foreword

The crucial stories of our time can be written in many ways, and each region of the world offers its own set of challenges. That is especially true for the Near East where the speed of events often supercedes the most cautious predictions. *The Gulf and International Security – the 1980s and Beyond*, edited and co-authored by Professor M. E. Ahrari, however, is a rare and brilliant collection of essays which not only gives a thorough historical background of the Persian Gulf region, but also provides an excellent analysis of the present. It advances a basic understanding of the region under observation, striving for a dramatic dynamic, rather than a static, delineation of events.

The co-authors of this study have given particular attention to the origins and traditions of the conflicts, tracing the sources of instability in the Gulf region. Understandably, the work focuses on security issues, not only from the Iranian and Iraqi perspective, but also from the vantage point of Saudi Arabia and other Gulf states. To make the picture complete, special emphasis is given to an analysis of the rather complex American and Soviet interests in the Gulf. The contents of the different essays sometimes manifest diverse views and opinions. Yet, the authors have sought to achieve the highest standards of scholarly objectivity. Last but not least, the work helps alike both laymen and students of the Near East to understand how finally, after eight years of fighting and one million victims, the hope of peace is on its way to the Gulf.

Professor M. E. Ahrari and his multi-disciplinary team of social scientists – Professors Mark N. Katz, Shirin Hunter, James Noyes, J. E. Peterson and Gregory F. Rose – worked diligently together. They produced a work which will contribute not only to a better understanding of the problems involved in the making of foreign policy in the Near East, but also to the prevention of future conflicts in the region.

The Center for International Security and Strategic Studies at Mississippi State University is honoured to be the sponsor of this study. As director of the Center, my special thanks go to Professor M. E. Ahrari, a Senior Fellow of our organisation. I am grateful for the cooperation and efforts of the members of this distinguished study group. I owe a debt of gratitude to the President of our university, Dr Donald Zacharias for his continuing support. The

National Strategy Information Center, Inc., the Earhart Foundation and the American-Arab Affairs Council awarded generous research grants which made possible the completion of this study. To all these institutions and persons I wish to express my most sincere appreciation.

JANOS RADVANYI
Professor of History
Director of CISS

Acknowledgements

A project of this nature is more a product of joint endeavours than meets the eye. My most heartfelt acknowledgement goes to my family members. The physical distance between us never lessened their constant encouragement and support while I was coming to grips with a string of personal problems and professional adjustments during the course of working on this book. The end result of their unflinching faith in my capabilities is in your hands.

A special mention should be made of Donna Janette Kittrell who helped in more ways than she would ever realise. I also wish to thank Cathy Vellake, Administrative Assistant at the Center for International Security and Strategic Studies (CISS), for providing me with editorial assistance on short notice, and Mary Catherine Carmichael for being a reliable secretary.

Last but not least, I wish to acknowledge my three colleagues Edward Clynch, Head, Department of Political Science, for his cooperation in the past two years of my stay at Mississippi State University; Ralph Powe, Vice-President for Research, and Janos Radvanyi, Director, CISS, for jointly providing a grant for my research in West Asia during the Summer of 1987.

Starkville, MS   M. E. AHRARI

List of Abbreviations

AWACS   Airborne Warning and Control System
CIA   The Central Intelligence Agency
CENTO   The Central Treaty Organisation
CPSU   The Communist Party of the Soviet Union
GCC   The Gulf Cooperation Council
NATO   The North Atlantic Treaty Organisation
NSC   The National Security Council
OAPEC   The Organisation of Arab Petroleum Exporting Countries
OPEC   The Organisation of Petroleum Exporting Countries
PDYR   People's Democratic Republic of Yemen
RDJTF   Rapid Deployment Joint Task Force
UAE   United Arab Emirates
USCENTCOM   United States Central Command
YAR   Yemen Arab Republic

Notes on the Contributors

M. E. Ahrari is an Associate Professor in the Department of political Science and a Senior Research Fellow in the Center for International Security and Strategic Studies at Mississippi State University. As a specialist in the American policy process, superpower relations and the Middle East, he has written three books: *Ethnic Groups and US Foreign Policy* (1987), *OPEC – the Failing Giant* (1986) and *The Dynamics of Oil Diplomacy: Conflict and Consensus* (1980). His numerous articles and book reviews have appeared in the *American Political Science Review*, *Political Science Quarterly*, *British Journal of Political Science*, *SAIS Review*, *Washington Quarterly*, *International Affairs* (London), *Presidential Studies Quarterly*, the *Middle East Review*, and the *Journal of Energy and Development*.

Shirin Hunter is the Deputy Director of the Middle East Project at the Center for Strategic and International Studies. From 1966 to 1978 she served as a member of Iranian foreign service in Tehran, London and Geneva. She is the author of *OPEC and Third World: Politics of Aid* (1984), and editor and contributor to *Politics of Islamic Revivalism: Diversity and Unity* (1988). Her forthcoming book is *Foreign Policy and the Islamic Republic of Iran: Continuity and Change* 1989.

Mark N. Katz is an Assistant Professor of government and politics at George Mason University. Until recently, he served as a Research Associate at the Kennan Institute for Advanced Russian Studies at the Woodrow Wilson Center for Scholars. His extensive research record includes *Russia and Arabia: Soviet Foreign Policy Toward the Arabian Peninsula* (1986). He has also contributed a number of articles in such journals as *Orbis*, *Problems of Communism*, and *Current History*.

James Noyes is a Research Fellow at Hoover Institution of War, Revolution, and Peace, and also serves as Middle East editor of *The Yearbook of International Communist Affairs*. His recent publication is the revised edition of *The Clouded Lens: Persian Gulf and US Policy* (1982). Noyes also served as Deputy Assistant Secretary of Defense for Near Eastern, African, and South Asian Affairs under Nixon and Ford Administrations.

J. E. Peterson is a Washington-based writer, a consultant on Middle East Affairs, and an adjunct Fellow at the Center for Strategic and International Studies. He is a specialist on the Gulf affairs. His most recent books include: *Security in the Arabian Peninsula and Gulf States: 1973–1984* (1985), *Defending Arabia* (1986), *The Arab Gulf States: Steps Toward Political Participation* (1988), and *Crosscurrents in the Gulf: Arab, Regional and Global Interests* (co-editor) (1988). He is now writing a book on comparative political change in the Arabian Peninsula.

Gregory F. Rose is an Assistant Professor of Political Science at the University of North Texas. His publications include, 'Factional Alignments in the Central Council of the Islamic Republic Party: A Preliminary Taxonomy', in *The Iranian Revolution and the Islamic Republic* (1982) and 'Revolution, Culture, and Collective Action', *Journal of Political Science*, Spring 1986. He is also a co-author of *The Balance of Power: Stability and Instability in the International System* (forthcoming).

Prolegomenon
M. E. Ahrari

THE PARAMETERS OF GULF SECURITY ISSUES

This book is aimed at examining the dynamics of security issues in the Persian/Arabian Gulf in the 1980s and beyond as they affect the political fortunes of the regional actors and the strategic interests of the United States and the USSR. Since the ouster of Shah Mohammad Reza Pahlavi from Iran in 1979, the Gulf has become an extremely volatile area, with the Shah's regime being replaced by the stridently anti-American Islamic regime of Ayatollah Rouhollah Khomeini. Iran has not only become an Islamic Republic but has also threatened to export its Islamic revolution to the pro-American Gulf states. The resulting turmoil and conflict in the Gulf region, coupled with its vital geopolitical and strategic importance, makes the outcome of these events of critical importance to the global security of the Western alliance.

As a direct response to the Khomeini revolution, the Gulf states have established a security-oriented Gulf Cooperation Council (GCC). The Carter Administration, although crippled by its inability to resolve the hostage crisis with Iran, viewed the threats posed by the Islamic Republic of Iran to the neighbouring Gulf as being serious enough to warrant a warning to the Khomeini regime and the Soviet Union that the United States will use force in order to prevent these countries from destabilising the Gulf states. This policy, referred to as the Carter Doctrine, stands today as an expression of American resolve to sustain political stability in the Gulf. The United States has backed this pledge by establishing the Rapid Deployment Force, which was later expanded into the United States Central Command (USCENTCOM). President Ronald Reagan has continued to reiterate American determination to protect the Gulf from external and internal threats.

In December of 1979, the Soviet Union invaded Afghanistan and its troops have remained an occupying force in that country ever since. The Soviet invasion of Afghanistan was viewed by the United States as an ominous act for three reasons. First, the Soviet occupation of Afghanistan refreshed memories of a similar Soviet action in northern Iran in 1941. The American decision-makers felt that a weak Iran under Khomeini would be easy prey should the Soviet Union decide to extend its grip from Afghanistan to Iran. Second, the massive influx of the Afghan refugees into Pakistan and the Pakistani willingness to serve as a conduit for guerrilla activities into Afghanistan made Pakistan open to Soviet retaliatory actions. Naturally, the United States cannot afford to stand by and watch Pakistan absorb the brunt of Soviet military might. As a precautionary measure, the United States initiated a massive military and economic assistance programme for Pakistan.

The third reason for American concern about the Soviet occupation of Afghanistan is that as a result of this move, the Soviet Union appeared to be consolidating its military presence around the Gulf. The Soviet strategic advantages in Afghanistan appear even more threatening when one considers the fact that this superpower also maintains a naval presence around Ethiopia and South Yemen. By utilising its naval facilities in those countries, the Soviet Union has an unprecedented potential for closing the Gulf of Hormuz and even the Bab Al-Mandab choke point.

These are the dynamics of superpower interests in the Gulf. In addition, however, the intricacies of conflicts that are indigenous to that area must also be examined. These conflicts have the potential for further complicating the strategic involvement of the United States and the Soviet Union by altering the local strategic balance through events over which the superpowers have little if any direct control.

First and foremost is the Iran–Iraq war which is in its eighth year. From 1980 until November of 1986, the United States maintained a public posture of neutrality. We learned later on that at least since 1985, the United States was selling arms to Iran while supplying intelligence data on the Iranian troop movement to Iraq. The Soviet Union maintained a slight tilt toward Iran during the initial phase of the Iran–Iraq war. By doing so, that country wanted to win the friendship of the Khomeini regime. When this policy did not bear results to the Soviets' liking, they reverted back to supplying arms to Iraq. Iran has also been receiving Soviet arms through indirect channels, such as Libya, North Korea, and Czechoslovakia, all of whom are Soviet allies. The Iran–Iraq war has proven that neither of the antagonists is dependent on either superpower to maintain its military strength. This reality has serious implications in the sense that neither superpower has the ability to de-escalate the level of violence. This inability to control events promises to make future military conflicts between minor states in the region even more intractable and complex.

The second intra-Gulf security issue is the conflict between the Khomeini regime and the Gulf states. There is a traditional rivalry between Iran, Saudi Arabia, and Iraq to dominate the politics of the Gulf. The rivalry between the two Arab states has been set aside temporarily because of the Iran–Iraq war, in which Saudi Arabia has been supporting the latter country. The Saudi-Iranian rivalry has been intensified. Under the Shah, as well as under Khomeini, Iran aspired to dominate the Gulf. As an imperial power, it championed, *inter alia*, Western interests. As a republic, however, Iran aspired to establish in the area an Islamic order in its own image. This aspiration comes into direct conflict with Saudi ambitions to dominate the region, and it also threatens the American-oriented status quo in the Gulf. Despite their differences, both Iran and Saudi Arabia practised Machiavellian politics on oil-related matters. Since the summer of 1987, however, because of the escalation of the Iran–Iraq war and due to the sustenance of a worldwide soft oil market, the relationship between Iran and Saudi Arabia has been coming under growing tensions.

The third intra-Gulf security issue is frictions between the Arab states of the Gulf. Kuwait, the United Arab Emirates (UAE), Oman, and North Yemen have been fearful of what they perceive to be Saudi hegemonic ambitions. Such a fear is reportedly responsible for the traditional Kuwaiti balancing act between the Soviet Union and the United States. The Omani decision to establish military ties with the United States is reported to be an outcome of similar feelings toward the Saudis. Kuwait has also been fearful of the irredentist ambitions of Iraq. These frictions seemed to have temporarily subsided because of the more serious threat that Khomeini's Iran poses to the security of the Gulf states. As the war-related violence threatened the security of the states of the Arabian Peninsula, Kuwait widened the scope of its balancing act by asking both superpowers to protect its ships. Given that the conservative GCC states operate based on a consensus forged behind closed doors, it is prudent to state that the Kuwaiti action has been approved by all the GCC states.

With the dissipation of the Iranian threat, the intra-Arab insecurities are likely not only to resurge, but also to affect the dynamics of superpower involvement in the Gulf. Even in the sustenance of the threats posed by Iran, conflicts between the states of the Arabian Peninsula are likely to result in varying policies toward Iran, especially if that country were to emerge victorious from the Iran–Iraq war. Such policy divergence, in all likelihood, is potentially detrimental to the sustenance of the GCC as a viable alliance.

This study goes beyond an examination of the immediate crisis in the Gulf to an evaluation of the broader underlying geopolitical and strategic issues that simmer just below the surface of the current conflict. Inevitably, these issues will rise to the surface and determine the conflict polarities that will emerge in the next decade. Thus, by examining the cumulative effects of all these variables on the security of the Gulf, this book looks to the future by examining such questions as:

1. What is the nature of the power game in the Gulf from the perspectives of the Gulf states, and how is the power game likely to change in the near future?
2. What is at stake for the superpowers (i.e., what is the nature of their strategic, political, and economic advantages and disadvantages) in the Gulf?
3. What are the underlying patterns of conflict and cooperation among the Gulf states that, in the absence of the Iran–Iraq war, are likely to emerge to unite them?
4. What policy options are likely to be adopted by both superpowers to sustain their strategic dominance in the Gulf, and how would these policies affect the nature of security issues and stability in the Gulf?

FRAMEWORK OF THE STUDY

This book is comprised of eight chapters. Given that Iran is perceived as a chief threat to the security of the Gulf in the 1980s and beyond, the first four chapters of this book are devoted to the Iranian role.

Ahrari's first chapter, 'Khomeini's Iran and Threats to the Gulf Security', sets the tone for the rest of this book. He argues that the manifest intent of Iran-related (or Iran-sponsored) turbulence in the 1980s is to create in various countries of the Gulf a political order that either resembles the Islamic Republic of Iran or is acceptable to the Khomeini regime. The Iran-centered political order that the Islamic Republic has been trying to establish is so radical from the perspectives of both the Arab states of the Gulf and the superpowers that any semblance of stability and lowering of the level of turbulence may only be the result of a *rapprochement* between these actors. Ahrari's essay describes the nature of the political intransigence of the Khomeini regime that is causing fear and consternation among the Arab states of the Gulf; Iranian attempts to neutralise the strategic interests of both superpowers as a precursor of establishing an Iran-centered order in the Gulf; and the reasons underlying the unacceptability of the Khomeini regime's version of power relations by both superpowers.

Shirin Hunter's chapter, 'Gulf Security: An Iranian Perspective', presents an Iranian view of Gulf security. After refuting the threat perception of the Gulf states *vis-à-vis* Iran, she states that with the Iraqi invasion of Iran on 22 September 1980, it is Iran that has become the subject of a full-scale Arab military attack. The author states that Iran's relations with the Gulf Arab states should be analysed and understood within 'the context of its relations with the broader Arab world, and the impact of the intra-Arab politics of Iran–Gulf Arab relations'.

Iranian behaviour, according to Hunter, should be understood by focusing on the historical importance that country attaches to the Gulf. During periods of instability and weakness, Iran was forced to retreat; however, when it became strong and stable, it has made its presence felt in the Gulf. Iran has always maintained that the security of the Gulf should be the responsibility of the riparian states and has opposed the presence of foreign forces. There has been a feeling among its leaders, both imperial and revolutionary, that because of its size Iran should have a dominant influence and a strong naval force in the Gulf. This strategic objective, notes Hunter, has become one of the chief reasons for consternation among the Arab states of the region, especially Saudi Arabia and Iraq. This objective has also forced the United States to enhance its naval presence as long as the congruities between the Iranian and American strategic objectives remain a world apart. She also points out other variables, such as Arab claims on Khuzistan, clashing and conflicting nationalistic feelings among Arab states, and the shifting ideological factor, which also affect security relations between Iran and the Arab states of the Gulf.

The third chapter of this volume, 'Saudi Arabia, Iran, and OPEC: The Dynamics of a Balancing Act', is an overview of the shifting relationships between the two chief rivals for the leadership of the Gulf. For Saudi Arabia, writes Ahrari, oil became one of the chief bases for its claim of leadership over the Organisation of Petroleum Exporting Countries (OPEC) and, by extension, over the Gulf. As the world's largest owner of proven oil reserves, Saudi Arabia remained adamantly opposed to unrealistic increases in the prices of oil in the 1970s. Yet as one of the leading members of the Organisation of Arab Petroleum Exporting Countries (OAPEC), Saudi Arabia opted for the oil embargo in 1973–4. The combination of oil wealth that the Saudis accumulated in the sellers' market of the 1970s and their sophistication of applying the oil weapon for political purposes (yet remaining cognizant of the limitations of oil power) enabled Saudi Arabia to emerge as one of the leading states of the Middle East. In the 1980s, the Saudi leadership remained preoccupied in its quest for strategies that would firm up the prices of oil and enable OPEC to regain its influential status of the 1970s.

The Iranian revolution of 1979, which brought to power a stridently anti-American leadership, notes Ahrari, provided an opportunity for Saudi Arabia to emerge as a dominant actor, with tacit American support for their role. Obviously, Saudi ambitions are in conflict with Iranian ambitions to dominate the region. Until 1987, the tensions emanating from the conflicting Saudi and Iranian security interests remained manageable. Since the summer of 1987, however, with the escalation of the Iran–Iraq war, Saudi Arabia and Iran are likely to find less grounds for cooperation, with oil being the only reason (though not a very promising one because of the continued oil glut in the world market).

Chapter 4 is Rose's 'Fools Rush in American Policy and the Iraq–Iran War: 1980–1988'. The tone of analysis in this essay is quite sympathetic to Iran, a portrayal that is very uncommon, if not unique, to most Western scholarly or journalistic literature. Despite its tone, the analysis itself is based on political realism. The author deals with five phases of the US treatment of this war. In 1980–1981, according to him, the Carter Administration was delighted by the Iraqi invasion of Iran, hoping that it would 'hasten the willingness of Iran to negotiate a settlement to the hostage crisis'. The newly-elected Reagan Administration manifested little interest in the war between 1981–3, according to Rose. When the Iranian offensive in 1983–5 drove Iraq out of the territory it occupied in the early stage of this war, a number of officials in Washington argued for 'a strong US tilt toward Iraq'. The United States took a number of measures, writes Rose, which were aimed at helping Iraq win the war. These included: resumption of diplomatic ties with Iraq, which were severed in the aftermath of the 1967 Arab-Israeli war; US involvement in arranging large loans for Iraq; American encouragement of France and other countries to arm Iraqis and dissuasion of its allies from selling weapons to Iran. Toward the end of 1985, notes the author, the US abandoned the pro-Iraq tilt and initiated a reassessment of its relations with Iran. A negotiated release of American hostages held in Lebanon was on top of the list of reasons, though by no means the only reason, for such a reassessment. The 1987–8 phase, the most recent in US treatment of this war, culminated in the American decision to reflag Kuwaiti oil tankers.

Peterson's Chapter 5, 'Security Concerns in the Arabian Peninsula', deals with the dynamics of security-related frictions among the states of the Arabian Peninsula, and between these states and Iran. Internally, despite the occurrence of isolated terrorist acts and sabotage against vulnerable oil installations, according to Peterson, 'there is little evidence that the majority of the population is sufficiently alienated to actively subvert still-legitimate political systems'. In the 1980s, the states of the Arabian Peninsula have been excessively preoccupied with security concerns. The only potential security threat to the GCC from within the Peninsula comes from the two Yemens. But, by and large, according to him, political and economic differences far outweigh the need and desire for cooperation.

The Islamic Republic of Iran has been the most ominous threat to the security of these states in the 1980s. The states of the Arabian Peninsula have taken effective measures, writes Peterson, to acquire the ability to buy time until outside help arrives in case of external threats. They are fully capable of responding to potential threats from within. The security of the Gulf, in his view, essentially depends on a partnership between the GCC and the West, principally the United States. Under such an arrangement, 'the US or western role is one of backup, to be invited in when the GCC states cannot handle a threat on their own'. He regards the 'over-the-horizon' presence of the United States as 'less than ideal' but 'workable'.

In the next two chapters, 6 and 7, an examination is made of the strategic concerns of superpowers in the 1980s and beyond. In Chapter 6, 'American Perceptions of Iranian Threats to the Gulf Security', James Noyes examines American perceptions and misperceptions concerning Iran. The misperceptions, notes the author, may be the outcome of changes that are 'so profuse that analysts of the Gulf are like physicians asked to prescribe for patients they

hardly know'. Another reason for misperception is that 'the American view of Iran has lông contained elements of distortion and
exaggerated expectation wherein the slightest missteps would propel
Iran into the Soviet camp or, on the other hand, a friendly Iran could
solve all US problems'. These distortions, which continue to linger,
were quickly recognised and continue to be exploited by the
Khomeini regime. The United States appears to have an exaggerated
view of the Iranian revolutionary potential. There is little evidence,
in his view, that Iran as a revolutionary state holds wide appeal even
among the Shia. He does not believe that Khomeini has made
ideological headway in the Gulf region itself. 'Iran is too close and
the regime's problems too visible.'

Regarding the growing American concern over possible Soviet
domination of the Gulf, Noyes notes that the Soviet Union may be in
a position to have a dialogue with both Iran and Iraq, but that
superpower's 'already poor reputation for reliability as a partner',
and its continued delaying tactics regarding a UN-sanctioned arms
embargo against Iran have caused considerable bitterness among the
Arab states of the Gulf. He rejects the two extremist scenarios of
either wooing Tehran or militarily intervening against Iran in the war.
Instead, he argues for a middle course of burning 'as few bridges to
Iran as possible', promoting arms sales proposals for GCC states, and
articulating consistent support for GCC security without locking into
a confrontational approach toward Iran.

The dynamics of Soviet involvement in the Gulf, Iranian threats to
these interests, and the Soviet responses to the Iranian manoeuvres
are discussed by Katz in the seventh chapter, 'Soviet Interests in the
Gulf'. Katz notes that Soviet interests in that region are both
offensive and defensive in nature. 'The reduction of American
influence is an offensive goal while preventing its growth is a
defensive one.' The Soviet Union, according to Katz, is interested in
both preventing the growth and reducing where possible the American interests in the region. The USSR would like to gain access to
the warm water ports of the Gulf. It even would like to obtain the
Gulf oil, but is not willing to the extent of going to war in pursuance
of any of these interests.

The Soviet Union has focused its attention on the anti-American
posture of the Khomeini regime despite the fact that the Islamic
Republic has also consistently maintained an anti-Soviet attitude.
The Soviets, notes Katz, hope that 'their friendly policy toward
Tehran combined with the continuation of Iranian-American hostility

will improve their ability as well as further reduce American opportunities to gain influence there in the future'. The USSR prefers to have the Arab-Israeli conflict as the focus of attention of the Arab states and not Iran. When the former is the focus of Arab attention, writes Katz, the Soviet Union hopes to rally the entire Arab world in opposition to America and Israel. On the contrary, when Iran is the focus of Arab attention, the moderate Arab states tend to envision the United States as their potential protector. Surmising the shape of strategic affairs, Katz observes that Iranian threats to Soviet interests in the Gulf would be greater if Iran defeats Iraq.

In the concluding chapter, the focus analysis will revolve around the future-oriented questions raised in this chapter.

1 Khomeini's Iran and Threats to Gulf Security

M. E. Ahrari

Since the accession of Ayatollah Rouhollah Khomeini to power in Iran the politics of the Gulf region has been quite turbulent. Examples of political violence since 1979 include an attempted coup in Bahrain, the takeover of the Grand Mosque in Saudi Arabia, a series of attacks on US diplomatic facilities and personnel in the Gulf area, and the assassination attempt on the Emir of Kuwait. The manifest intent underlying these events is to create a political order in various countries in the area that either resembles the Islamic Republic of Iran, or, at least, is acceptable to the Khomeini regime.

The Iran-centered political order that the Islamic Republic has been trying to establish is so radical from the perspectives of the Arab states of the Gulf and both superpowers that any semblance of stability and the lowering of the level of turbulence may only be followed by a *rapprochement* between Iran, Arab states of the Gulf, and the superpowers. At the present time, the chances of *rapprochement* are minimal because of the continued insistence of Iran on altering the existing power relations in the Gulf, the growing fear of the Gulf states that they might become victims of revolutionary violence sponsored by the Khomeini regime, and the unacceptability of the Khomeini regime's version of power relations in the Gulf by both superpowers.

This chapter will describe the nature of political intransigence of the Khomeini regime that is causing fear and consternation among Arab states of the Gulf; Iranian attempts to neutralise the strategic interests of both superpowers as a precursor of establishing an Iran-centered order in the Gulf; and reasons underlying the unacceptability to both superpowers of the Khomeini regime's version of power relations.

POLITICAL INTRANSIGENCE OF THE KHOMEINI REGIME

From the very beginning, the Khomeini regime has invested considerable energy in delineating the 'evil' nature of both superpowers, thereby declaring its unwillingness to cooperate with them on political issues.

The foreign policy of the Islamic Republic is based upon the Iranian experience, especially under the Shah. Iran encountered brief Soviet occupation, and most recently it has been ruled by 'America's Shah'.[1] Its experience with both superpowers has been bitter and has caused considerable resentment. Consequently, the Khomeini regime emphasised the belief that the true path to the success of the revolution and to the establishment of Islamic government is through non-alignment with either superpowers since alignment would be tantamount to 'subservience'. Expounding on this theme, Khomeini states that under his rule Iran will neither became an American base in the region, nor will it provide such facilities to the Soviet Union, since his regime regards the former to be a 'colonialist power' and considers the latter covets its territories.[2]

The chief contribution of the Islamic Republic to the well-known position of the non-aligned movement is the Islamisation of the slogan 'neither East nor West'. By Islamising this slogan, the Khomeini regime underscores various aspects of superpower involvement in the Middle East that are deleterious to the interests of Muslim countries. For instance, regarding the American association with Israel, the Islamic Republic points out that American arms are freely used by Israel to dictate its will on, and to carry out some of the most outrageous actions against the Arabs (Muslims). These include: the invasion, destruction, and carnage in Lebanon; the annexation of the Golan Heights; and the bombing of the PLO headquarters in Tunisia. Iran under Khomeini also points out that the continued US military support of Israel and its expansionist policies are only used to thrust political solutions on the Arabs that are aimed at guaranteeing the existence of Israel without necessarily making an attempt to resolve the Palestinian question. Naturally, argues the Khomeini regime, such solutions blatantly violate the aspirations of the Palestinians and the Arabs.

By the same token, Iran points out that the Russian role in the Middle East has not worked to the advantage of Muslims either. The Iraqi treaty of Friendship and Cooperation with the Soviet Union did not protect that country from the Israeli raid on its nuclear facility. In addition, the Israelis have declared a policy of disallowing the possession of nuclear technology to any Arab state which remains hostile to Israel while they themselves are quietly enhancing their own nuclear capability.[3] Similarly, the Syrian friendship treaty with the USSR did not enable it to win back the Golan Heights from Israel.

Iran is also wary of Soviet hegemonic ambitions in the Gulf area. The USSR has been in occupation of Afghanistan for seven years where it is busy 'Sovietising' that country (i.e., building the Afghani political and economic infrastructure along the Soviet line). South Yemen, the only Marxist state in the Middle East, has already become a Soviet dependency and, according to all indications, the Russian grip on that Arab state is likely to be even firmer in the future. Even if the Soviets were to withdraw from Afghanistan, as they recently stated, Iranian wariness concerning the Soviet hegemonic ambitions is likely to remain virtually intact.

A viable alternative to aligning oneself with either superpowers, according to the Khomeini regime, is the adoption of the Islamic version of 'neither East nor West'. Two important principles of this slogan are anti-imperialism and Islamic unity. Anti-imperialism is interpreted as freedom from dominance by either superpower. Khomeini states that Muslim countries must reject all military assistance from the alliances that are designed by foreign powers. Instead, they should pursue foreign policies that are supportive of liberation struggles such as the Palestinian liberation movement, and other 'just' causes all over the world.[4]

The tacit basis of Islamic unity, the second principle of 'neither East nor West', is the acceptance of the Khomeini interpretation of international relations. Even though acceptance of such by other states in the region promises to assign them a lesser status, the Khomeini regime argues that these countries should, however, have no fear of Iran which, as a sister Islamic state, poses no imperialistic threats to any country.

In addition to exhorting the Gulf states (and Muslim countries in general) against holding allegiance to any superpower, Iran has been insisting, with equal fervour, on both the universality of Islam for the Muslim world and on the necessity of the establishment of Islamic government. Khomeini states, 'We must exert serious efforts to form the Islamic government and we must begin our work with propaganda activity and must develop this activity.' On another occasion, Khomeini states that endless efforts may be made to 'enlighten' the people of the 'criminal plans' and 'deviations' of the existing temporal authorities. Through this enlightenment, continues Khomeini, the masses should be gradually polarised toward the establishment of

Islamic government.[5] An assumption here is that the creation of Islamic government will be carried out by overthrowing the 'criminal' and deviant regimes. For the heads of Muslim states, Khomeini also offers an olive branch by inviting them to 'understand' and 'accept' the programme of Islamic government. If these heads accept the 'truth' as enunciated by Khomeini, then he and his followers promise to leave them in their places.[6]

In principle, the establishment of an Islamic government is not likely to receive strong opposition in the Muslim world. The modality of such a government, however, is a chief source of contention among Muslim scholars as well as among groups advocating its creation in various Muslim countries. Saudi Arabia claims to be an Islamic government; and Pakistan under General Zia ul-Haq laid a similar claim. What sets these governments apart from the Islamic Republic of Iran is the fact that both Saudi Arabia and Pakistan are part of the Sunni tradition. But, more important, neither Saudi Arabia nor Pakistan are tacitly or manifestly interested in exporting Sunni puritanism. Iran under Khomeini, on the contrary, claims to have established a pure version of Islamic government. Since a 'purer' version of Islam by definition is 'superior' to ones established in the Gulf countries, Iran insists that these countries emulate its example. This last characteristic makes the Islamic Republic a threat to the political status quo in the region.

The exportability principle not only exhorts Muslims to be proud of their faith but also to proclaim it loudly to the whole world. Khomeini's writings and speeches are full of statements that declare Islamic government to be inherently superior to all other forms of government, past or present. It is by ignoring their religious past and by emulating alien traditions and philosophies, states Khomeini, that the Muslims have allowed themselves to be enslaved and exploited by the West and the superpowers. It is through the practice of Islam and through the creation of Islamic governments in their respective countries that the Muslims will regain their honour.

For the exportability of Islam to other countries of the Gulf, Iran has adopted a rather sophisticated strategy of communicating with the masses of the Muslim (and especially of the Gulf) countries through a number of symbols. Edward Sapir writes, 'It is customary to say that society is peculiarly subject to the influence of symbols in such emotionally charged fields as religion and politics.'[7] It is through the use of what Murray Edelman calls 'condensation symbols' that Khomeini's exportability principle becomes most potent against the superpowers and against those Gulf regimes that maintain friendly relations with them. Condensation symbols, according to Edelman, 'condense into one symbolic event, sign, or act, patriotic pride, anxieties, remembrance of past glories or humiliations, promises of future greatness: some of these or all of them'.[8] Since the Soviet Union does not have strong ties with any Gulf country except South Yemen, the pro-American policies of the states of the region serve as the chief targets of Khomeini's condensation symbols.

Islamic Republic's most potent condensation symbol is the phrase 'enemies of Islam'. Even though these 'enemies' are identified primarily in the light of Iran's historical experience, the Islamic context of this phraseology is readily recognised throughout the Muslim world. All enemies are not lumped together. This author has developed a 'hierarchy' of 'enemies of Islam' from examination of a wide variety of sources.

The actors in the uppermost echelon of the hierarchy are the 'imperialists', notably the two superpowers. Since the United States has been identified as the 'Great Satan', its allies are, at least, tacit partners to the 'crimes' committed by that superpower in the Islamic countries. The Soviet Union is viewed with no less disdain. As far back as 1963 Khomeini declared, 'I make clear the fact that Americans are more evil than the English, the English are more evil than the Americans, and Russians are more evil than both of them. Each one of them is more evil and more wicked than the other.'[9]

The second echelon of the 'enemies of Islam' is occupied by the Jews, particularly the Zionists, personified by Israel. Here again, the Khomeini regime relies heavily on an 'anti-Islamic' portrayal of the Jews. In his *Islamic Government*, Khomeini states:

> We see today that the Jews . . . have meddled with the text of the Quran and have made certain changes in the Qurans they had printed in the occupied territories. It is our duty to prevent this treacherous interference with the text of the Quran. We must protect and make the people aware that the Jews and their foreign backers are opposed to the very foundation of Islam and wish to establish Jewish domination throughout the world.[10]

The third echelon of the 'enemies of Islam' is occupied by the pro-Western Arab regimes of the Middle East and especially of the Gulf. Regimes which have adopted a friendly posture toward the United States and which might also be persuaded by the United

States to accept a negotiated solution of the Arab-Israeli conflict are readily judged as anti-Islamic and became targets of the Khomeini propaganda. The lack of unity among Muslim governments and their pro-Western policies are not only branded as antithetic to Islam by Khomeini, but these characteristics are also related to the inability of these governments to have the Palestinian problems resolved.[11]

In summary, 'neither East nor West' should be viewed in tandem with the exportability principle. The first principle declares illegitimate the political orders affiliated with both superpowers since these orders, according to Iran, are essentially 'anti-Islamic' in nature. The second principle exhorts the Muslim, and especially the Gulf, countries to adopt an Islamic order that is either similar to the one established in Iran, or, at least, acceptable to the Islamic Republic. These two principles contribute to the intransigence of the Khomeini regime. The predominantly religious character of this intransigence does not leave any room for negotiations and political compromises which are integral aspects, and also cardinal principles, of relations among nations. From the perspective of the Khomeini regime, how can the Islamic Republic, the defender of Islamic order, compromise with forces of evil, the two superpowers? Similarly, the establishment of Islamic order, as envisioned by Khomeini, is an equally noble issue. In principle, compromise on this issue is unthinkable.

IRANIAN ATTEMPTS TO NEUTRALISE THE STRATEGIC INTERESTS OF THE UNITED STATES

An Iran-centered political order in the Gulf, as the Islamic Republic perceives it, may only be established by bringing about noticeable, if not radical, changes in the established political order. But these changes do not necessarily have to be brought about by overthrowing the existing regimes (even though such an option is not completely ruled out). As long as the existing regimes are willing to change their pro-American policies or at least neutralise their pro-American posture, the Khomeini regime would be willing to live with them.

The response of the Gulf states to the Khomeini regime will be divided into two phases: the appeasement phase, which lasted between 1981 and the summer of 1987, and confrontational phase, which began when Kuwait approached the superpowers during the summer of 1987 to enhance their naval presence in the Gulf. It should be emphasised that at no time during these phases the Gulf states adopted either purely appeasing or confrontational policies toward Iran.

The appeasment phase

Since the Soviet Union does not have a strong military or diplomatic presence in the Gulf, despite its decision to lease three tankers to Kuwait and its success in establishing diplomatic ties with Oman and the UAE, the main focus of Iranian manoeuvres in the Gulf is aimed at altering the pro-American policy posture of the Gulf states without necessarily providing diplomatic or military openings for the Soviet Union in that region.

As Iran perceives it, the Gulf states are likely to accept the Khomeini version of the Islamic order only when the Islamic Republic emerges as a regional power. In other words, unlike its role under the Shah – when Iran served as the gendarme of the Western and especially American interests in the region – Iran under Khomeini must be viewed as a defender of the Islamic order. In the latter role, however, the Islamic Republic is bound to come into conflict with the order preferred by the United States under the Shah as well as with the order desired by the Soviet Union since his ouster.

Of the two superpowers, the US response to Iran is seen as potentially more harmful because the former was most comfortable with the political order under the Shah. Iran flexed its muscles on a number of occasions to safeguard its own as well as Western interests. For instance, the Shah, by demonstrating his military superiority, seized three Gulf islands – Abu Musa and the two Tumbs – near the Strait of Hormuz in 1971; his armed forces dealt a crippling blow to the communist insurgency in the Dhofar province of Oman in 1975; and his military might also enabled him to extract a humiliating agreement from Iraq in 1975 which declared the deep-water line in Shatt al-Arab as the boundary line between the two countries. All Gulf states, except South Yemen, were considered friendly to the United States. When the Shah was overthrown in 1978, American strategic dominance in the region sharply eroded.

The stridently anti-American posture held by the Islamic Republic since almost its very inception, and the possibility that other Gulf countries might also experience Islamic revolutions, provided reasons for antagonism between the United States and Iran. The hostage crisis added intensity to this antagonism. The United States, through the Carter Doctrine stated in 1980, expressed its willingness to take military actions against 'any outside force to gain control' of the Gulf. Even though this declaration was made in the immediate aftermath of the Soviet invasion of Afghanistan, it was clear that any attempts by Iran to export its revolution to other Gulf countries would also invoke a retaliatory American response. After absorbing a sizeable erosion in its strategic position stemming from the ouster of the Shah, the United States was willing to save the remainder of the status quo in the Gulf (and also to retain its credibililty *vis-à-vis* the Arab states in the region) through the promise of use of its military might. The creation of the Rapid Deployment Joint Task Force (RDJTF), which was later expanded into the US Central Command (USCENTCOM), was the most visible military step taken by the United States since the signing of the Baghdad Pact in 1955 (which was renamed as the Central Treaty Organisation – CENTO – in 1959). In order to provide teeth to the RDJTF, the United States also obtained facilities access agreements from Somalia, Kenya, and Oman.

In a major action that was related to regional security, the rulers of six Gulf states – Saudi Arabia, Kuwait, the UAE, Qatar, Oman, and Bahrain – created the Gulf Cooperation Council (GCC) in May 1981. It is important to note that while the USCENTCOM was aimed at militarily tying various Gulf countries in a US-centred order, the *raison d'être* of the GCC was not so straightforward. In this arrangement, the Gulf states had emphasised Islam as the basis of their unity, obviously a measure aimed at preempting potential charges from Iran that GCC was in any way anti-Islamic.

Concerning military cooperation with superpowers, in the early phase of its creation, the GCC agreed to postpone its decision because of conflicting positions taken by Kuwait and Oman. While Oman preferred a collective defence agreement between the Gulf countries and the United States, Kuwait advocated a balanced relationship with both superpowers. However, the GCC later succeeded in developing a sophisticated position on this issue. According to the Secretary General of the GCC, Abdallah Bishara, the member states did not want either superpower to gain a foothold in the Gulf area, What the GCC preferred was 'Gulfanisation' of Gulf security – i.e., an arrangement based upon cooperation among the Gulf states on matters of internal security and external threats. The GCC, continued Bishara, did not envision the use of RDJTF – as proposed by the United States – as a preferable option to guarantee the flow of oil since it might invoke a direct or indirect intervention from the

Soviet Union. At the same time, stated Bishara, the GCC rejected the Soviet Union's proposal to neutralise the area while it continued to occupy Afghanistan and maintained military presence in the Indian Ocean and the Red Sea through its use of military facilities in South Yemen and Ethiopia.[12]

The real policies of the GCC countries, however, have been more congruent with the strategic objectives of the United States in the region in the following ways:

1. Both the GCC and the United States strongly favour the present political status quo in the Arab states of the Gulf.
2. Both the Gulf states and the United States envision the GCC as a legitimate vehicle for promoting political stability and order in the region.
3. The GCC members continued their heavy reliance on Western military equipment and on the use of Western military advisers to build their armed forces and military infrastructures, respectively.

From the perspective of the GCC, the 'Gulfanisation' of Gulf security not only was in harmony with the 'neither East nor West' principle espoused by the Islamic Republic, but it also appeared to soothe whatever fear Iran might have about the potential reliance of the Gulf states on American military might to overthrow the Khomeini regime. The Gulf states also hoped that their stated policies would serve as a carrot for Iran in calming its revolutionary fervour. If that failed, they could always use US military intervention to protect themselves from covert or overt attempts of the Khomeini regime to overthrow them.

The confrontational phase

The escalation of the Iran–Iraq war brought about in the summer of 1987 a significant and radical change in the policy posture of the GCC states, from appeasement to that of confrontation with Iran. The carrot aspect of the Gulfanisation policy alluded to above was at least temporarily deemphasised as Iran increased its hostile acts against the Gulf sheikhdoms, especially Kuwait and Saudi Arabia.

Kuwait, in keeping with its balancing act, asked Washington to reflag its tankers and approached Moscow to lease Soviet tankers. The GCC states were politically and economically supporting Iraq in the war. The implications of a potential Iranian victory over Iraq were nightmarish for these states. Until the tide of war turned against Iran, they were not about to lower the level of their support for Iraq. The Arab sheikhdoms envisioned being overwhelmed by the snow-ball effects created by a potential Iranian victory. They have preferred Iraq over Iran as the lesser of the two evils during the entire course of this war. Accordingly, in the summer of 1987 they have turned toward both superpowers when their appeasement of Iran did not lower its threat potential to their security.

Even in their decision to confront the Khomeini regime, by seeking the protective shields of superpowers, the GCC countries sustained their quest for a negotiated solution to this war by enticing Iran with offers of economic reconstruction. Moreover, even in inviting the US navy in the Gulf, the GCC states preferred that this presence remain 'over-the-horizon'.

From the perspective of Iran the political and strategic contradictions between the United States and the Gulf countries made their relationship quite nebulous. By underscoring these contradictions through verbal barrages, Iran anticipated keeping these states from getting any closer to the United States in the short run than they already were. In the long run, the Islamic Republic hoped that a *rapprochement* with the Gulf states might be reached on Iranian terms. The outcome of the Iran–Iraq war was also to determine the terms of this *rapprochement*. For this reason, while Iran continued its war with Iraq, it also periodically assured the Gulf states that it has no intention of creating turmoil within their borders. Even during the confrontational phase, Iran reiterated such reassurances. At the same time, the potential for turmoil was also used to keep the issue of *rapprochement* on the front burner.

Attempts to neutralise the US interests

In order to underscore why the Islamic Republic of Iran considers the relationship between the Gulf countries and the United States so nebulous and so easy a target for its attack, it is important to examine American strategic objectives in the Gulf. The dynamics of American involvement are aimed at the fulfilment of the following three strategic objectives: (1) that the Gulf states continue to supply oil to the Western alliance; (2) that the threats to stability of these countries from within and without remain minimal; and (3) that these states be persuaded to strive for the creation of an Arab consensus that is aimed at finding a political solution to the Palestinian question and thereby recognising Israel.

Iran has no particular quarrel concerning the first American strategic objective, for it recognises the significance of oil, not only for the economies of the Western European countries and Japan, but, more important, for the fulfilment of its own regional political and strategic objectives. Consequently, despite fighting a war with Iraq, Iran continues to participate, alongside Iraq and its Gulf supporters, in OPEC meetings. It is by underscoring the 'anti-Islamic' aspects of the second and third American strategic objectives in the Gulf that the Khomeini regime is attempting to undermine a possible resuscitation of an American-centred political order and to maximise the potential for the creation of an Iran-centred order.

President Ronald Reagan's corollary to the Carter doctrine which stated that the United States will not tolerate any threats to the stability of the Gulf regimes either from within or without, committed America to the maintenance of political status quo in that region. If there were any doubts that the Carter doctrine did not include potential regional troublemakers in its admonition, the Reagan corollary clarified it. From the American perspective, Iran has the potential of triggering turbulence from without by attempting to invade the Gulf sheikhdoms, as well as fomenting insurgencies from within.

The Islamic Republic of Iran, however, describes the US resolve to ensure a political status quo in the Gulf as an American design to reestablish its 'hegemony' by using the Gulf states as instruments, as it used the Shah until 1978. The reestablishment of the American hegemony in the Gulf, according to the Khomeini regime, only serves the fulfilment of its third strategic objective, i.e., using the moderate Gulf countries to create an Arab consensus aimed at finding a solution to the Palestinian question preferred by Israel. A solution preferred by the Israelis, as the Islamic Republic envisions it, is to become the basis of Arab recognition of the Jewish state. Thus, argues, Iran, by cooperating in the reestablishment of the US hegemony in the Gulf, the states in the region are serving as pawns in the hands of the United States toward the legitimation of Israel and the betrayal of the Palestinians. All of these acts, as previously noted, are regarded by Iran as grossly 'anti-Islamic'.

Whether or not Iran poses an internal or external threat to any Gulf regime is likely to be determined by the Khomeini regime on the basis of how cooperative these countries are with the United States. In order to pass the Iranian 'litmus test', the Gulf countries must at best renounce their friendship with the United States, or at least sustain a neutral stance. Neutrality means that they must refrain from establishing a military partnership with and providing military facilities to the United States. Their failure to do so 'qualifies' them to be labelled as friends of the 'Great Satan' and as 'enemies of Islam'. Once so branded, they may be overthrown by the 'defenders' of Islam – i.e., the pro-Khomeini forces – by applying the exportability principle.

The adoption by the Gulf sheikhdoms of a stated neutral posture toward both superpowers was an acceptable, though not an optimal, option to Iran. It is easier to seek a *rapprochement* with the Gulf states when they maintain a more or less neutral *modus vivendi* with the United States than when most or all of them become signatory to an American-centred military alliance. In the view of the Islamic Republic, the emergence of an Iran-centred regional order is only natural since it has the largest population and one of the largest oil reserves in the area. Ironically, the Iran-centred order in the region under the Shah serves as a precedent for an order sought by the Khomeini regime. As Iran envisions it, as long as the Gulf sheikh-doms continue to maintain a neutral posture toward the United States, the chances of reestablishment of an Iran-centred political order remain quite real.

In view of the preceding analysis, political developments since the summer of 1987 only escalated the chances of political turbulence in the Gulf. The GCC states' decision to increase security-related cooperation with the US as manifested in the Kuwaiti invitation to both superpowers is bound to make them an increased target of Khomeini's exportability principle. The action of the GCC countries, while a deliberate one, also underscores a sense of collective desparation. Appeasement of the Islamic Republic did not work. Attempts for a negotiated settlement with Iran failed to bring about a cessation of hostility. The attempts to confront Iran appear to be measures of the last resort. But there is a serious problem associated with the GCC states' opting for a high profile American military presence in the Gulf. This problem is associated with the overall American involvement in the Middle East.

The United States is perceived as a staunch supporter and an ally of Israel. It is generally believed in the Arab world that the Palestinian question could be resolved only if the United States were to show its resolve. The Khomeini regime has been harping on this point. No

Arab state of any political leaning would deny the perceived American influence with Israel. The fact that the Arab-Israeli conflict remained unresolved unquestionably raises serious doubts about the friendly relationship that prevails between the Gulf monarchies and the United States. The new wrinkles associated with this conflict – such as the Israeli invasion of Lebanon, and the so-called 'iron-fist' policy of Israel against the political protest in the occupied West Bank and the Gaza Strip – put the Gulf and other moderate Arab states not only in a tenuous position, but also tend to erode their political stability from within. Undoubtedly, the Khomeini regime not only understands this reality, but has, on occasions, demonstrated its willingness to exploit the dissenting forces in the neighbouring states to destabilise the political order.

If a negotiated solution of the Iran–Iraq war is to emerge, an important aspect of this negotiated package between Iran and the Gulf states is most likely to be the neutrality of the latter *vis-à-vis* the superpowers, especially the United States. As the Khomeini regime perceives it, this neutrality is a vital precursor to the establishment of an Iran-centred political order in the Gulf, in the long run.

Iran and the Soviet strategic interests in the Gulf

At the time of the political revolution in Iran, the Soviet Union had very good diplomatic relations with the Shah's regime. As Rubinstein notes, 'The border was quiet, with no large-scale deployments on either side; defectors were returned with quiet regularity; Soviet propaganda was restrained and said little to embarrass the Shah's persecution of local Communists.' The Soviet Union built one steel plant and a natural gas pipeline; the Shah purchased one billion dollars worth of light arms during the 1967–78 period; and he sold natural gas to the Soviet Union.[13] Despite a prolonged effort by the Shah to serve as the gendarme of the Western interests in the Gulf, the Soviet Union – as a result of a personal assurance from the Shah that Iran would never allow its territory for the launching of an attack on its Communist neighbour – did not feel threatened by his role.[14] Indeed the Soviet Union was even reported to have instructed the Tudeh (Communist) party of Iran to support the monarchical regime.

The Soviet Union, undoubtedly, applauded the uprooting of the Shah's rule since it also brought about a significant erosion of the American strategic dominance in the region. It hoped that the anti-American posture of the Islamic Republic would become the basis for the establishment of strong friendly ties with Iran. When Khomeini continued the reiteration of his long-declared characterisation of Russia and the United States as equally evil, the Soviet Union was forced to rethink its strategy toward his regime. Two events enormously complicated the Soviet endeavours to build friendly relations with Iran. The first one was the Russian invasion of Afghanistan in December 1979. Iran not only allowed the Afghan refugees to settle in the border areas, but also provided them with military equipment to launch guerrilla attacks into Afghanistan. Moreover, condemning the Soviet occupation, Khomeini drew parallels between the anti-Shah and anti-American struggles in Iran and the struggle of the Afghan insurgents, and proclaimed that the latter would be similarly victorious.[15] The sustained Soviet occupation of Afghanistan remained one of the major sources of irritation and contention between Iran and the USSR.

The second event which served as a major obstacle in the Soviet efforts to create close ties with Iran was the Iran–Iraq war. The Soviet involvement in this war has been a complicated one, and has undergone changes in response to such variables as: the Russian ambitions toward the Gulf; the Gulf regimes' perception of the Soviet intentions in the Gulf; and the sustained desire of the USSR to have the best of both worlds: not allowing the level of hostility to be so escalated that Iran would be forced to restore friendly ties with the United States, at the same time not jeopardising its alliance with Iraq.

When the Iran–Iraq war broke out in September 1980, the Soviets adopted a neutral stance. Even though the Soviet decision-makers were not known for their risk-taking characteristic, this neutrality was indeed a daring one since it was also fraught with considerable risks. The 1972 friendship treaty between USSR and Iraq not only made it a partisan to any conflict Iraq might develop with other nations, but also committed it to supply military equipment. Any other policy posture was to damage the Russian credibility which was not unblemished during its military alliance with Egypt in the 1970s. However, the neutrality decision toward this war only underscored the significance the USSR attached to winning the Iranian friendship. During late 1982, when the Iran–Iraq war appeared to be favouring Iran, the Soviet Union adopted a slight but definite shift toward Iraq since the emergence of either nation as a decisive winner was not in the best strategic interest of that superpower.[16]

By late 1982, the Soviet Union was convinced that its decision to refrain from supplying arms to Iraq was not about to win Iran to its side. Thus by early 1983, it resumed military shipments to Iraq. Even in opening the military supply lines to Iraq, the Soviets made sure that the pace of war did not inordinately favour that country. Iran was also allowed to receive military supplies from Russian allies such as North Korea, Syria, and Libya. Between 1986 and 1988, the Soviet Union appeared to be continuing the policy of sufficiently supplying military hardware to both antagonists – direct supplies to Iraq and indirect supplies to Iran – and thereby assuring the continuation of the war, its public pronouncements to the contrary notwithstanding.

It can be argued that by prolonging the war, the Soviet Union might be keeping both Iran and Iraq preoccupied. The preoccupation of these antagonists would keep them from competing in the Gulf as the Soviet Union continues its efforts to expand its sphere of influence. Furthermore, the constant concern about the deleterious effects of this war would make the Gulf states more receptive to Soviet diplomatic overtures in the area as evidenced by the decision of Oman and the UAE to establish diplomatic contacts with the USSR in 1985 and the Kuwaiti decision to lease Soviet tankers in the summer of 1987. The Soviet preference concerning the prolongation of the war also stemmed from the fact that it was well aware of a similar preference being strongly shared by Iran, Iraq and Saudi Arabia: 'that regional affairs should be managed autonomously'.[17] Of the three regional actors, the Islamic Republic was too threatening to the Soviet objectives. Aside from being armed with Islamic ideology, Iran is also stimulated by a zeal to reinvigorate Islamic internationalism. The decisive victory of Iran in this war would enable it to create an Iran-centred military order in the Gulf, and mobilise the Muslim population of Russia.

Despite its preoccupation with the Iran–Iraq war, Iran continues to serve as the chief regional threat to the Soviet objectives in the Gulf. From Iran's perspective, of the two superpowers, it is considerably easier to convince the Gulf states of the Soviet menace to regional stability than of the threats emanating from the American presence for several reasons. First, the Gulf states have been considerably suspicious of the Soviet Union, a proximate superpower with a long history of absorbing Muslim territories and subjugating Muslim populations. Second, South Yemen and Afghanistan continue to serve as prime examples of the capability of the Soviet Union to dominate Muslim states. Third, the atheistic nature of the Soviet Union has always been repugnant to the Gulf regimes.

At this point, it is important to examine the nature of Soviet objectives in the Gulf and their relationship with attempts of the Khomeini regime to establish an Iran-centred political order. The most important Soviet strategic objective is to break the Western political and military monopoly in the Gulf. In order to attain this, the Soviet Union has adopted a three-pronged approach. The first prong was the Soviet proposal to make the Gulf a nuclear free zone and an area free of superpower rivalry.[18] Since it regards the Gulf states to be very pro-American, the neutrality offer of the Soviet Union was aimed at dissolving American strategic advantages. The second prong of the Soviet attempt to break the Western monopoly has been to gain access to the Gulf countries through establishing diplomatic contacts with them. In the strategic thinking of the Soviet decision-makers, a string of bilateral agreements thus reached with other Asian countries – as exemplifed by Soviet-Iraqi and Soviet-Indian treaties – would enable the USSR to emerge as 'the principal participant in the continental affairs' and 'the power that must be consulted on all issues affecting Asia'.[19]

The third prong of the Soviet strategy has been the use of its diplomatic presence in the Gulf to exploit the recurrence of internecine internal conflicts or inter-Arab rivalry. It hopes to accomplish this by serving as a mediator and a supplier of military weapons at any time one of the Gulf states either becomes disillusioned with the American policies in the region or deliberately adopts policies to balance the influence of both superpowers.[20] An example of internal conflict was witnessed in the violent outbreak of civil war in South Yemen which reportedly resulted in more than 12 000 deaths. The potential for internal conflict also exists in Iraq and Bahrain with majority Shiite populations. The potential for other inter-Arab conflicts are also considerable. For instance, Omani and North Yemeni concerns over the alleged hegemonic ambitions on the part of the Saudis, and the protracted conflict between the two Yemens (which already enabled the Soviet Union to supply arms to both parties). Kuwait is a prototype of a Gulf state that has been performing the balancing act between both superpowers. One of the reasons underlying this Kuwaiti policy is its fear of Iraq. By sustaining diplomatic contacts and purchasing arms from the Soviet Union, Kuwait hopes to rein the potential revival of irridentist designs of Iraq. At the same time, Kuwait views the 'over-the-horizon' American presence in the Gulf as a deterrent against possible mischief-making behaviour by the Soviet Union in the region.[21]

As previously noted, despite Kuwaiti balancing act, the rest of Gulf sheikhdoms maintained an overall pro-American posture, including a decisive preference for American military hardware. Even though the United States officially maintained a neutral position on the Iran–Iraq war, in view of worsened US-Iranian relations, the Arab states were periodically assured of American sympathies. Then came the disclosure that the Reagan Administration was involved in trading arms for hostages with Iran. This disclosure, while jolting the Gulf states into rethinking whether they want to put all their eggs in the American basket, provided new openings for the Soviet Union in that region.

The strategic realities of the Gulf are also favouring the Soviet Union. Under Mikhael Gorbachev, the Soviet Union is working hard on a new image. Some scholars label the Soviet behaviour under Gorbachev as a 'shift to the right'. Since such a shift has been noted under the reigns of a number of other Soviet leaders, the implication is that this might not be a 'new' image after all. When the Soviet Union takes a rightward shift, according to Francis Fukuyama, its foreign policy 'initiatives are likely to be directed toward strengthening ties with geopolitically important Third World states, even if they are capitalist oriented'.[22] An important elaboration on the shift toward right is reflected in the writing of Alexsander Yakovlev, a member of the Politburo and Secretary of the Central Committee of the Communist Party of the Soviet Union and an influential theoretician of foreign policy under Gorbachev. Yakovlev proposed a 'multipolar strategy' for his country, under which that country 'broaden its range of contacts and cultivate important capitalist allies of the United States in Western Europe and Asia'.[23] This is marked deviation from a traditional and narrow bipolar approach practised under the foreign ministership of Andrei Gromyko. There have been a number of significant Soviet moves underscoring the implementation of the multipolar strategy in the Middle East. These include: the establishment of diplomatic ties with Oman and the UAE in September and November of 1985 respectively; increasing contacts between the Soviet Union and Saudi Arabia; the USSR's willingness to lease Soviet-flagged tankers to Kuwait in conjunction with a low level of naval presence in the Gulf; a sustained widening of economic ties between the Soviet Union and the Islamic Republic of Iran; and the growing Soviet willingness to reestablish its diplomatic ties with Israel. Obviously, there is no suggestion that, because of these new developments in the foreign policy behaviour of the USSR, the Arab states have either forgotten the historical record of Soviet empire-building, or have ignored the atheistic character of communism. Since the Western press portrays Gorbachev as a leader preoccupied with establishing *glasnost* and *perestroika* within the Soviet Union, reestablishing *détente* with the United States by signing a medium- and short-range nuclear missile reduction treaty, negotiating closer ties with the Peoples Republic of China, and, most important, declaring the Soviet willingness to withdraw from Afghanistan, the Gulf states appear to be increasingly curious about the purported changing character of the Soviet international involvement.[24] The USSR's decision to lease ships to Kuwait – a measure aimed at soothing the security-related fears of the GCC states, and attempts to maintain a low naval profile – a step clearly aimed at not antagonising Iran, are bound to be beneficial to the strategic objectives of that superpower in the Gulf.

Ironically, the 'exportability of Islamic revolution' in conjuction with the 'neither East nor West' principle of the Islamic Republic appeared to have originally forced the Gulf states to adopt a more pro-Soviet policy than they otherwise would have adopted. Countries which maintained diplomatic ties with both superpowers could more persuasively argue that they are non-aligned than those who have strong ties with the United States and none with the USSR. However, the escalation of war forced the Gulf states to opt for the presence of both superpowers, a positive development indeed from the perspective of Soviet strategic interests in that region.

CONCLUSION

No matter what dynamics the Soviet-American relations undergo in the future, the USSR, in its quest for dominance in the Third World areas vital to the United States, will continue to seek, in the words of Christopher Bertram, 'clarification of what the United States is up to'.[25] Such clarification, in turn, might be used to set the parameters of its own strategic policies in those areas.

While the Carter doctrine and the Reagan corollary warned against the destabilising forces in the Gulf, these pronouncements appear less relevant under the current strategic realities of the Gulf. The shift to the right in the Soviet foreign policy behaviour in tandem with its withdrawal from Afghanistan – if that indeed materialises – will definitely lower the Arab perception of the Soviet threat potential.

Under such a circumstance, the US strategic objectives toward the Gulf must be be redefined. As the threat potential related to the Soviet Union is lowered, the chief thrust of the Carter doctrine/ Reagan corollary, at least in the near future, is on the strategic manoeuvres of Iran as it affects the regional status quo. Since the Soviet naval presence is an outcome of the Kuwaiti invitation, the United States has to reexamine the nature of its own responses to the Gulf security.

Despite the fact that Iran is opposed to the presence of the United States and the USSR in the Gulf, the superpowers have been unable to develop much common ground concerning that country. Both superpowers have been on the record in their preference for a political solution to the war, but the Soviet Union has been unwilling to give a green signal to the proposed UN-sponsored sanctions against Iran for its refusal to cease hostilities against Iraq.

The fact also remains that an escalation of Iran-backed political turbulence aimed at overthrowing any government in the Gulf may still be seen as a new opening by the Soviet Union to enhance its strategic presence, the new shift to the right in the foreign policy of that superpower notwithstanding. So, even if the Soviet Union under Gorbachev were to publicly condemn such Iranian manoeuvres, one cannot categorically state that the heightening of political turbulence in the Gulf would be damaging to the Soviet interests. One may also want to argue that, because of its spill-over effects in the Islamic region of that country, a potential escalation of political instability in the Gulf may not be in the best interests of the Soviet Union. However, given the past Soviet record of crushing domestic dissent of any magnitude, the Soviet leaders, including Gorbachev, may be taking little risk in not appearing to be eager to cooperate with the United States in discouraging Iranian manoeuvres aimed at changing the political status quo in the Gulf.

There is an additional variable to be considered. The Soviet Union, because of its proximity to Iran, envisions that country and its contiguous areas as vital to its own security interests. Indeed in November 1978, the USSR issued a statement to that effect, when Iran was undergoing the early phases of its revolution. The United States during the Carter Administration, by assuring the Soviet Union that it had no intention of invading Iran to restore the monarchy, and later – during the hostage crisis – by providing similar assurances, has established precedents of being sensitive to the primacy of the Soviet security-related concerns regarding Iran. Two important questions should be raised here. First, is the United States likely to manifest similar sensitivity toward Russian security interests in the future? The limited nature of American military action against Iran, which was necessitated as a response to the Iranian attack on a reflagged Kuwaiti ship, was convincing evidence that the United States is likely to express similar prudence in any future military action against that country. The second question here is whether the United States is willing to accord similar recognition to Soviet security concerns in the Gulf. The United States has accepted the Soviet military presence in the Gulf as a *fait accompli* since the summer of 1987. How permanent this *modus vivendi* is likely to be in the future depends largely upon the outcome of the Iran–Iraq war and the dynamics of the Khomeini revolution in Iran. In the long run, a superpower *rapprochement* must be reached regarding their respective concerns in the region. Until then, each superpower is likely to serve as a deterrent against the other's ambitions in the Gulf.

The Islamic Republic of Iran remains the chief beneficiary of any superpower deterrent in the sense that it is largely free to sustain its threatening posture through verbal barrages on the Gulf governments or even by trying to foment insurgencies within their borders. Short of an Iranian attack on the Gulf states of the Arabian Peninsula, the United States will think about the Soviet reaction in formulating the scope of its response to the Khomeini regime. Similarly, Iran can continue its attacks on the evil nature of communism and on the hegemonic character of the Soviet Union. The latter country's response to anti-Soviet activities of the Khomeini regime is also likely to be most measured as a result of the Soviet concern regarding the possible American reaction.

The mutual restraint of both superpowers toward Iran is also likely to provide the latter ample opportunity to create an Iran-centred political order. Such an order may not necessarily be created by overthrowing the existing regimes (which the US would not allow), even though Iran would prefer to have such threats hanging, like the Damocles' sword, over the heads of rulers of Gulf sheikhdoms. The Khomeini regime is most likely to keep the exportability principle very much alive. At the same time, 'neither East nor West' is also likely to be used to condemn both superpowers, their designs in the Gulf, and those Gulf regimes who dare to cooperate with them.

The outcome of the Iran–Iraq war will have a tremendous impact on Iranian ambitions to create its version of an Islamic order. The continuation of this war may turn out to be a deadly gambit for Iran.

Its escalation has already forced the Gulf states to request a high military visibility of both superpowers. If the pendulum of advantage in this war is to continue to swing in favour of Iran, the Gulf states may also raise the level of their confrontational policies, a scenario inherently detrimental to the strategic objectives of Iran. Often it seems that the Iranian conduct of this war is guided more by an ongoing struggle between the ideologues and pragmatists than by an astute reading of regional realities. The former group, led by Ayatollah Montazari who is to succeed Khomeini, appeared to be too dedicated to the exportability principle. The pragmatists, under the leadership of the Speaker of the Iranian parliament, Rafsanjani, seem to continue their quest for a political solution to this war. If the war indeed is guided by the struggle between these groups, its outcome is also likely to be determined by which group becomes victorious. In the meantime the level of political turbulence in the Gulf is likely to escalate.

Notes

1. Richard Cottam, 'Goodbye to America's Shah', *Foreign Policy*, Spring 1979, no. 34, pp. 3–14.
2. J. S. Ismail and T. Y. Ismail, 'Social Change in Islamic Society: The Political Thought of Ayatollah Khomeini', *Social Problems*, June 1980, no. 5, pp. 601–19.
3. Ironically, the Soviet decision to remain neutral during the first two years of the protracted Iran–Iraq war, which was based on its desire not to antagonise Iran, worked to the advantage of the IRI, and proved Khomeini's argument that the Soviet Union would readily abandon its allies or friendship treaties when they would not suit its strategic interests in the region.
4. Ismail and Ismail, op. cit., note 2, pp. 615–16.
5. Both quotes are from Ayatollah Rouhollah Khomeini, *Islamic Government* (New York, NY: Manor Books, 1979), pp. 93–4.
6. Hamid Algar (trans.), *Islam and Revolution: Writings and Declarations of Imam Khomeini* (Berkeley, CA: Mizan Press, 1981), p. 138.
7. Edward Sapir, 'Symbolism', *Encyclopedia of Social Sciences* (New York, NY: 1934), pp. 492–5.
8. Murray Edelman, *The Symbolic Uses of Politics* (Urbana, IL: University of Illinois Press, 1964). p. 6.
9. *Joint Publication Research Service (JPRS)*, 1979, 73794.
10. Algar, *Islam and Revolution*, op. cit., p. 127.
11. Ibid., p. 196.
12. For details see Emile A. Nakleh, *The Persian Gulf and the American Policy* (New York, NY: Praeger, 1982, pp. 43–61; also John Duke

Anthony, 'The Gulf Cooperation Council', in Robert G. Darious, John W. Amos II, and Ralph H. Magnus (eds), *Gulf Security into the 1980s: Perceptual and Strategic Dimensions* (Stanford, CA: Hoover Institution Press, 1984), pp. 82–92.

13. Alvin Z. Rubinstein, 'Soviet Policy Toward South and Southwest Asia: Strategic and Political Aspects', in A. Z. Rubinstein (ed.), *The Great Game: Rivalry in the Persian Gulf* (New York, NY: Praeger, 1983), pp. 81–114. Also Muriel Atkins, 'Soviet Relations with the Islamic Republic', *SAIS Review*, Winter/Spring 1983, pp. 183–94.

14. M. Reza Pahlevi, *Mission for my Country* (London: Hutchinson, 1961), p. 120.

15. Atkins, op cit., note 13, p. 186.

16. US Congress, *The Soviet Union and the Third World: 1980–85: An Imperial Burden or Political Asset?*, Report prepared by the Congressional Research Service of Library of Congress, 23 September 1985 (Washington, DC: Government Printing Office, 1985), p. 152.

17. Shahram Chubin, *Soviet Policy Toward Iran and the Gulf*, Adelphi Paper, no. 157 (London: The International Institute for Strategic Studies, 1980), p. 16.

18. Brezhnev proposed a neutralisation of the Gulf and Indian Ocean regions in December 1980 and reiterated it at the Twenty-Sixth Communist Party Congress in February 1981.

19. Chubin, op cit., note 17, p. 17.

20. Ibid., p. 14.

21. Almost all Gulf states prefer an 'over-the-horizon' American presence. For a detailed discussion of this point see US Congress, House of Representatives, *US Security Interests in the Gulf*, Report of a Staff Study Mission to the Persian Gulf, Middle East, and Horn of Africa to the Committee on Foreign Affairs (Washington, DC: Government Printing Office, 1981).

22. Francis Fukuyama, 'Patterns of Soviet Third World Policy', *Problems of Communism*, Sept.–Oct. 1987, pp. 1–13, XXXVI. Also, Samuel P. Huntington, 'Patterns of Intervention', *The National Interest*, Spring 1987, VII.

23. Fukuyama, op cit., note 22, p. 6.

24. For instance, see Jerry E. Hough, *The Struggle for the Third World: Soviet Debates and American Options* (Washington, DC: The Brookings Institution, 1986), especially chs 7, 8, and 9; Francis Fukuyama, *Soviet Civil-Military Relations and the Power* (Santa Monica, CA: The Rand Corporation, 1987); and Daniel S. Papp, *Soviet Policies Toward the Developing World during the 1980s: The Dilemmas of Power and Presence* (Mawell Airforce Base, AL: Air University Press, 1986), especially chs 8 and 12.

25. Christopher Bertram, 'Introduction', in *Prospects of Soviet Power in the 1980s* (London: The International Institute for Strategic Studies, 1979), pp. 1–4.

2 Gulf Security: An Iranian Perspective
Shirin Hunter

Since the advent of the Islamic revolution, Iran has become the number one security preoccupation of the Gulf Arab states. The Gulf Arabs' view of the Iranian threat is multi-dimensional. They view Iran as a potential source of direct military attack, and a source of internal subversion. In fact, they view the very existence of Iran and its current ideology of revolutionary Islam as a mortal threat to their security and survival.

Meanwhile, the Gulf Arabs believe that they do not pose any security threat to Iran. No doubt Iran's revolutionary rhetoric, its hostile propaganda and, at times, its involvement in subversion against the Gulf states to some extent justifies these fears.

However, lest the view of Iran as an imminent and deadly threat to the Gulf Arabs' security, and the lack of any Arab threat to Iran, is accepted at face value, the following points need to be stressed at the outset. First, the theme of an Iranian threat to the Gulf Arabs' security is not new, and did not originate with the Islamic revolution. The theme of a so-called 'Iranian hegemonic thrust' emerged in the late 1960s, when as a result of the 1968 British decision to withdraw its military presence from the Persian Gulf, Iran was propelled into performing a major security role in the region on behalf of the West, and ironically, also on behalf of the Gulf Arabs.

In fact, while currently the Gulf Arab states are harbouring a secret nostalgia for the Shah, in the 1970s they were concerned with what they saw as the Shah's desire to resurrect the Persian Empire. The most widely asked question by the Gulf Arabs at the time was 'Where and against whom does the Shah want to use all the weapons that he is accumulating?', thus betraying an anxiety that they might be Iran's potential targets.

Second, Iran's greater size, larger population, longer coastline, more diverse resource base, plus the Iranian leaders' – be it imperial or Islamic – tendency to use grandiose and often inflammatory language have lent credence to the view of Iran's hegemonist thrust and Arab vulnerability.

32

The same factors have also caused most neutral observers to overlook, or underestimate, Iran's security concerns and its fears of an Arab threat to its security and other interests. Yet it is Iran that in the last forty years has become the subject of a full-scale Arab military attack with the Iraqi invasion of Iran on 22 September 1980. This attack has since been supported by other Arabs, especially the Gulf Arabs. This last observation points to another vital, and yet generally overlooked, fact that Iran's relations with the Gulf Arab states cannot be analysed, or understood, outside the context of its relations with the broader Arab world, and the impact of intra-Arab politics on the Iran–Gulf Arab relations.

A further point needing stress is that while certain common factors have applied to Iran's relations with the Gulf states, other factors of a more specific nature have governed Iran's relations with individual Gulf states. For example, the element of competition for regional power has greatly affected the nature of Iran's relations with Saudi Arabia. The presence of Arab nationalist elements within Kuwait's Palestinian and other non-indigenous Arab populations was a main cause of strain in Kuwaiti-Iranian relations under the Shah. Since the Islamic revolution, the existence of a large Shiah population in Kuwait, Bahrain, and Saudi Arabia has contributed to tense relations between Iran and these countries.

By contrast, Iran has had basically friendly relations with the UAE, and especially Dubai, both in the pre- and post-revolutionary periods. The existence of a large Iranian community there, and the historically benevolent attitude of Dubai's ruling family toward this community have been among the reasons for this situation. There is, however, some evidence that the new generation of Dubai's rulers may not share these friendly sentiments toward Dubai's Iranian community. Thus, Iran's relations with the Gulf Arabs should be looked at on an individual as well as collective level.

Similarly, there has not been adequate understanding of the vital importance of the Gulf to the very existence of Iran as an independent national entity. Yet this fact has made the Iranians extremely sensitive to any actual, or perceived, threats to their security and other interests in the Gulf.

This Iranian sensitivity should also be understood within the context of Iran's historical experience. In this respect, it is important to note that in the past two hundred years, particularly during the period of British dominance, Iran has faced constant pressures and encroachments on its interests and sovereignty not only in the Gulf but also in its southern provinces. In fact, an important aspect of British policy was to weaken the control of Iran's central government over these provinces and bring local tribal chieftains under British control.[1]

In sum, the vital importance of the Gulf to Iran, and Iran's historical experience in the region have generated deep-rooted views and perceptions among the majority of the Iranians regarding Iran's interests and role in the region. These perceptions have remained remarkably constant over the years, including during the post-revolutionary period. In fact, the degree of continuity in the views and policies of the Islamic regime *vis-à-vis* the Gulf with those of the previous regime is remarkable, although the current regime uses Islam, at time ingeniously, as its rationalising and legitimising ideology.[2]

Thus, a correct analysis of Iran's current relations with the Gulf Arab states can only be done by placing them within the context of Iran's historical exeperience in the Gulf, the importance of the Gulf to Iran, and Iran's relations with the broader Arab world.

A further point to be kept in mind is that in the post-revolutionary period, Iran's relations with the Gulf Arabs, as with the rest of the world, have been affected by factors related to political developments inside Iran, especially factional rivalries and power struggles within its leadership.

IRAN AND THE GULF: HOW IMPORTANT IS IT?

The importance of the Gulf to Iran can only be appreciated by looking at it within the context of Iran's geostrategic location. All across its northern borders, Iran faces the Soviet colossus.[3] Should the Soviet Union succeed in establishing a Soviet-dominated regime in Afghanistan, Iran will also face the USSR in parts of its eastern borders. To the east, Iran faces the vast expanses of the Indian subcontinent and its nearly one billion population. To the west of Iran are Turkey and Iraq.

What this situation means is that Iran has no direct access to the outside world except through the Gulf, with all the other access routes being controlled by countries which have been, are, or could be hostile to Iran. In other words, without its Gulf ports, Iran would be a land-locked country similar to Afghanistan.

Economically, Iran's oil resources in the Khuzistan region, as well as in the continental shelf of its Gulf coast, constitute the backbone of its national economy and its only hope for achieving some measure of economic development and self-sufficiency.

Without its southern oil fields, Iran would be a country almost as economically worse off as Bangladesh. Thus, it is in this context that Iran's view of the importance of the Gulf to its national survival, and its sensitivity to an actual, or potential, Arab challenge to the Khuzistan Province or to an Iranian presence in the Persian Gulf should be appraised.

IRAN'S HISTORICAL EXPERIENCE IN THE GULF

The history of Iran's interaction with the Gulf is as old as the country itself. This history reflects the rising and falling fortunes of Iran over its long and turbulent past. In periods of strength and stability, Iran has exerted effective control over its southern shores and has made its presence felt in the Gulf. Periods of decline and political instability and, at times, foreign occupation have forced Iran's retreat from the Gulf.

What has, however, remained constant all through Iran's long history is that the Iranians have always viewed retreat from the Gulf as a forced one, and thus, only temporary in nature. Consequently, every time that after a period of decline Iran has managed to achieve some degree of order and physical and political unity, it has turned its attention toward the Gulf and has tried to control its shores and to reestablish its presence. The most dramatic illustration of this persistent Iranian attitude is the successful efforts of the sixteenth-century Safavid king, Shah Abbas, to retake Bandar Abbas (then named Gombrun) from the Portuguese. Later, in the late eighteenth century, when, after a period of turmoil following the fall of the Safavids, Nader Shah Afshar stabilised Iran and restored its borders, he turned his attention to the Gulf and tried to build a viable naval force.[4] These efforts, however, were interrupted by his death. The next two hundred years saw Iran at the mercy of expanding European powers – Russia in the North and East, a British maritime empire in the South.

The period of British supremacy in the Gulf witnessed the most dramatic and, as it was proved later, irreversible decline in Iran's presence in the Gulf. British policy aimed not only at eliminating any remnants of Iran's military and political presence in the Gulf, but also to eliminate its cultural influence.[5]

Historically, Iran's interaction with the Gulf region was not limited to political, economic, or military spheres. Rather, human and cultural interaction have always been very important. Iranian communities have existed in other parts of the Gulf since pre-Islamic times and are not solely the creation of recent migrations. Yet the trend in the last two hundred years has been one of steady decline of Iran's cultural presence in the region.

However, as with other aspects of Iran's interaction with the Gulf region, the Iranians have never accepted this situation as the natural state of affairs.

British supremacy in the Gulf also resulted in its encroachment on Iran's southern provinces and the gradual loss of effective control of Iran's central government over these regions. Moreover, the British used their naval supremacy in the Gulf to pressure Iran in relation to other issues.

The psychological legacy of this experience for Iran has been feelings of extreme vulnerability to threats emanating from its southern shores as a result of the presence of outside military forces in the region.

Thus the Shah's – and the current regime's – policy that the security of the Gulf should be the responsibility of the riparian states, and opposition to the presence of outside forces in the region are derived from this experience. Obviously, the fact that in the absence of foreign forces, Iran as the largest country would have a dominant influence in the region has not escaped the attention of its leaders. However, the element of fear of outside pressure and feelings of insecurity on Iran's part should not be underestimated.

Another legacy of this experience has been a deep-rooted belief on the part of the Iranians that Iran must have a strong naval force. Iran's inability to adequately defend its shores and other interests in the Gulf has always been blamed on its lack of naval power. The following statement by Moshir-ed-Dowleh, the nineteenth-century Iranian prime minister, in answer to a complaint by Iran's ambassador to the Ottoman Court regarding the latter's designs in the Persian Gulf at Iran's expense, clearly illustrates this belief:

The right you are talking about is based on equity and justice and does not exist in the world. As I have told you before, the maintenance or restoration of rights depends on power *and military and naval force* [emphasis added]. Knowing Iran's naval weakness, today Medhat Pasha is infringing on our rights. Tomorrow the Sheikh of Kuwait or Emir of Muscat will have the same ambitions.[6]

Nevertheless, it would be a mistake to assume that only the negative aspects of Iran's historical experience have affected its perceptions of this region. On the contrary, memories of periods when Iran has had an important, if not dominant, influence in the Gulf, and those times when it had succeeded in restoring its presence, have had a lasting impact on its perceptions of its place and role in the Gulf. In fact, most Iranians view the latter as more in the natural order of things, and the first situation as the result of actions by foreign enemies, or the inadequacies of their national leaders.

From the Iranian perspective, it was only natural that the Shah, who saw himself as the restorer of Iran's strength and unity, should also try to build a viable naval force, and to assert Iran's presence in the Gulf. Thus, rather than viewing this as evidence of Iran's hegemonist intentions, the Shah saw himself as following an old Iranian tradition of restoring Iran's presence in the Gulf after a period of decline and retrenchment.

The advent of the Islamic Revolution, despite appearances, has not drastically altered these deep-rooted views and perceptions regarding the Gulf. Indeed, nowhere has the continuity in the Iranians' underlying attitudes and perceptions in the pre- and post-revolutionary periods been greater than in regard to the Gulf. The statements by the military and political leaders of Islamic Iran bear striking resemblance to those of the Shah, as illustrated by the following. Note, for example, the remarks by the commander of the Iranian navy which were provoked by the visit of the commander of the US Rapid Deployment Force to the Gulf Arab states:

The Islamic Republic of Iran has repeatedly said that maintaining security in the Persian Gulf is the responsibility of the countries of the region . . .

As the strongest country in the region, Iran is determined to safeguard the region's security with all its might, just as we have defended the security of the Persian Gulf waters especially the strategic strait of Hormuz.[7]

The speaker of Iran's parliament, Ali-Akbar Hashemi Rafsanjani, echoes the same sentiment when he says that the security of the Gulf

has been 'the responsibility of our valiant and courageous navy'.[8]
What the above imply is that Iranian views of the Gulf and its
importance to Iran's security and economic interests, as well as the
legitimacy of Iran's claim to an important, if not dominant, presence
in the Gulf commensurate to its size and population are very deeply
rooted and are not easily altered even by strong ideological shifts. To
have the legitimacy of this presence acknowledged by the Arab states
has been, and continues to be, an important aspect of Iran's policy in
the Gulf.

IRAN AND THE ARAB WORLD: IMPACT ON IRAN–GULF RELATIONS

As noted earlier, an understanding of the dynamics of Iran's relations
with the Gulf Arabs is not possible without placing them within the
context of Iran's relations with the Arab world in general, for the
following reasons. First, certain underlying factors which have traditionally determined the state of Iran's relations with the Arab world
in general also affect its relations with the Gulf Arabs. Second,
dynamics of intra-Arab politics affect Iran–Gulf Arab relations by
often limiting the extent to which the Gulf Arabs could befriend Iran.
This is also in part because of the very nature of these countries which
are small, rich, and of heterogeneous ethno-religious make-up, and
thus vulnerable to a wide range of pressures from stronger Arab
states or radical forces in the Arab world.

Over the last forty years that Iran and the Arab countries have
been interacting as independent states, the following factors have
largely determined the state of their relations.

Ethno-religious differences

Ethno-religious differences have always coloured Arab-Iranian relations, although their policy impact has either been mitigated or
reinforced by other factors.

These differences are rooted in the Arab defeat of Iran in the
seventh century AD. Although conquered militarily and politically,
Iran was not assimilated in the Arab-Islamic empire and it retained a
high degree of cultural and ethno-linguistic distinctiveness. Iran's
Islamisation, instead of bringing the Arabs and the Iranians closer

together, drew them further apart since Iran embraced Shiahism which is considered heretical by the Sunni Arabs, some of whom perceive it as 'an Iranian conspiracy against Islam'. Moreover, since Islam was first revealed to the Arabs, they believe that they have a special status within the Islamic world. Since the Iranians have also had a more or less similar view of their own place within the Islamic community, religion has become a dividing rather than a unifying factor in Arab-Iranian relations.[9] The divisive impact of ethno-religious differences on Arab-Iranian relations has traditionally been exacerbated by cultural competition between the Iranians and the Arabs within the context of the Islamic civilisation. The Arabs' proprietary attitude toward Islam's cultural legacy including the part contributed by non-Arabs has been a particular bone of contention in view of Iran's significant role in this regard.[10]

These differences, in turn, have created a psychological barrier for cooperation between the Arabs and the Iraninians. For example, over the years most Arab states, including those in the Gulf, have found it more difficult to accept, let alone request, Iranian assistance, at least in an open manner. The Shah was rebuffed by Kuwait when he offered support against the Iraqi attack on Kuwait in 1972. He was also attacked by other Arabs when he tried to help Sultan Qabus against the Dhofari rebels at the Sultan's request, even though the Arab states could not offer Oman a viable alternative to Iranian aid. By contrast, the Saudis, until recently, have had little difficulty accepting Pakistan's military contribution to their security.[11]

Similarly, Iran's *de facto* relations with Israel became a major cause of Arab animosity and even subversion against Iran. Yet Turkey, which recognised Israel *de jure* and established full diplomatic relations with it, has received much less blame and criticism. The Gulf Arab states have also found it very difficult to enter into any kind of security, or other formal cooperative, arrangement with Iran.

The divisive impact of ethno-religious differences has also been felt in the post-revolutionary period, since ethnic particularism and nationalism have remained strong forces both in Islamic Iran and in the Arab world.

Iran's revolutionary leaders have espoused a universalist Islamic ideology which transcends, at least in theory, ethnic and sectarian divisions. In Iran, the Islamic regime has embarked on a systematic campaign against the so-called nationalist tendencies (Meligarai), and has consistently denigrated Iran's pre-Islamic culture.

However, both Iran's efforts to eliminate nationalist tendencies and to portray itself as a universalist Islamic power have been only marginally successful. Internally, the popular reaction to the most extreme aspects of the regime's anti-nationalist campaign has been negative.[12] This, in turn, has forced the regime to somewhat relent on its campaign. Moreover, after the start of the Iran–Iraq war, the regime has found it necessary to appeal to nationalist feelings as well as to Shiah Muslim symbols in order to gain popular support. Thus the regime has increasingly acquired an Iranian Shiah, rather than a universalist Islamic, character.

Consequently, Islamic revolution in Iran, rather than eliminating sectarian-based friction between the Arabs and the Iranians, has in some ways exacerbated them. This has been particularly true in the Gulf region where Shiah activism encouraged by Iran has increased animosity between the two communities.[13]

In the Arab world as well, ethnic particularism and nationalist tendencies have remained strong despite the growing appeal of Islam. As a result, while Iran's emphasis on Islamic brotherhood and unity, and downplaying of Iranian nationalism have appealed to some Arabs, the persistence of Arab nationalism has limited Iran's ability to reach significant segments of Arab populations. Indeed, Iran's opponents in the Arab world have used Arab nationalism to harness support for themselves against Iran. Iraq, in particular, has resorted to this factor and has consistently portrayed its war against Iran as the defence of 'Arabism against the racist, fire-worshipping Persians'.

Competing nationalisms

The underlying ethno-religious differences and rivalries in Arab-Iranian relations acquired concrete political dimensions with the rise of modern nationalism after the Second World War, both in Iran and in the Arab world. For more than thirty years, the Gulf has been the battleground for competition between Arab and Iranian nationalisms although, since the Islamic revolution, Iranian aspirations in the Gulf are not gauged in nationalist terms. The rise of nationalism in Iran meant that the Iranians would pursue with greater vigour a policy of restoring Iran's presence in the Gulf.

Arab nationalism, in turn, became highly focused on the Gulf, given the fact that foreign presence on the Arab side of the Gulf lasted longer than in other parts of the Arab world. The oil riches of the Gulf Arabs were also viewed by the Arab nationalists as belonging to the so-called Arab nation, and were the Arabs' main hope for achieving socioeconomic development.[14] From the Iranian perspective, however, it was the expansionist and exclusivist aspects of Arab nationalist ideology as expounded by Jamal Abdul Nasser and later the Ba'athists which was threatening to its interests.

For example, one of Nasser's aspirations was to create what he called a united Arab nation stretching from the Atlantic to the Gulf. Egypt, followed by other Arab nationalists, embarked on an extensive campaign to change the Persian Gulf's historic name into the [Arabian] Gulf.[15] During the 1960s, Egypt launched an extensive campaign against Iranian communities on the Arab side of the Gulf. It also attacked Iranian immigration to the Arab side of the Gulf and accused Iran of wanting to create 'another Palestine' in the Gulf, and tried to prevent Iran's economic interaction with the Gulf Arabs.[16]

Needless to say, these actions prompted Iran to take measures in defence of its interests, including pointing to its good intentions and Egypt's less than noble ambitions in regard to the Gulf Arabs.[17]

The Gulf Arab states, for reasons of geographical proximity and the inevitability of Iran's physical presence, have generally been more willing to strike some kind of *modus vivendi* with Iran and, at times, they have even cooperated with it. But the impact of Arab nationalist ethos have complicated their relations with Iran for the following reasons. First, the Gulf Arabs themselves ascribe to certain basic tenets of Arab nationalism, including the Arabism of the Gulf. Moreover, given the influence of Arab nationalist ethos among Arab populations, no Arab government can afford to at least not pay lip service to nationalist goals without rendering itself vulnerable to charges of treason against the Arab nation, and thus providing its enemies with ammunition to justify their subversive and other inimical actions against it.

Over the last forty years, the Gulf Arab states, with their vast resources, large non-indigenous populations, limited military capabilities, and conservative political leadership, have been particularly vulnerable to these pressures.

Another significant tenet of Arab nationalism has been the economic and political integration of the so-called Arab nation. While this is a perfectly legitimate aspiration, in the Gulf it has meant the effective exclusion of Iran from regional groupings. During the 1960s and 1970s Iran's proposals for regional security arrangements were refused by the Arabs. Iran, for its part, has looked with disfavour at exclusively Arab groupings, and has viewed such exclusively Arab groupings as a threat to its legitimate presence in the Gulf.

The advent of the Islamic revolution has not changed Iran's basic perceptions of the importance of the Gulf and its interests in the region. Despite official denigration of the so-called nationalist tendencies, Iran has followed a nationalist policy in the Gulf. In fact, the new Iranian regime is as sensitive to the maintenance of the historic name of this body of water as was the Shah's regime. The Iranians are also still suspicious of exclusively Arab groupings in the Gulf, and perceive this as an essentially anti-Iranian force. Iran's view of the Gulf Cooperation Council (GCC) reflects this deep-rooted perception.

Territorial disputes

It is impossible to understand Arab-Iranian relations in the past, as in the present, without adequately taking into account the territorial disputes which have opposed them to one another. The most important of these disputes have been the long-standing Arab claim to Khuzistan and Iran's historic claim to Bahrain. The discussion of the historical or legal validity of these claims and counterclaims is beyond the scope of this Chapter. What we are concerned with here is their practical impact in shaping Arab-Iranian relations.

The Bahrain dispute was settled in 1970 when Iran gave up its claims to the island. However, as Iran's alleged support for a coup in Bahrain in 1981 illustrates, many Iranians have not yet quite come to terms with the loss of Bahrain. They feel that, at least, Iran should have had a strong presence there. Iran's lack of influence in Bahrain is a particularly sore issue when compared to the dominant Saudi presence in that country. In fact, Bahrain, particularly after the completion of the causeway linking it to Saudi Arabia, has become a Saudi appendage in all but name.[18] Another Iranian complaint in this regard is that the Arabs regarded Iran's relinquishing of its claim as a vindication of Arab rights, and not only did not show any appreciation for this conciliatory gesture, they interpreted Iran's assertion of its other rights as evidence of its hegemonic intentions. The Arab claim to Khuzistan, however, has really never been clearly settled. Of course the Arab governments have legally recognised Iran and have established diplomatic relations with it, an act which has implied their recognition of Iran's legal borders. However, in practice, the Arab countries – including those friendly to Iran – have kept their claim toward Khuzistan alive.

For example, while during the Shah's time Jordan maintained close relations with Iran, Jordanian maps and schoolbooks showed Khuzistan as part of the Arab world. Naturally, Arab governments hostile to Iran have used the Khuzistan issue to justify their anti-Iranian attitudes or actively subvert the Iranian regime. For example, during the 1970s the Iraqis established and used the so-called 'Front For the Liberation of Ahwaz' as part of their anti-Iranian strategy. The Front is still active in Baghdad.[19]

But the most dramatic example of the impact of territorial disputes on Arab-Iranian relations has been the Iraqi invasion of Iran on 22 September 1980. No doubt a variety of reasons contributed to Iraq's decision to invade Iran. But the desire to vindicate the Arab claim to Khuzistan was one of the most powerful causes of Iraq's action, as will be discussed later.

Similarly, despite some apprehension over growing Iraqi power, during the early days of the war many Gulf Arabs were happy about the so-called liberation of Khuzistan.

Other territorial disputes affecting Arab-Iranian relations are the Arab claim to the three Gulf islands of Abu Musa and the Greater and Lesser Tumb and Iraq's claim to total sovereignty over the Shat-al-Arab (Arvand Rud). However, although territorial disputes – particularly the Arab claim to Khuzistan – constitute a significant underlying irritant in Arab-Iranian relations, they have not been the determining factors in shaping these relations. Whether or not they have been used actively by individual Arab governments against Iran, or they have been conveniently ignored, has depended on other factors and the overall state of Arab-Iranian relations.

Thus, for example, in 1971 Libya was in the forefront of Arab attacks against Iran's military takeover of the two disputed islands. However, since the revolution, Libya has not mentioned these two islands. Nevertheless, it is very significant that neither Libya nor Syria, currently Iran's closest allies, have renounced Arab claims either to Khuzistan or to the islands. By contrast, Jordan, which in the past had turned a blind eye to these issues, has made several references to Khuzistan's Arabness since the revolution. Despite these tactical shifts, however, latent territorial disputes, unless finally resolved, will remain a significant irritant in Arab-Iranian relations.

The impact of ideology

Important as the above factors have been, in the final analysis they have not determined the shape of Arab-Iranian relations. Of far more importance have been factors such as ideological affinity – or its lack – and the respective positions of Iran and the Arab countries toward the East–West conflict.

Over the last thirty years, ideological factors, including respective Arab-Iranian attitudes on the East–West conflict, have to a great extent determined the state of Arab-Iranian relations. Thus, during the Shah's rule, given Iran's anti-Communist ideology and its alliance with the United States, it maintained essentially cooperative relations with those Arab countries that shared its anti-Communist and pro-Western stands. By contrast, during this period Iran's relations with those Arab countries and groups which, for a variety of reasons, adopted a pro-Soviet stand and advocated revolutionary change – as was the case with Nasser's Egypt, Syria, Iraq, and the PLO – were highly strained.

Nevertheless, ideological affinity has not always been enough for harmonious and fully cooperative Arab-Iranian relations. On the contrary, the divisive factors discussed earlier, plus competition for power, have continued to exert a powerful influence in determining the nature of Arab-Iranian relations. However, shared ideological preferences and common positions *vis-à-vis* the East–West conflict have often created enough incentive for both sides to gloss over other differences. For example, while both Iran and Iraq were ruled by monarchies, and especially after both of them became members of a US-sponsored defence pact (the Baghdad Pact, later renamed the Central Treaty Organisation), they maintained friendly relations and began a determined effort to resolve their disputes. The nature of Iraqi-Iranian relations changed drastically after the 1958 revolution in Iraq and later, the Ba'athist takeover and adoption by Iraq of a pro-Soviet stand.

Similarly, Egyptian-Iranian relations were extremely tense while Nasser was in power, but the shift in Egypt's attitude in a pro-West and pro-status quo direction under Sadat brought Egypt and Iran closer together. The shift in the pattern of Arab-Iranian relations since the Islamic revolution demonstrates the continued importance of the ideological factor, especially respective positions on the East–West conflict and the inherent conflict between the forces of change and those of status quo.

In view of the shift in Iran's position from that of a US ally to a staunchly anti-American position, as well as Iran's advocacy of revolutionary change, the pattern of its relations in the Arab world has also been altered. Thus, currently, Iran has friendly relations with Syria, Libya, Algeria, and South Yemen, while its relations with the rest of the Arab countries are strained. There are, however, certain differences between the current situation and that of the Shah's time.

For example, what today links Iran's Islamic regime to Syria and Libya is their common anti-Americanism rather than their common liking for the USSR. In fact, although the Islamic regime has maintained reasonable relations with the Soviet Union, it cannot exactly be characterised as pro-Soviet. During the Shah's rule, however, in addition to common friendship with the United States, shared animosity toward the USSR largely tied Iran to the conservative Arab regimes.

The other distinction between the present and the past is that in the past there was a higher degree of commonality of view between Iran and the conservative Arab governments – many of which are monarchies like Iran under the Shah – regarding the structure of their domestic societies. By contrast, Iran currently has deep ideological differences with its Arab allies as far as the structure of their respective societies is concerned.

For example, the ideology of Iran's Islamic Republic based on a revolutionary interpretation of Islam and that of the Ba'athist Syria based on a blend of secular socialism and extreme Arab nationalism are totally incompatible.

Similarly, the Ayatollah Khomeini's brand of revolutionary Islam and that of Libya's Muammar Qaddafi are completely different. Nevertheless, the by and large common views of Islamic Iran and its Arab friends in regard to regional and global issues, and especially their common animosity toward the United States, have been enough to bring them together, albeit in an uneasy alliance.

Similarly, the Gulf Arabs' close ties with the United States has been one of the reasons for strained relations with Iran. As the Shah in the past was perceived as a US client and thus abhorred by Arab radicals, the current Iranian regime perceives the Gulf Arab governments as agents of the United States.

In fact, currently, as in the past, the impact of these factors on the state of Arab-Iranian relations has been so strong that it has even submerged issues such as Iran's attitude *vis-à-vis* Israel, territorial disputes, and difficulties arising from clashing nationalisms. For example, prior to the Shah's fall, Iran's relations with Israel, though a serious irritant, were not an insurmountable obstacle for its friendly relations with like-minded Arab countries. Nor have Iran's militant anti-Israel policies in the post-revolutionary period been enough to ensure good relations with conservative Arab regimes.

On the contrary, these countries have emphasised the fact of Iran's willingness to obtain arms in the black market through the intermediary of Israeli arms dealers as evidence of continued cooperation between Iran and Israel and proof of Iran's enmity toward the Arabs. Needless to say that this view ignores the fact that if Iran was forced to buy arms from Israel, it was because Iraq, an Arab country, had invaded Iran.

SYSTEMIC FACTORS

In the last thirty years, the nature of Arab-Iranian relations has been greatly influenced by changes which have taken place in the international political system, and more importantly, in the Middle East regional subsystem. These systemic changes have dramatically increased the level of Arab-Iranian interaction, thus profoundly affecting the nature of their relations.

Of all the systemic changes, as far as Arab-Iranian relations are concerned, the most significant has been the total integration of the Arab side of the Gulf into the rest of the Arab world. This process, which began in the mid-1950s and has since steadily accelerated, was partly due to the shift of Arab nationalist focus to the Gulf, leading to the active involvement of Arab nationalists in Gulf politics during the 1960s and the 1970s.

For the larger part of the 1960s and the 1970s, the Arab nationalists and other radical Arabs viewed the Gulf as a bastion of Western influence and the Gulf regimes, both Arab and Iranian, as the instruments of Western policy. The Arab radicals also believed that Western domination of the Gulf had deprived the Arabs of their most valuable resource – oil – whose revenues should have been used for the Arabs' economic and social development.[20] Thus, the elimination of Western influence from the Gulf became a primary objective of Arab radicals. And since they viewed the Gulf governments as the West's clients, they considered a change in the nature of these governments as a necessary part of their regional strategy.

Nasser's intervention in the Yemeni civil war and Iraq's assistance to the 'Front for the Liberation of Oman and the Occupied Arab Gulf' were some of the practical consequences of this approach by Arab nationalists.

Given the radicals' frame of reference, Iran, the largest Gulf country and a member of a Western-sponsored alliance, became relevant to the calculations of Arab radicals. The Arab radicals viewed Iran as an obstacle to the realisation of their objectives, and thus a change in its leadership was seen as equally necessary.

Iran, for its part, viewed the Arab radicals as a serious threat to its security and that of the region, and tried to combat their influence. Thus during the 1960s, the Gulf became an arena of Egyptian-Iranian conflict. The underlying conflict between the Arab radicals and conservatives greatly impacted Arab-Iranian relations in the Gulf with an alliance emerging between Iran and Saudi Arabia against Nasser's Egypt. The net result of these developments was a greater linkage between events in the Gulf and the rest of the Middle East, and an increase in the level of Arab-Iranian interaction.

The process of regional linkage was accelerated by the events of the late 1960s and especially after the 1973 war and the ensuing oil shock.

First, the 1967 Arab-Israeli war shifted the intra-Arab balance of power against the radicals by reducing Egypt's influence and its ability to use military force in pursuit of its objectives. Parallel with this development, the financial position of a number of conservative Arab regimes, such as Saudi Arabia and Kuwait, was improved due to changes in the energy markets and in the producer-country/oil company relation.

The result was an increase in the political power of conservative Gulf Arabs, their greater involvement in the management of conflict with Israel, and thus, the further integration of the Gulf into the rest of the Arab world.[21]

The oil-generated development in the Gulf Arab countries which led to a massive influx of Palestinian and other Arabs to the Gulf states further increased the interaction between the Gulf and other Arab states, and contributed to the integration of the Gulf into the rest of the Middle East.

Meanwhile, improvements in Iran's military and economic conditions had led to an expansion of its regional and international relations, and had increased its regional significance, thus making it even more relevant to intra-Arab politics. Britain's decision in 1968 to withdraw from the Gulf by 1971 and Iran's assumption of aspects of Britain's old role in the region made it the principal force for the maintenance of the status quo and the protector of Western interests in the Gulf region, and thus, an even greater factor in intra-Arab calculations.

The twin process of greater intra-regional linkage and Iranian involvement in Arab politics accelerated after the 1973 oil revolution. Enriched by its oil wealth, Iran adopted a very activist foreign policy in the Middle East through the use of financial aid and military power.

Iran assisted Egypt financially – which contributed, albeit to a much lesser extent than Saudi and Gulf assistance, to Sadat's ability to move toward the United States and the West and to negotiate with Israel. It also intervened militarily in Oman in defence of Sultan Qabus against the leftist Dhofari rebels.

In general, Iran tried to create and maintain a regional environment congenial to its own interests and those of the West and its conservative Arab allies. As a result, the radical Arabs came to see Iran as an even greater obstacle to the realisation of their regional objectives, and they intensified their subversion against Iran. Libya and Iraq financed Iranian opposition groups and many of the Iranian opposition groups were trained in Palestinian camps in Lebanon.[22]

Since the Islamic revolution, Iran's interaction with the Arab world intensified and acquired a new popular dimension. Iran's anti-Israel policy, its anti-Zionist, imperialist rhetoric, its emphasis on Islamic brotherhood, its downplaying of Persian nationalism, and its encouragement of the use of Arabic has enabled it to reach Arab masses to a large degree. This factor indeed has been the main cause of Arab anxieties, particularly in the Gulf, which fear the contamination of their societies by Iran's revolutionary ideology.

However, the essence of Iran's foreign policy in the Gulf and the Middle East has remained the same although its manifestations have obviously changed. Even today Iran wants to safeguard its shores in the Gulf, to maintain an adequate economic, commercial, and political presence on the Arab side of the Gulf, and to create a regional environment congenial to its interests, or at least non-hostile to them. This, however, now means reducing Western influence in the Gulf and trying to establish like-minded regimes in the Gulf and the rest of the Middle East. These policies have brought Iran into conflict with conservative Arab regimes and closer to the radical forces, especially Islamic militants. As a result, while Iran is now encouraging radical forces and anti-regime elements within conservative Arab countries, it has itself become the target of subversion by conservative regimes who are now helping and financing its opposition groups.

INTRA-ARAB POLITICS: IMPACT ON ARAB-IRANIAN RELATIONS

Systemic changes discussed above have made Arab-Iranian relations vulnerable to the ebb and flow of intra-Arab relations, particularly its ever-shifting alliances and enmities.

The impact of Arab nationalist ethos on Arab-Iranian relations was discussed earlier. Of more practical consequence for the state of Arab-Iranian relations has been the divided nature of the Arab world along ideological and other lines, and deep-rooted rivalries among Arab states for prestige and the Arab world's leadership. In fact, this aspect of intra-Arab politics, together with the ideological factors has, in the final analysis, determined the state of Arab-Iranian relations.

In the last thirty years, Iran, although on the periphery of the Arab world, has, because of systemic changes, become far more relevant to intra-Arab politics. The Arab states have used Iran to affact intra-Arab balance in their own favour. Iran, for its part, has used tactical alliances with Arab countries to create a regional environment more congenial to its own interests. Thus, for example, during the Shah's time, Iraq's cooperation with Iran within the framework of the Baghdad Pact was in part because of Egyptian-Iraqi rivalry for the Arab world's leadership.

Similarly, Saudi Arabia cooperated with Iran to limit Nasser's influence in the Gulf and the rest of the Middle East. In fact, one of the Middle East's oddest couplings occurred when the Shah of Iran and King Faisal of Saudi Arabia joined hands to form the Islamic Conference and used Islam to combat Nasser's Arab nationalism and socialism. In the 1970s as well, Saudi Arabia and Iran pursued more or less parallel policies in the Middle East as far as helping the conservative Arab regimes were concerned. But this did not lessen their competition for power in the Gulf. In fact, Saudi Arabia tried to limit Iran's influence in Bahrain, Oman, and the United Arab Emirates. In the UAE, the Saudis used their influence with Abu Dhabi to check Iran, while Iran used the rivalry between Abu Dhabi and Dubai to maintain its presence and influence there.[23]

The result of Iran's tactical alliances with conservative Arab countries during the 1970s was the heightened animosity of Arab radicals which by manipulating factors discussed earlier, plus active subversion, tried to limit Iran's influence in the Gulf and elsewhere in the Middle East.

This basic situation has not changed since the Islamic revolution, although Iran's partners in the Arab world have changed. For example, Syria's alliance with Iran is essentially prompted because of its rivalry with Iraq. Since the 1982 Israeli invasion of Lebanon and the introduction of an Iranian presence into Lebanon, the Syrians used Iran to check Israeli and PLO influence in Lebanon, and to extend their own control. The Syrians and the Libyans also used Iran in order to somewhat strengthen the position of the so-called rejectionist Arab front within the context of the Arab-Israeli conflict.

Similarly, they have found the Gulf Arabs' preoccupation with Iran convenient since this prevents them from putting pressure on Syria on matters related to the Arab-Israeli conflict. However, the Syrians have not helped Iran expand its influence in the Gulf. Rather, they have made it clear to Iran that they oppose any Iranian military actions against the Gulf countries. The Syrians do not even want to see Iran win the war against Iraq since this would shift the regional balance far too much in Iran's favour. Rather, what they want is to use Iran to topple Saddam Hussein's regime and to establish a pro-Syrian Ba'athist regime in Iraq which would serve Syria's regional goals. Nor do they want to see Iran expand its influence in Lebanon, and they have, in fact, actively sought to limit Iranian influence there. Moreover, in the event of Saddam's fall, present Syrian-Iranian cooperation will inevitably turn into acute rivalry over the future leadership of Iraq.[24]

Similarly, Egypt and conservative Arab regimes have used the pretext of an Iranian threat to bring Egypt back into the Arab world. These countries have argued that the Arab world needs Egypt as a counterweight to Iran. This indeed was the dominant theme of the Arab summit held in Amman in November 1987.[25]

THE EVOLUTION OF IRAN–GULF RELATIONS IN THE POST-REVOLUTION PERIOD

The foregoing has illustrated that Iran's basic perceptions of the importance of the Gulf to its security and economic well-being, and its own role and place in the region have over the years remained remarkably constant.

It has also illustrated that, despite drastic changes in the pattern of Iran's friendships and enmities in the Arab world, as in the past, the same fundamental forces are still shaping Arab-Iranian relations. Therefore, the remainder of this chapter will focus on the evolution of Iran–Gulf relations since the revolution within this general framework, and in light of the evolution of Iran's domestic political scene.

Since the revolution, like any other aspect of Iran's foregin policy, Iran–Gulf relations should be looked upon within the context of two distinct periods: the period from February 1979 until September 1980 when Iraq attacked Iran – an event which contributed to the final defeat of secular forces; and the period since September 1980.

During the first period, Iran's political scene was characterised by a duality of power centres and the weakness of official government. Consequently, Iran's policy *vis-à-vis* the Gulf, as indeed with regard to other aspects of its foreign and domestic policies, was carried out at two levels: at the level of the official government and at the level of a variety of revolutionary committees, personalities, and groupings which had mushroomed in post-revolutionary Iran.

The government of Mehdi Bazargan, and to a great extent the government of President Bani-Sadr, subscribed to a nationalist, non-aligned foreign policy stressing Iran's independence from both superpowers and advocating the maintenance of reasonable relations with all countries, and especially with Iran's neighbours.

In the Gulf, this meant a reversal of Iran's policy under the Shah, which was viewed by many Iranians as serving Western, especially American, interests rather than those of Iran. In fact, shift in policy in this regard had already taken place before the total collapse of the Shah's regime. And the Shah's last prime minister, Shahpour Bakht-iar, had said that Iran would no longer play the role of the policeman of the Gulf. This change in Iran's policy was welcome news to the Gulf Arabs, who were also pleased by the shift in Iran's policy toward Israel. In their most optimistic moments, the Gulf Arabs even expected that Iran would return to Arab sovereignty the three islands of Abu-Musa and the Greater and Lesser Tumbs. However, this expectation was more representative of Arab wishful thinking than of Iranian realities.

As it would transpire clearly later, opposition to the Shah's Gulf policy was not due to any doubts regarding the legitimacy of Iranian claims, or to any questioning of the necessity for Iran to play a central role in the Gulf. Rather, the opposition related to Iran performing this role on behalf of Western interests. Beyond this fundamental change, as long as the Bazargan government lasted, and even to some extent under Bani-Sadr, Iran's official policy toward the Gulf Arabs was one of neighbourly coexistence. This basic policy orientation even applied to relations with Iraq.[26]

However, the official aspect of Iran's foreign policy represented only part of the whole picture. Bazargan and his colleagues, and even to a great extent Bani-Sadr and other secular figures in Khomeini's entourage such as Sadeq Qotbszadeh, ascribed to a nationalist, non-aligned, and pragmatic foreign policy.

The Islamic revolutionary forces, by contrast, saw the spread of Islamic revolution as the main goal of Iran's foreign policy. Thus, parallel with waging a campaign internally against secular forces, they also embarked on their own foreign policy, trying to stir up Islamic movements in the Gulf states.

A number of clerical figures became particularly active in this regard and created difficulties in Iran's relations with the Gulf states. For example, an Iranian cleric named Ayatullah Sadiq Ruhani created an uproar when he said that he would lead a movement to annex Bahrain unless its rulers adopted an Islamic form of government similar to that of Iran.[27]

This statement, while expressed in religious terms, in fact reflected the Iranians' unhappiness with the Shah's decision to relinquish Iran's historic claim to Bahrain. The Iranian government, however, was quick to reassure Bahrain and other Gulf states of its intentions. To ease Bahrain's anxieties, Bazargan sent a special envoy to that country and other Gulf states, and reassured them of Iranian intentions. Since then, none of the Iranian officials, within or without the government, have repeated such views. Rather, they have stressed that Iran does not have any territorial claims on any of the Gulf states. Yet the Gulf states have generally ignored Iran's official assurances and actual behaviour. Few other clerics such as Hodjat-al-Islam Hadi Mudarisi and Hodjat-al-Islam Muhri in Bahrain and Kuwait in their speeches and sermons advocated the creation of Islamic governments. Most Gulf states attributed the outbreak of Shiah disturbances in their countries to these and other Iranian instigations.

No doubt, these activities encouraged the Gulf Shiahs to express their pent-up resentments. But more than Iranian words or actions, it was the example of Iran and what was perceived to be the victory of a revolutionary brand of Islam which inspired the Gulf Shiahs. And ultimately it is this subversion by example that is the real cause of concern for the Gulf Arabs rather than any specific act of sabotage by Iran. This is so because of the specific socio-political conditions of these countries, and especially the position of the Shiahs within their societies.

A detailed discussion of the Gulf states' Shiah problems is beyond the scope of this chapter. Suffice it to say that the Gulf Shiahs have deep-rooted and legitimate social, economic, and political grievances against their governments. Some of the Gulf states such as Bahrain have had a long history of Shiah unrest. Moreover, some of the Shiah protest in the early 1980s in the Gulf was prompted by the Iraqi government's arrest and execution of that country's foremost Shiah leader, Imam Muhammad Baqir al-Sadr, and was unrelated to any Iranian instigation.

In short, given the depth of Shiah grievances, it was inevitable that sooner or later they would come to the fore. Moreover, greater Shiah activism in the Gulf should be seen as part of the broader and growing Shiah consciousness as manifested by the Shiah movement in Iraq and Lebanon, a development which long preceded the Iranian revolution, although the latter intensified it and accelerated its course. Given this state of affairs, the Iranians have resented the accusation that they are at the source of the Gulf States' Shiah problems. Admittedly, Iran's insistence on revolutionary propaganda, which they view as a religious duty deriving from the Quranic injuction of 'Amr Bi'l Ma'ruf va Nahy Men al Munkar' (enjoining to good and warning from evil) has exacerbated the Gulf States' problems. But this must also be seen against Arab propaganda and acts of subversion against Iran.

In this respect, Iraq was the main culprit. For example, as early as 1979, the Iraqis were subverting Khuzistan's Arab minorities and distributing arms among them. The Iraqis were also encouraging and assisting Iranian opposition abroad. For example, many observers have maintained that faulty advice by some Iranian exiles regarding Iran's internal conditions contributed to Saddam Hussein's decision to invade Iran. Of course, it could rightly be argued that the Gulf Arabs should not be held responsible for Saddam's actions.

However, the fact also remains that, for a number of reasons related to the dynamics of intra-Arab relations, during the period between 1979 and 1981, the Gulf Arabs basically followed the Iraqi line in regional matters and did not do much to dissuade Saddam from attacking Iran, and after he did so they supported him.

The most important reason was that Egypt's isolation following its peace treaty with Israel, and Syria's growing sense of vulnerability *vis-à-vis* Israel following the Egyptian-Israeli peace treaty, had left Iraq as the dominant force in the Middle East. And Iraq, seizing this opportunity, was trying to impose its leadership on the rest of the Arab world. For example, Iraq organised the two Baghdad summits aimed at harnessing Arab opposition to Egypt, and initiated a so-called Arab charter. Given Iraq's proximity to the Gulf states and its military superiority and extreme nationalist ideology, combined with the Gulf Arabs' inherent vulnerabilities, they could not have challenged Iraq.

However, there was more than just the element of fear in the Gulf Arabs' support for Iraq. The Gulf Arabs shared Iraqi sentiments *vis-à-vis* Khuzistan, and although they may not have been happy with Iraq becoming the dominant force in the Gulf, they welcomed the idea of the so-called liberation of Khuzistan. There was in the Gulf a sense of jubilation – albeit mixed with apprehension – when Iraqi troops moved into Iran and initially seemed to be winning the war.

In addition, the Iranians have claimed that some Arab Gulf states such as Kuwait have been financing some Iranian opposition.[28]

The above observations prove the point that Iran's relations with the Gulf Arabs cannot be analysed outside the context of intra-Arab politics and Iran's relations with the Arab world as a whole. The Gulf Arabs did not initiate the military attack against Iran, nor did they encourage Iraq to invade Iran. But neither did they do anything to dissuade Iraq. Later, when Iraq began to falter, the Gulf Arabs actively supported it through financial assistance and by allowing the use of their territory for the transport of war material to Iraq, and for Iraqi attacks against Iranian targets. In this sense, they themselves became part of the broader Arab threat to Iran's security.

It is, however, important to note that not all of the Gulf states have followed this line of policy. On the contrary, such Gulf states as Oman, Qatar, and the UAE have adopted a more neutral posture *vis-à-vis* the war and have consistently argued for a policy of keeping the channels of communication open to Iran. Consequently, they have maintained relatively friendly relations with Iran.

Nevertheless, there has been a steady Arabisation of the Iran–Iraq war in the sense that the Gulf Arabs have been financing Iraq's war effort, while Egypt, Jordan, and others have been contributing manpower and advisers. In the latest Arab Summit on November

1987, some Arab states were even advocating the development of a common Arab defence against Iran, or the activation of the 1950 Arab defence pact against Iran.[29]

THE IRAN–IRAQ WAR AND IRAN–GULF RELATIONS

The Islamic revolution, despite the Gulf Arabs' earlier expectations, created new tensions and difficulties in their relations with Iran. However, as long as the Bazargan government was in power, it tried its best to keep Iran–Gulf relations from deteriorating, and endeavoured to undo the damage done by the actions and statements of a number of revolutionary clerical figures as well as members of revolutionary committees which had mushroomed in Iran. Had Iran's internal evolution taken a different course and had the more moderate Islamo-nationalist elements retained their influence, Iran–Gulf relations might have settled into a reasonably stable and even friendly state.

However, this was not to be. Factors, mostly related to Iran's internal dynamics, and whose discussion is beyond the scope of this chapter, led to the elimination of the more secular, nationalist-oriented elements and the victory of the Islamic forces.

Given the fact that significant elements of Islamic forces favoured a more aggressive export of revolution, their ascendancy raised the level of tension in Iran–Gulf relations. However, it must be noted that not all Islamic elements favour aggressive export of revolution. On the contrary, a significant percentage of Islamic elements favour a more pragmatic and non-confrontational foreign policy, and insist that the export of revolution should be done peacefully and by the force of example, and through the propagation of ideas.[30]

The Iranian political scene in the last seven years has been deeply affected by the tension between these two tendencies. Seemingly inexplicable contradictions and changes in Iran's foreign policy reflect this underlying tension, as well as the relative shifting of power between the proponents of these tendencies. Understandably, Iran–Gulf relations have also been affected by this factor. However, since 1983, increasingly more pragmatic considerations have determined Iran's foreign policy. This more pragmatic line was sanctioned by the Ayatollah Khomeini himself in a famous speech in 1984 which ushered in Iran's so-called 'open door' foreign policy.

Iran's policy *vis-à-vis* the Gulf Arab states has been characterised by a far greater degree of restraint and pragmatism than is generally realised. This Iranian restraint becomes particularly significant if judged against the Iraqi invasion of Iran and the Gulf Arabs' financial and other support to Iraq.

As noted earlier, when the Gulf war first broke out with Iraq's invasion of Iran on 22 September 1980, the Gulf Arabs did nothing to dissuade Iraq. Moreover, as long as Iraq seemed to be winning the war, the Gulf Arabs, while apprehensive about growing Iraqi power, were happy about the prospects of a second Arab victory over Iran. After all, Saddam Hussein called this war against Iran the second Qadisiyah, the first being the historic Arab victory over Iran in the seventh century AD.

Much has been said about the element of fear in prompting Saddam Hussein to attack Iran. Yet, while fear played a role in Iraq's decision, it was Iraq's unbridled ambition and the power vacuum created by Iran's chaotic conditions and international isolation which led to the Iraqi attack. The following points will support this contention.

As far as the threat of military attack is concerned, in 1980, Iran, gripped by political chaos, and its military establishment seriously disrupted as a result of wide-ranging purges and desertions, was in no position to attack Iraq. As far as the contamination of Iraqi society by Iran's revolution is concerned, certainly the threat existed. But the threat was not of a magnitude to justify a full-scale invasion.

First, Iraq's Shiah problems and its Shiah movement started long before the Iranian revolution. Moreover, by September of 1980 the Iraqi regime had the movement effectively under control, largely through harsh measures including the arrest and execution of its leader Imam Muhammad Baqir-al-Sadr.[31] As far as the impact of the element of ambition and an irresistible urge to take advantage of seemingly unique circumstances on Iraq's decision is concerned, the evidence shows that they were stronger motives.

To fully understand this dimension, it is important to understand both the Ba'athist ideology and Saddam Hussein's personality, as well as statements made by him and actions taken by Iraq prior to its fateful decision to invade Iran.

The Ba'athist ideology as elaborated by its principal theoretician, Michel Aflaq, has extreme Arab nationalist dimensions. In fact, the ideas of a rebirth of the Arab nation, the restoration of its rights, and the achievement of its economic and political unity constitute the central themes of Ba'athism. Saddam Hussein subscribed to these ideas. Moreover, like other Arab leaders before him, such as Nasser, he sought prestige and influence for himself and his country through manipulating Arab nationalism.

Another important point to be noted is that many Arab nationalists, including many Ba'athists, equate Arabism with Islam and believe that the Arabs have a superior claim to Islam. In fact, Saddam Hussein betrayed this basic bias when in an interview he warned Iran's Islamic revolutionaries by stating that

the Islamic Revolution should be friendly to the Arab Revolution; any revolution that calls itself 'Islamic', but contradicts the Arab Revolution would not be Islamic at all.[32]

In short, Saddam Hussein, both for ideological reasons and by temperament, was committed to fulfilling what he saw as his Pan-Arab duties.

In 1979, a unique set of circumstances had created for Iraq a golden opportunity to settle old scores, assert its leadership in the Gulf and the Arab world, and to cut a larger profile in the Third World. These included the fall of the Shah, the isolation of Egypt as a result of the Camp David process, and the tremendous increase in Iraq's financial resources, as well as its military potential. Taking advantage of these circumstances, Iraq moved to establish itself as the leader of the Arab world and the dominant power in the Gulf.[33] In the Gulf, however, Iraq had to do away with Iran once and for all in order to become the undisputed leader.

Thus, Iraq more openly championed the cause of the so-called Arabs of 'Arabistan', the Arabs' name for Khuzistan. Saddam Hussein began sending arms to them, and he demanded the return of the three disputed islands of Abu-Musa and The Greater and Lesser Tumbs to Arab sovereignty. He tore up the Algiers agreement under the pretext that Iran had not lived up to its terms, and also that it was demeaning to Iraq, even though earlier Hussein had hailed the agreement as being in Iraq's interests.

More ominous from Iran's point of view, Hussein championed the cause of all of Iran's minorities, saying that Iraq's war aim was the restoration of the rights of Iran's oppressed minorities. Similarly, while he thought he was winning the war, Saddam Hussein made it clear that he had no intention of returning Iranian territories.

In an interview with the Baghdad radio on 12 November 1980, when Iraq seemed to be winning the war, Saddam Hussein said,

Those who are involved in the war should accept its consequences. Therefore, how can the people who have been defeated in the war be told to come and take back their homeland? How can you tell them now that we have defeated you, here you are, this (once again is a part of) your country?

The territory Saddam Hussein was talking about was of course Khuzistan.

In turn, the separation of Khuzistan, and the establishment of full sovereignty over the Shat-al-Arab would ensure Iraq's total dominance in the Gulf. In short, the threat Iraq posed to Iran was nothing short of that to its territorial integrity and national survival. And yet the Gulf Arabs – or other Arabs, for that matter – did not utter a word against this clear threat to Iran's national survival. Moreover, although worried about the prospect of Iraqi domination, they favoured what they saw as the restoration of Arab rights. It is, therefore, because of this underlying agreement in the Arabs' view of Iran that it was argued at the outset that Iran's relations with the Gulf Arabs cannot be separated from its relations with the rest of the Arab world.

Admittedly, the Arab states feared the spread of Iran's revolution. But at no time in recent Middle East history had a country been invaded because of its revolutionary ideology by its neighbour. Neither Egypt, Iraq, Syria, nor Libya had suffered Iran's fate, although they had, at different times, been at least as active as Iran in spreading their particular revolutionary message.

GULF ARAB ASSISTANCE TO IRAQ'S WAR EFFORT AND THE FORMATION OF THE GCC

Iraq's dream of a quick victory over Iran, however, did not materialise. The basic reason for this was that the Ba'athists had come to believe in their own propaganda and thus had seriously misread Iranian realities. For example, believing in the Arabness of Khuzistan, they expected an uprising by Arabic-speaking Iranians which did not occur.

Similarly, falling in the ideological trap expounded by some that Iran is not a nation, rather it is a hodgepodge of different ethnic and linguistic minorities, they underestimated the strength of nationalist feeling in Iran, and the will of the Iranians to defend their country. The Iraqis also relied too much on advice given by Iranian exiles, which proved to have been wrong, as well as other faulty intelligence. The result was that an intended blitzkrieg turned into a trench war.

Since the turning of the war's fortunes against Iraq, the Gulf, as well as other, Arabs' economic, logistical, and military support has made the continuation of the war possible. There is no accurate estimate of the total amount of financial assistance given to Iraq, but it is believed to be well over the $50 billion mark. Other Arab countries like Egypt and Jordan have provided military assistance both in the form of hardware and experts.[34]

In addition, two million Egyptians working in Iraq have eased that country's manpower problem. Also a number of Arab volunteers from as far away places as Sudan have fought against Iran. But it has been the financial support of the Gulf Arabs, especially Saudi Arabia and Kuwait, that has enabled Iraq to pursue the war. Kuwait and Saudi Arabia have also become major conduits – by land and by sea – for the supply of war-related material to Iraq. In addition, Saudi Arabia has provided Iraq with vital information gathered by its AWACS planes.

The Gulf Arabs' assistance to Iraq might have gone further than this. The Iranians have alleged that the Kuwaitis have on occasion allowed Iraq's air force to use their territory for refuelling and other purposes in their attacks on such Iranian targets as its makeshift oil terminal in Sirri Island.

The element of fear from possible Iraqi reprisal has certainly played a role in the Gulf Arabs' – especially Kuwait's – assistance to Iraq. But that does not make much difference from Iran's perspective. Moreover, the Gulf Arabs have justified their assistance to Iraq on the basis of fear of Iranian intentions and the requirements of Arab solidarity. The Gulf Arabs' contribution to Iraq's war efforts has been complemented by other efforts to pressure Iran. For example, the Gulf Arabs have lobbied in the West, in the United Nations, and elsewhere for Iran's economic isolation and an arms embargo against Iran. According to some reports, Saudi Arabia, for example, tried to persuade Turkey to stop trading with Iran and offered to compensate for any losses that Turkey might suffer as a result.[35]

In the summer of 1986, following Iran's success in the capture of Faw Peninsula, Saudi Arabia effectively used its oil power to pressure Iran. Saudi Arabia's policy of so-called defending OPEC's market share which led to a sharp fall in the price of oil, coupled with Iraqi bombings of Iran's oil terminals, put the latter in extremely difficult economic conditions. Admittedly, other factors such as the desire to affect the pattern of oil consumption in the industrial countries, and to discipline non-OPEC producers, also affected Saudi policy. Nevertheless, the devastating impact of this policy on Iran could not have escaped Saudi attention.

Judged in the light of the above, Iran's reaction to the Gulf Arabs' policies has been mild. Admittedly, Iran has been engaged in propaganda against some Gulf regimes, and it may also have been indirectly involved in certain subversive actions. Iran has, on a few occasions, bombed Kuwaiti territory and attacked Kuwaiti tankers.

Also, no doubt there are still elements within the Iranian regime that favour a more aggressive export of revolution. But the fact is that since 1983–4, and especially after Khomeini's famous speech on foreign relations in 1984, Iran has adopted an essentially pragmatic foreign policy.

This pragmatism has applied to relations with the Gulf states. For example, despite tensions, Iran has not severed diplomatic relations with the Gulf states, including Saudi Arabia, even after the killing of Iranian demonstrators by the Saudi security forces during the Hajj ceremonies in the summer of 1987. Rather, it has shown considerable willingness to compromise, as illustrated by the understanding reached with Saudi Arabia over oil prices in August of 1986. Iran has also maintained relatively friendly relations with those Gulf states which have not been too closely identified with Iraq, such as Oman and the UAE, particularly Dubai and Sharja. Iran has also on many occasions tried to separate the issue of Gulf security and the war with Iraq, and has suggested the working out of security arrangements with its Gulf neighbours.

In addition to a basic shift in Iran's foreign policy in favour of pragmatism, the lack of any serious Iranian military response to the Gulf Arabs' extensive and multi-dimensional assistance to Iraq has derived from its military shortcomings and a determination to avoid provoking the Gulf Arabs' Western allies, or antagonising other Arabs.

Since 1983, Iraq, and lately its Gulf allies such as Kuwait, have tried to internationalise the war by provoking Iran into actions which would trigger a Western military response against Iran. Kuwait's request to the United States and Soviet Union in 1987 to reflag Kuwaiti tankers and offer them naval protection was the latest in efforts to internationalise the Gulf war. However, Iran has very carefully avoided falling into these traps.

For example, following the Iraqi-initiated tanker war, since 1984 there has been a great deal of anxiety regarding the possibility of Iran closing the Strait of Hormuz. Yet the Iranians have repeatedly said that they have a greater interest in keeping the strait open than anybody else, and as long as they can export their oil they will keep the strait open. In fact, at one point the speaker of the Iranian Parliament, Ali-Akbar Hashemi Rafsanjani, stated that even if Iran could export half of its oil it would not close the Strait of Hormuz. In fact, the threat to the freedom of shipping in the Gulf has come from the Iraqi efforts to strangle Iran economically, and as noted earlier, to internationalise the conflict.

Last year Rafsanjani, in a meeting with the visiting Omani foreign minister, even conceded that both Iran and Oman are jointly responsible for the security of the Strait of Hormuz.[36] Consequently, Iran has basically resorted to warning the Gulf Arabs to stop helping Iraq, coupled with propaganda, but also giving assurances that Iran does not have any territorial or other claims toward the Gulf Arabs, or even Iraq.

For example, as early as 1982, the Majlis speaker Rafsanjani, during a Friday prayer sermon referring to the Gulf states, said:

They can even benefit from the AWACS planes in defending their skies. *We do not mean to attack them* [emphasis added]. We would not even allow Iraq to attack Kuwait's borders; we would break that hand. We defend Kuwait.[37]

Similarly, in a commentary during a GCC summit meeting in 1982, Tehran radio said that

The Islamic Republic announced from the very beginning that *it does not want to undermine the dignity of any Gulf state* and the war which took place and is still continuing was not initiated by the Islamic Republic.[38]

Despite some relatively minor incidents, Iran has managed to avoid a head-on collision with US naval forces protecting the American-flagged Kuwaiti tankers in the Gulf.

However, Iran's conciliatory gestures and statements have gone mostly unheeded, although diplomatic contacts between Iran and the

Gulf states have continued. The lack of significantly positive Gulf response has been attributed to Iran's lack of sincerity and its subversive actions. The yardstick with which Iran's sincerity has been measured has been its willingness to accept negotiated peace with Saddam Hussein without any conditions. However, the Gulf states have not been willing to consider Iran's point of view which maintains that the beginning of the war cannot be separated from its end, and that making peace with an aggressor without even a verbal condemnation will only encourage more aggressions.

Nor have they been willing to understand Iran's fear of future Iraqi designs on Iran. The following commentary clearly illustrates Iran's fears. The commentary was prompted by the enunciation of a peace proposal in 1985 by Iraq. The following are the relevant parts of the commentary:

> No doubt, this 'comprehensive peace' proposal of the Iraqi Ba'athist regime will also entail the annexation of all the Iranian territories occupied by the Iraqi aggressors in Khuzestan province as well as in the west of the country and will be included in maps of Iraq . . . This is nothing new . . . In the early days of the war, the Iraqi ruler also announced that their advance into Iran was aimed at liberating 'Arabistan', a misnomer used by the Iraqis to refer to the Iranian province of Khuzestan and reaching the Straits of Hormuz.

> The inclusion of parts of Iran in Iraqi maps, referring to Khuzestan Province as Arabistan and many other such instances show that the present call for returning to international borders is a sign of Iraqi regime, *a regime which if it becomes strong again, will not hesitate to violate international borders* [emphasis added].

The commentary further continues that not long after the war Tariq Aziz, the then Deputy Prime Minister, said publicly that 'if peace is not feasible, then Iraq will agree to the division of Iran into a number of smaller nationalities'.[39]

The Iranians also point to the fact that as long as Iraq seemed to be winning the war, there was no call from the Gulf Arabs, or others, for Iraqi withdrawal from Iranian territory or return to international borders. More importantly, none of the Gulf States, Iraq, or any other Arab state, including Iran's so-called allies such as Syria, have unequivocally recognised Iran's sovereignty over Khuzistan. Rather, the Gulf Arabs are insisting on Iran's acceptance of a negotiated peace without any recognition of Iraq's initial aggression. They are also insisting on a United Nations Security Council-imposed arms embargo on Iran.

IRAN'S VIEW OF THE GCC

Iran has also perceived the creation of the Gulf Cooperation Council in May of 1980 as both a security threat to itself and as a manifestation of Arab desire to exclude Iran from decisions regarding the future of the Gulf. They have also perceived the GCC as a vehicle for the expansion of Saudi influence in the Gulf, as well as a cover for US assistance to the Arab states, including Iraq, against Iran. This Iranian view of the Gulf Cooperation Council is not quite justified.

The creation of the GCC was prompted by a desire on the part of the Gulf Arab states to pull their resources together in order to balance the superior forces of both Iran and Iraq. The existence of common economic concerns and extensive cultural ties among the Gulf states were other contributing factors to the creation of the GCC.

Nevertheless, with Iraq's invasion of Iran and growing GCC support for Iraq, the organisation has acquired an essentially anti-Iranian character. The Iranians have thus begun to ask what is this threat against which the Gulf states are organising. After refuting that the GCC is designed to meet the Israeli and US challenge, the following commentary continues:

The reactionary group which believes the Islamic government and the Islamic Republic of Iran constitute a danger threatening the region must be told the following: The Iranian Islamic revolution regards the question of establishing peace and security in the world, and particularly in the Persian Gulf, as one of the most important basic issues . . . In the event the other countries in the region favor tranquility and peace, the Iranian Islamic Republic – as the strongest and the largest country in the region, particularly in the Persian Gulf – is prepared to cooperate with them in the direction of this objective. However, *if a number of small regimes in the region wish to make decisions concerning the waters of the Persian Gulf without attaching any importance to the Islamic Republic of Iran, their initiative will undoubtedly be regarded as a conspiracy against the interests of the Muslim Iranian people* [emphasis added].[40]

The last part of the Iranian commentary reflects Iran's main concern over purely Arab groupings in the Gulf, namely the exclusion of Iran from Gulf affairs.

The Iranian concern over the exclusion from Gulf affairs and decisions regarding the Gulf's security, political and economic future becomes more understandable if it is realised that the GCC was conceived as a step toward broader Arab economic and political integration. The Gulf Arabs made this very clear when, at the birth of the organisation, some Arabs referred to it as a 'rich man's club' and criticised it for going against the goal of Arab economic unity. Moreover, while currently Iraq is excluded from the GCC, voices have been heard in favour of including Iraq in the GCC. For example, the Kuwaiti diplomat, Abdullah Hussein, in an article in the Kuwaiti newspaper, *Al-Anbaa*, called for the inclusion of Iraq in the GCC and argued:

> If we do not consider seriously the inclusion of Iraq in the Council and the formation of a unified Arab army to be deployed along the Gulf shores to confront the Islamic revolution, then any talk about Arab security is without avail.[41]

Moreover, Iraq – and other Arab states – are already involved in a number of multi-lateral Gulf Arab economic and cultural projects.

Thus, there is an organic link between collective Gulf Arab institutions and the rest of the Arab world, while Iran is totally excluded. The Gulf Arabs may have valid reasons for this, but they should at least make an effort to understand how these activities affect what Iran considers as its legitimate interests. If Iran objects to the gradual turning of the Gulf into an exclusively Arab region, it should not be characterised as hegemonic thrust. This is particularly so in light of the fact that even the historic name of the Gulf is challenged by the Arabs.

The Iranian regime also objects to the GCC as being an instrument of US policy, and since it believes that part of US strategy is to eliminate the Islamic regime, it views the GCC as an essentially anti-Iranian force.

They believe the GCC was created to play the role of US surrogate in the Gulf, a role that the Shah played in the pre-revolution days and was pilloried for by Arab radicals.

In addition, Iran perceives the GCC as a vehicle for the expansion of Saudi influence, and even control, in the Gulf. While the Iranian view of Saudi control of the GCC is somewhat exaggerated, there is no doubt that Saudi Arabia, the main inspiration behind the creation of the GCC, also constitutes the core component of its economic and military power.

Also, there is no secret that Saudi Arabia considers the Arabian peninsula as its sphere of influence. Saudi Arabia, since 1973, has been a main competitor for influence in the Gulf and in the Arab world. The Saudis have also exerted considerable influence over domestic policies of such Gulf states as Kuwait and Bahrain, which has often been resented by many groups in these countries.[42] The Saudis have also always tried to limit Iran's influence among the Gulf states. Therefore, there is some justification to the Iranian view of Saudi Arabia's role in the GCC.

However, despite these more basic reservations, the current Iranian problems with the GCC derive from its members' support for Iraq, rather than from the creation of the organisation.

CONCLUSIONS

The foregoing has illustrated that a number of underlying factors which determine Iran's relations with the Arab world in general also affect its relations with the Gulf Arabs. Thus, it has also been clearly demonstrated that Iran's relations with the Gulf Arab states cannot be analysed in isolation from its relations with the rest of the Arab world. The Iran–Iraq war has clearly demonstrated this. Massive financial and military assistance of Arabs to Iraq has indeed made the Iran–Iraq war an Arab-Iranian war. Moreover, the preceding analysis has shown that Iran's so-called hegemonic thrust in the Gulf and the threat it poses to Arab security has been highly exaggerated. It has also shown, particularly in light of the Iraqi attack against Iran, that there indeed is an Arab threat to Iran's security and territorial integrity. This threat will continue to exist as long as the Arabs will not give up their claim to Khuzistan, will accept the legitimacy of Iran's presence in the Gulf, and will not pursue an exclusivist Arab approach toward the region's security or its economic and cultural life.

Finally, the problem of security in the Gulf is not one of Iranian hegemonist thrust. The problem of security in the Gulf is far more complicated and derives from diverse sources including the clash of competing nationalisms, ideologies, and competition for power and even superpower rivalry.

But most important, the core security problem in the Gulf is that of conflict between the forces of social and political change and those of status quo. In the past, the Arab world represented the main forces for change and now they are represented by Iran. Thus the security challenge of the rest of the 1980s and beyond in the Gulf will continue to be how to deal with and accommodate inevitable forces of change so as to prevent violent eruptions.

Notes

1.   For example, British support for the Al-Khalifa family in Bahrain was primarily responsible for Iran's loss of influence in Bahrain. See Fereydoun Adamiyat, *Bahrain Islands: A Legal and Diplomatic Study of the British-Iranian Controversy* (New York: Praeger, 1955). Similarly, British support enabled Sheikh Khaz'al to develop a semi-autonomous position in the Khuzistan Province.

2.   For example, in a recent commentary, Tehran Radio, complaining that the president of the United States had referred in a speech to the Persian Gulf as the 'Gulf', said that: 'The historic name of the Persian Gulf is related to Salman Farsi [Salman the Persian], one of the first few disciples and companions of Prophet Mohammad. Needless to say, this assertion ignores a thousand years of pre-Islamic history and Greek and Roman historical works.' See *Foreign Broadcasting Information Service (FBIS)*, South Asia (SA), 27 January 1987.

3.   Iran has a 2500 kilometre border with the USSR.

4.   See R. K. Ramazani, *The Persian Gulf: Iran's Role* (Charlottesville: The University of Virginia Press, 1973). The book contains an excellent bibliography on Iranian sources.

5.   In Bahrain, for example, the British closed Iranian schools and imported teachers from Iraq – which was under the British mandate – and embarked on a policy of total Arabisation. See Adamiyat, *Bahrain Islands*, op cit., note 1.

6.   Quoted in Fereydoun Adamiyat, *Andisheh-e-Taraghi Va Hokoumat Ghanoun* (The Idea of Progress and the Rule of Law) (Tehran: Intesharat Kharazami, 1351, 1973).

7.   *FBIS*, SA, 24 October 1984.

8.   *FBIS*, SA, 24 October 1984.

9.   See Hamid Enayat, 'Iran and the Arabs', in Sylvia Haim (ed.), *Arab Nationalism and a Wider World* (New York: American Association for Peace in The Middle East, 1971).

10.   See A. J. Arbery (ed.), *The Legacy of Persia* (Oxford: The Clarendon Press, 1952).

11. See William B. Quandt. *Saudi Arabia in the 1980s: Foreign Policy, Security and Oil* (Washington, DC: The Brookings Institution, 1981). However, this cooperation has run into some problems because of Pakistan's refusal to alter its friendly relations with Iran, or allow its troops to take part in any military action against Iran. As a result, according to some reports, the Saudis are sending the Pakistani contingent home. See *The Washington Post*, 29 November 1987.

12. For example, there was a strongly negative popular reaction to the government's efforts to discourage the people from celebrating Iran's pre-Islamic new year, Now Rouz. Finally, the government had to somewhat relent on this and other anti-nationalist campaigns.

13. For example, in Kuwait Sunni fundamentalists have attacked the offices of Iran's national airline. See Joseph Kostiner, 'Islamic Revivalism in Bahrain and Kuwait', in Shirin T. Hunter (ed.), *The Politics of Islamic Revivalism* (Bloomington, Indiana: Indiana University Press, 1988).

14. See Emile Boustani, *Marche Arabesque* (London: Robert Hale, 1961). Also see David Hirst, *Oil and Public Opinion in the Middle East* (London: Faber & Faber, 1966).

15. See R. K. Ramazani, *The Persian Gulf*, op. cit., note 4.

16. For example, Abd-al-Khaliq Hassouna, the Egyptian Secretary-General of the Arab League, said in a speech that the fresh fruit that Iran was exporting to the Gulf states were products of Israel. See ibid.

17. The Iranians, for example, pointed out that there were Iranian communities in the Gulf Arab states before a drop of oil was discovered there, whereas Egypt's interests began because of the oil riches of the Gulf.

18. The Iranian news media in discussing the causeway has characterised it as the annexation of Bahrain by Saudi Arabia. See *FBIS*, SA, 28 January 1982.

19. See R. M. Burrell and A. J. Cottrell, *Iran, Afghanistan, and Pakistan: Tensions and Dilemmas* (Washington, DC: The Center for Strategic and International Studies, Georgetown University, 1974). The Leaders of the Front recently gave an interview to the *Arab Times*. See *FBIS*, SA, 21 August 1985.

20. For an excellent discussion of these issues see David Hirst, *Oil and Public Opinion in the Middle East* (London: Faber & Faber, 1966).

21. See Nazli Choucri, *International Politics of Energy Interdependence: The Case of Petroleum* (Lexington, Mass.: D. C. Heath, 1976).

22. One of those trained in the AMAL camps was Mustapha Chamran who, after the revolution, became Iran's Minister of Defence.

23. On Saudi-Iranian cooperation against radicalism and competition for power, see Judith Perrara, 'Together Against the Red Peril: Iran and Saudi Arabia Rivals for Superpower Role', *The Middle East*, no. 43, May 1978.

24. See Shirin T. Hunter, 'Syrian-Iranian Relations: Alliance of Convenience Or More?' *Middle East Insight*, May/June 1985.

25. See various issues of *The Washington Post* and *The New York Times* of November 1987.

26.   For a full and excellent discussion of these issues, see R. K. Ramazani, *Revolutionary Iran: Challenge and Response In The Middle East* (Baltimore: The Johns Hopkins University Press, 1986).
27.   For details, see ibid.
28.   See Ayatullah Montazeri's remarks. *FBIS*, SA, 14 January 1987.
29.   Egypt, for instance, has said that it would be willing to activate the 1950 Arab Defence Pact should Iran threaten any of the Gulf states. See *New York Times*, 11 November 1987, and 'Saudis Seeking an Arab Alliance Against Iran', *New York Times*, 16 October 1987.
30.   See Shirin T. Hunter, 'After the Ayatullah', *Foreign Policy*, no. 66, Spring 1987.
31.   See Chibli Mallat, 'Islamic Revivalism in Iraq', in Shirin T. Hunter (ed.), *The Politics of Islamic Revivalism*, op. cit., note 13.
32.   See R. K. Ramazani, *Revolutionary Iran*, op. cit., note 14.
33.   See Shireen T. and Robert E. Hunter, 'The Post-Camp David Arab World', in Robert O. Freedman (ed.), *The Middle East Since Camp David* (Boulder, CO: Westview Press, 1985).
34.   See various issues of *FBIS*, SA, on Egyptian, Jordanian, Sudanese, and other Arab aid to Iraq, including 15 April 1982 on Egypt's aid and 15 October 1982 on Sudan's aid.
35.   See *Middle East Economic Digest* (MEED), vol. 30, no. 6, 19–25 Aprial 1986.
36.   See *MEED*, vol. 31, no. 21, 23–29 May 1987.
37.   *FBIS*, SA, 29 January 1982.
38.   *FBIS*, SA, 10 February 1982.
39.   *FBIS*, SA, 14 May 1985.
40.   *FBIS*, SA, 29 January 1982.
41.   As reported in the *Financial Times*, 19 March 1984.
42.   For example, after the closure of the Kuwaiti Parliament in 1986, a Kuwaiti delegate said that 'We are now really part of the Gulf Cooperation Council' implying other Gulf, especially Saudi, pressure on Kuwait. See *MEED*, vol. 30, no. 28, 12–16 July 1986.

3 Saudi Arabia, Iran and OPEC: The Dynamics of a Balancing Act

M. E. Ahrari

The beginning of the Khomeini era gave a different twist to Iran's relations with the countries of the Arabian Peninsula in the form of heightened security-related concerns. Within the framework of the Organisation of Petroleum Exporting Countries (OPEC), however, this relationship remained essentially very similar to the one that prevailed between Iran and the OPEC states during the days of the Shah. As the war between Iran and Iraq heated up since the summer of 1987, Iran's ties with Saudi Arabia and the other Arab states of OPEC have been under tremendous strain. This chapter is aimed at an examination of the dynamics of the relationship between these two countries.

Both Saudi Arabia and Iran have been trying to emerge as the dominant actors of the Gulf. Iran's claim to this dominance has been the precedence of its military preponderance during the days of the Shah. Saudi Arabia has been vying to dominate the region largely as a result of its significance within OPEC in the 1970s. Militarily speaking, Iran made a more persuasive claim to be the dominant regional actor under the Shah. But under Khomeini, the Iranian claim has been on shaky grounds. From the perspective of oil power, Saudi Arabia made a more persuasive claim to dominate the Gulf in the 1970s. In the 1980s, under a prolonged worldwide oil glut, the Saudi claim to dominate the region has been equally murky.

In part one of this chapter, the focus of inquiry will be the conventional aspects of the conflict between Iran and Saudi Arabia over the leadership of OPEC. The issues of contention between these two actors in the 1970s were the timing and amount of price escalations. In the 1980s, production-programming (i.e., the adoption of a policy of reduced oil production by all members on the basis of allocation of individual production quotas that were to be adhered to by all participants) added a new dimension to this struggle. An evaluation of the security-related aspects of the conflict between these two countries will be made in the second part. In the concluding portion, some observations will be made on the implications of the future dynamics of the balancing act between Saudi Arabia and Iran for regional stability and for the survival of OPEC.

THE ANALYTICAL FRAMEWORK

In the Gulf there are three actors who aspire for hegemony and regional dominance. The first of these is Iran with population 48 million, an area of 636 296 square miles, total armed forces of 704 500, and proven oil reserves of 51 billion barrels (1985 figure). It is continguous to the Soviet Union in the north, to Turkey and Iraq in the west, to Pakistan and Afghanistan in the east, and to the Gulf and the Gulf of Oman in the south. Iran under the Shah played the role of a hegemonic actor. Under Khomeini that country envisions the continuation of this role except that the Islamic Republic of Iran aspires to be the leader of an Islamic international subsystem in the Gulf.

Saudi Arabia, the second actor aspiring to dominate the Gulf, is the largest country of the Arabian Peninsula, occupying four-fifths of the Peninsula, with a population of a little over 10 million, an area of 864 869 square miles, armed forces of 67 500 men, and proven oil reserves of 66 billion barrels.[1] In the 1970s, within the framework of OPEC, Saudi Arabia remained the leading voice of moderate increases and made sure that the rest of the OPEC membership towed the line by going along with its preferences. However, within the Organisation of Arab Petroleum Exporting Countries (OAPEC), Saudi Arabia was the chief architect of the oil embargo of 1973, which was quite an anathema to the traditional Saudi predilection for moderation. The complexity of Saudi policies within OPEC and OAPEC made that country a legitimate claimant to the leadership of the former organisation. This claim and the implementation of the oil embargo also collectively became the basis for Saudi aspirations to emerge as the dominant power in the Gulf.

The rivalry between Iran and Saudi Arabia became significant in the 1970s as oil emerged as the potent weapon along with the growing effectiveness of OPEC to introduce intermittent increases in the prices of oil. As the owner of the largest proven oil reserves in the world, Saudi Arabia looked with askance at the periodic demands by certain oil states, frequently led by Iran, to introduce unrealistic price increases. These demands by the price hawks – so called because of the nature of their price-related demands – and a combination of reluctance and refusal by the Saudis, defined the parameter of conflict between Iran and Saudi Arabia in the 1970s.

The oil market of the 1980s was characterised by a prolonged oil glut. The challenge for OPEC in this decade was how to keep the prices from falling. Saudi Arabia, once again, had to bear the burden of leadership with Iranian challenges to its position being governed by its ever-growing need for capital to bankroll the intractable war with Iraq. In the 1970s as well as in the 1980s, Iran remained a leading price hawk and manifested its aspirations for the leadership of OPEC.

Any nation state's ability to emerge as the dominant actor in the Gulf is largely dependent on its military capability, its size, population, and, most important, a credible record of flexing its muscle as a military actor. On the last variable, the pendulum of advantage has been swinging in favour of Iran both during the Shah's regime and under the Khomeini rule.

In the 1980s, the conflict over the pricing of oil and the leadership of OPEC became less significant because of the prolonged slump in oil prices. The security-related issues, however, became an integral part of the 'high politics' with the continuation of war between Iran and Iraq.[2] Iran especially targeted Saudi Arabia for its verbal barrages that were also marked by instances of hostile acts. The security-related conflict between Iran and Saudi Arabia became a dangerous new wrinkle, and also an unconventional aspect, to an already strained relationship. The issue of regional dominance is far from settled. The jury is still out. A detailed examination of these dimensions is in order.

Iraq, the third nation with ambitions to be the dominant factor in the region, is excluded from the scope of this chapter. The on-going Iran–Iraq war appears to have damaged the chances of the emergence of a dominant Iraq in the foreseeable future, unless that country decisively wins the war. The chances of such a happenstance, however, are minimal at this time.

THE ECONOMIC ASPECTS OF THE IRAN-SAUDI OPEC'S LEADERSHIP

The pricing of oil

Saudi Arabia played a crucial role during a number of negotiations that were quite significant for the emergence of OPEC as the price-setting cartel. Even though Colonel Muammar Qaddafi of Libya emerged as the pace-setter of price negotiations with the Western oil companies, it was under the careful leadership of Ahmad Zaki Yamani, the former oil minister, that Saudi Arabia not only set the parameters of a series of highly intricate negotiations but also put the weight of its oil reserves to force the oil companies into yielding to the demands of the OPEC states.

For both Iran and Saudi Arabia, the Tehran negotiations of January 1971 served as a forum for the nurturing and growth of the aspirations for the leadership of OPEC. Resolution XXI.120, which was passed by the Twenty First Conference of OPEC, became the basis for a unified pricing strategy. The framework of this strategy was 'regionalisation' or a regional cooperative approach. The principle involved was to treat separately the price problems of each region within OPEC jurisdiction. The negotiated increases in the prices of oil in one region would serve as the basis for ensuing negotiations aimed at incorporating these increases in the other regions. For instance, any agreement between the oil industry and the Gulf states to raise the price of crude oil would become the basis of renewed negotiations for more price hikes by the Mediterranean states, and vice versa. Three regional committees were established to deal with the price issues: the Gulf states committee, made up of Iran, Iraq, and Saudi Arabia; the Mediterranean committee, including Saudi Arabia, Libya, Algeria, and Iraq; and a third committee comprised of Venezuela and Indonesia.[3]

In the Gulf committee, both Iran and Saudi Arabia played an important role as OPEC leaders. The oil companies deftly tried to pit price moderates against price hawks by inviting OPEC to conduct joint negotiations. OPEC declined and opted to play a consultative role. It asked the Gulf and Mediterranean committees to directly negotiate with the oil companies.

After failing to conduct joint negotiations with OPEC members, the oil industry focused on ensuring the longevity of any agreement reached with OPEC. On this point, the Gulf states gave assurances of their willingness to enter into and abide by a five-year agreement. On the recommendations of the US State Department, the oil industry initiated parallel negotiations, which were labelled as 'separate but necessarily connected negotiations', with Libya and the Gulf states. This decision ended all realistic possibilities for the prolonged sustenance of any agreement. The Tehran agreement, signed on 14 February 1971, was an enormous victory for both Saudi Arabia and Iran.[4]

It was during the pricing negotiations between the Mediterranean committee and the oil industry and during negotiations leading to the participation of oil states in upstream (i.e., exploration and production) operations that the Saudi leadership played a crucial role in bringing about a solution desired by Libya. During the course of these negotiations, Saudi Arabia did not try to be the pace-setter. Instead, by going along with extreme demands forwarded by Libya, and by not publicly dissociating itself with the radical negotiating tactics used by that country to force concessions from the oil companies, such as threats to introduce production cutbacks or outright nationalisation, the Saudi leadership made its mark on OPEC in the early 1970s.

During these negotiations, the oil ministers of the Mediterranean committee, with the visible participation of Saudi Arabia, authorised Libya to negotiate separately with each company operating in that country. If the companies rejected the 'minimum demands' agreed upon by these ministers, they were to face a Mediterranean embargo. The Saudi decision to go along with as drastic a move as an embargo was a clear undermining of good faith and a violation of the assurances it had given to oil companies in its capacity as one of the prominent members of the Gulf committee. The companies had no choice but to concede.

During the participation negotiations, Saudi Arabia, once again, sustained its preference for moderation.[5] It was best reflected in the negotiated formula governing the takeover of upstream operations by the oil states. This incremental formula allowed for an initial 25 per cent participation by the governments concerned immediately after finalisation of the relevant agreements. This was to be increased to 30 per cent on 1 January 1979; to 35 per cent on 1 January 1980; to 40 per cent on 1 January 1981; to 45 per cent on 1 January 1982; and to 51 per cent on 1 January 1983. Thereafter, it was to remain at 51 per cent until the expiration of oil concessions. This formula was never implemented, however, because Libya concluded a far better deal with the oil companies operating within its border.

OPEC's success in introducing unilateral increases in the prices of crude oil, starting 16 October 1973, marked the beginning of conflict between Saudi Arabia and Iran over the twin-issues of pricing (i.e., the amount) and the timing of price increases. Between October and December of 1973, the Gulf states of OPEC raised the posted prices of Arabian Light, the key crude oil in the Gulf area, from $3.11 to $11.651/b (per barrel). This was a cumulative increase of more than 384 per cent.

Before the unilateral increase of 16 October, the oil companies served as moderators of OPEC's pricing behaviour. But the removal of these entities from exchanges did not eliminate the vital need for moderation on the issue of price increases. Starting in 1974, Saudi Arabia emerged as the leading force for price moderation within OPEC. The Saudi decision to adopt this role stemmed from the fact that their country had the largest quantities of proven oil reserves and in this capacity their economic prosperity was inextricably linked to the economic stability and a healthy growth of the Western industrial economies. A related and equally important factor was that the accumulation of petrodollars in the hands of the oil states, especially the Arab oil states, was causing enormous consternation in the Western industrial world.

The predominant feeling in the West was that the oil states could not be trusted to behave responsibly in the international money market, an opinion based on their continued disregard for the impact of their unrealistic and intermittent price increases on the world economy. If the oil states remained as oblivious to the implications of their economic actions in the international financial market as they had been about raising oil prices, the Western industrial states believed that the non-Communist economies would face an even more uncertain future. Such feelings were bound to complicate the recycling of petrodollars, which were viewed as crucial, not only to the survival of the Third World economies, but also to the potential growth of the industrial economies. Under these circumstances, Saudi Arabia, the possessor of the largest share of petrodollars, was in a mood to be cautious with the world economy by making it very difficult for its OPEC allies to continue introducing unrealistic price increases.

Beginning in 1974, OPEC meetings were marked by in-group squabblings between the price hawks, an informal and *ad hoc* coalition of Iran, Libya, and Algeria, which were frequently joined by Iraq and Nigeria, and the price moderates, led by Saudi Arabia and regularly joined by the UAE, Kuwait, and Qatar. The effect of quantum leaps in the prices of OPEC crude in October and December of 1973 emerged in the inability of that organisation to introduce further major increases in 1974 and 1975. The oil states could only bring about minor upward adjustments in royalties and taxes.

OPEC hawks went along with decisions to freeze prices between 1974 and 1976 under frequent Saudi threats to reduce prices unilaterally and to increase production if they raised prices. As the Western economies recovered from the great recession of 1974–5, a debate between hawks and moderates also initiated over further price increase. Toward the end of 1976, however, the magnitude of disagreement on the amount of price increase between these two groups of countries was quite divergent.

Saudi Arabia, supported by the UAE, favoured a continuation of the price freeze for another six months. The position of the price hawks on the amount of increase varied from a low of 10–15 per cent to a high of 26 per cent. Iran proposed a 15 per cent increase. In a radical departure from their past tradition of arriving at a compromise formula at the last moment, neither the price hawks nor the Saudis were willing to agree to a uniform price increase. In view of the acute variance between positions, both sides sought solace in 'agreeing-to-disagree', and this 'consensus' gave birth to a two-tier price system as a result of the December 1976 meeting of OPEC.

According to this arrangement, eleven oil states agreed to bring about an approximately 10 per cent increase in their prices from 1 January 1977, and an additional 5 per cent at mid-year, while Saudi Arabia and the UAE announced a 5 per cent increase for the entirety of 1977. As a tactical manoeuvre aimed at applying pressure on the price hawks, Saudi Arabia and the UAE announced the removal of their previous self-imposed production ceilings, thereby raising their combined production from the then prevailing rate of 11.1 million b/d (9.1 million for the Saudis and about 2 million for the UAE) to 12.5 million b/d (about 10 million for the Saudi and about 2.5 million for the UAE) or about 42 per cent of the total OPEC production, which remained at 32–33 million b/d. The Saudi hoped that the surplus thus created would produce downward pressure on the price scales adopted by the eleven other oil states and that the latter would be forced to realign their prices with those of Saudi Arabia and the UAE. The OPEC majority was equally determined to back its higher price tier, with coordinated production cutbacks if necessary, rather than succumb to the Saudi pressure.

As the realities of maintaining a two-tier price system were beginning to sink in, both price hawks and moderates were becoming increasingly aware of the practical difficulties of adhering to their respective positions. The Shah of Iran, in the wake of the Saudi estimate that the production of the eleven OPEC price hawks might drop by more than 25 per cent because of lower Saudi prices and increased production, stated that any attempt by the Saudis to use escalated production as a pressure tactic would be tantamount to an act of aggression.

By July of 1977, however, Saudi Arabia decided to unify prices by raising its own by a maximum of 5 per cent. A number of variables influenced the Saudis. These included an increasingly bouyant oil market, growing pressure by price hawks on oil companies operating within their border, the inability of Saudi Arabia and the UAE to raise their respective production levels, the high demand for the upper-tier Libyan and Algerian lighter low sulphur crudes, and, more important, behind the scenes diplomatic manoeuvres to find a common pricing formula by a number of oil states. The two-tier price system caused little damage to the OPEC price hawks. They learned to defy Saudi Arabia despite its role as a swing producer (i.e., a producer that was capable of bringing about necessary upward or downward swings in its production levels to alter the behaviour of oil states or companies), and the Saudis had to choose another occasion to demonstrate the potential power of their enormous oil reserves as a modifier of the pricing behaviour of other OPEC members.

The political revolution in Iran created a highly uncertain situation concerning the supply of oil. Toward the end of the first quarter of 1979, OPEC members convened a meeting to tackle the reports that the Western oil companies were reaping a bonanza from the Iranian oil shortfall. This meeting was marked by the now familiar positions taken by price hawks under the leadership of Iran and the moderates. The hawks envisaged the tight supply situation as a golden opportunity to restore the eroded purchasing power of their revenues and to reverse in real terms the decline in prices of crude oil. There was a vain hope that Saudi Arabia, whose surplus production capacity was no longer a deterrent to the tide of price escalations (since this capacity had its telling effect under surplus supply conditions), might be able to moderate some extreme pricing ideas put forth by the hawks. The outcome was another 'agreement-to-differ', a euphemism for the emergence of a multi-tier price structure.

This price structure enabled the hawks to reap a bonanza by diverting increasingly larger volumes of supplies to spot markets (i.e., markets for the sale of non-contract oil). Saudi Arabia unsuccessfully continued its advocacy of a unified price structure. Unbeknown to the price hawks, in allowing the spot market to set the prices of crude oil, OPEC was indeed abandoning its role as a price-fixing cartel.

In order to reunify the multi-tier price structure and also to ameliorate the chaotic supply-related market conditions, Saudi Arabia opted for raising its production levels. Despite this measure, the prices of crude oil in spot markets continued to escalate. That country also realised that despite its attempts to curb prices, the American partners of Saudi Aramco – Exxon, Texaco, Socal, and Mobil – were buying the Saudi oil at a cheaper rate but were selling at premium prices. In view of the preceding, Saudi Arabia, convinced that the chief beneficiaries of its lower prices and higher production were not the consumers of industrial nations but the treasuries of Aramco partners, raised its prices to those of other OPEC members. However, the vagaries of the oil market toward the end of 1979 were such that Saudi Arabia was forced to introduce two more upward adjustments in its futile endeavours to reunify prices and bring about order to the market.

In the first quarter of 1980, the oil market began to create a condition of oversupply due to a build-up of inventories and a slowing down of economic activities in the industrial countries. OPEC members remained oblivious to these signs, however. The sustained escalation of political tensions between the United States and the Khomeini regime stemming from the continuation of the hostage crisis only postponed the inevitable emergence of the softening of oil prices. By August 1980, it appeared almost certain that petroleum prices were moving downward.

By the beginning of 1981 predictions of the emergence of a soft market abounded, barring an unforeseen political crisis affecting either supplies or prices of crudes. Any scenario of a soft market automatically involved the reinstatement of Saudi Arabia as a swing producer, using its two-pronged strategy of production and pricing to bring about stability of prices.

During 1977 and numerous occasions in 1979 and in 1980, Saudi Arabia had unsuccessfully tried to reunify OPEC prices. In the first quarter of 1981, however, the chances of Saudi success appeared high. The Saudi insistence on price reunification grew almost in direct proportion to the increasing softness of the world oil market. As it appeared certain that the surplus supply situation would prevail at least through 1981, the OPEC price hawks clamoured for price and supply stability. The foremost expression of their concern was the sudden rejuvenation of their interest in the long-term strategy plan to stabilise oil prices, an issue that was of interest to this group only during oversupply market conditions. Saudi Arabia, however, wanted an OPEC-wide price unification as a precondition for its consideration of the long-term strategy plan.

Disagreeing with the Saudi position, the hawks adopted OPEC-wide cutbacks to firm up prices. The Saudis promptly dissociated themselves from this decision. Toward the end of October 1981, Saudi Arabia attained its long-cherished goal of subjugating the OPEC majority through its leverage as a swing producer. The continuance of a soft market throughout 1981 was the ideal circumstance for Saudi Arabia. At the conclusion of their 29 October meeting, OPEC members agreed to price reunification. As a compromise measure, Saudi Arabia raised the price of its marker crude from $32 to $34/b, while the remainder of OPEC states lowered their prices from $36 to $34/b.

Production programming

Despite undergoing a radical transformation from a monarchical to a revolutionary regime, the oil policy of Iran remained essentially the same. One significant difference was that the Islamic Republic announced its intention to introduce considerable production cutbacks, from around 6 million during the last days of the Shah to about 2 million b/d. However, on the issue of pricing Iran became more hawkish. Within OPEC, it continued to lead the debate on price escalation, and outside OPEC it sustained a policy of imposing surcharges and rerouting its contract crude into spot sale.

As the Khomeini regime was settling down in Iran, it faced two issues of considerable significance. The first one was how to come to grips with the growing supply surpluses and the related downward pressure on oil prices. The second problem emanated from the Iraqi attack on Iran in September 1980. The latter issue will be considered in the second half of this chapter.

In early 1982, the oil glut and a related price slump in the world oil market were causing consternation for both Saudi Arabia and Iran. OPEC emerged as a powerful price-fixing cartel in the 1970s, years marked by intermittent supply shortages. In the 1980s, the oil market was characterised by oversupplies, a situation that warranted production cutbacks and a price freeze, or even price reduction. As the organisation was gearing up to tackle new issues, the struggle between Saudi Arabia and Iran over the leadership of OPEC was to focus, aside from the pricing issue, on production programming.

OPEC never before seriously tried to adopt production programming. However, in 1982 it had to bite the bullet and adopt this measure. Saudi Arabia, as the largest owner of oil reserves, had to agree to play the role of a swing producer. The Saudi willingness to perform this role only solved a minor aspect of the problem related to production programming. Two additional, and quite obdurate, hurdles were: the basis for assigning the production quotas to the rest of OPEC membership, especially the warring Iran and Iraq; and the willingness of OPEC members to abide by production quotas and price scales that an incorporation of production programming was to entail.

The issue of allocating quotas emerged as an immediate problem when OPEC considered the adoption of production programming in 1982. Iran argued that quota allocation should be based on population and financial need. Such a formula clearly put Iran (with a population 48 million), Nigeria (80 million), Indonesia (150 million), and even Iraq (13 million) ahead of Saudi Arabia (10 million), since all populous states, as 'high absorbers' of capital, were also in acute need of capital. Needless to say, the populous oil states were quite sympathetic to the Iranian argument, especially when they considered that Saudi Arabia was one of the leading members of the 'low absorber' group of countries. Nevertheless acceptance of the Iranian position by Saudi Arabia would clearly enable Iran to regain within OPEC the role of contender for leadership it had enjoyed under the Shah. Moreover, the political implications of this role for Iran might further escalate the already threatening posture of the Khomeini regime in the Gulf, a horrifying scenario not only for Saudi Arabia but also for other oil monarchies.

When Iran was accused of violating its 1982 quota of 1.2 million b/d and undercutting other OPEC members by selling its crude oil at a lower price, the Iranian oil minister, Mohammed Gharazi, reminded his OPEC colleagues that they should, in fact, be grateful to Iran for drastically lowering the 6 million b/d production level from the days of the Shah to about 2 million b/d. Iran accused Saudi Arabia of unfairly expanding its own share at Iran's expense at a time when the latter was fighting a war with Iraq. Under such circumstances, argued Iran, it was left with no alternative but to exploit whatever opportunities presented themselves. Consequently, Iran remained the leading violator of OPEC-allocated quotas in 1982. When the March 1983 production ceiling agreement was negotiated, Gharazi publicly endorsed the move by accepting the OPEC-assigned quota of 2.4 million b/d. However, given the fact that the Iranian need for capital was growing in view of the continuing war, that country, along with a number of OPEC states, was expected to violate the assigned quota.

Throughout the 1980s, the issue of leadership over OPEC was put back on the back burner. The continued slump in the oil market forced OPEC to scramble for survival strategies. The adoption of production programming, which was incorporated quite frequently with little or no chance of it being adhered to seriously by the member states, was just one such strategy. One more reason for the failure of production programming in bringing about price escalation in the 1980s was the emergence of non-OPEC producers. These producers – such as Norway, Britain, the USSR, Mexico, Egypt, etc. – continued to raise production with little regard to its effects on prices. OPEC became the only group of oil producers to defend prices by lowering production. Under the Saudi leadership, OPEC members tried unsuccessfully in 1982 to involve Norway and Britain in production programming. In early 1987, Saudi Arabia also approached the Soviet Union to reduce production with little positive results from OPEC's perspective. Mexico and Egypt on a few occasions aligned their prices and production quotas with OPEC, but their own need for capital, a sustained lack of discipline by OPEC members, and the continued oil glut forced them to go their own way.

Toward the end of 1985, OPEC temporarily abandoned production programming and opted for the so-called 'fair share policy', which was essentially a price war with non-OPEC producers for a brief duration. As the chief architect of this controversial policy, Yamani lost his job. The Iranian sustained displeasure with the moderate policies of the capable Saudi oil minister was reported to have been one of the chief reasons underlying the sacking of Yamani by King Fahd. It was reported that the Saudi King, who himself was not happy with Yamani's policies, also wanted to appease the Khomeini regime. In March 1988, a possible adoption of yet another production programming schedule was bogged down because of the growing importance of non-OPEC producers. The OPEC states were afraid that if they adopted a proposed reduced production of 5 per cent, non-OPEC oil producers, whose production level was to reach 30 million b/d in 1988, would nullify that reduction. The OPEC states were seeking a commitment from their non-OPEC counterparts that they, too, would reduce their production.[7]

In 1988, the leadership of OPEC, though unresolved, is diminished in its significance because that organisation itself is experiencing a lowered international status and prestige. If the non-Communist world were to experience oil shortfalls in the coming years, undoubtedly both OPEC and Saudi Arabia would regain their political significance. Given a long-established predeliction for moderation, Saudi Arabia would, once again, be facing the price hawks under Iranian leadership.

THE MILITARY ASPECT OF THE IRAN-SAUDI CONFLICT

With the accession to power of the Khomeini regime in Iran, the military dimension of the Saudi-Iranian aspirations to dominate the region became of utmost significance. During the days of the Shah, Iran emerged as the dominant military actor. It flexed its muscles on a number of occasions, such as in putting down the communist insurgency in the Dhofar province of Oman, in seizing the Abu Musa and Tumb Islands in the Gulf, and in forcing Iraq to sign a peace treaty in 1975. The pendulum of advantage also swung in favour of Iran in the 1970s because the Shah was perceived as the protector of Western interests in the region.

The Saudi Arabian leadership emerged during the 1962 civil war in Yemen, which brought an end to the monarchy in that country. Saudi Arabia backed the pro-monarchical forces, while Egypt's President, Gamal Abdel Nasser, supported the anti-monarchical elements. The war was brought to a negotiated settlement in 1968, in the aftermath of the Arab-Israeli war of 1967. After encountering a humiliating defeat at the hands of Israel, Nasser was in no mood to sap Egyptian military resources fighting another Arab state.

In the early 1970s, Saudi Arabia was in the process of defining and expanding the scope of its leadership. The shortage of oil supplies worldwide and the growing importance of OPEC best suited the Saudi objectives. As was demonstrated in the preceding section, originally the focus of Saudi leadership was rather narrow – i.e., negotiating with multinational companies on oil prices. The participation negotiations were of considerable significance for two reasons. First, once these negotiations were concluded, there was no telling what other equally or more radical ideas the Saudis might propose that would further shift the economic balance of power in favour of the oil states. Second, any alteration of the economic balance of power, which would further enhance Saudi position in the Gulf region as well as in the Arab world, could very easily be utilised for the fulfilment of its regional political aspirations.

The Saudi success in implementing the Arab oil embargo was the ultimate transformation of economic power into political prestige. Prior to their willingness to use oil as a political weapon, Saudi Arabia succeeded in extracting an agreement with the front-line states (i.e., states bordering Israel) that they would do their share in bringing about an end to a long-standing impasse on the Arab-Israeli conflict by attacking Israel. Only after the front-line states gave such an assurance did the Saudis agree to use the oil weapon for political purposes.

This agreement with the major military actors of the Arab world – e.g., Egypt and Syria – enabled Saudi Arabia to emerge as one of the most significant actors of the Middle East. This clout was deftly utilised by the Saudis in giving or withholding their approval to the modalities of the withdrawal negotiations that were carried out by the US Secretary of State, Henry Kissinger, between the armed forces of Egypt and Israel and of Syria and Israel in the aftermath of the 1973 Arab-Israeli war. The Saudis also gave their nod of approval to Sadat's overtures toward the United States following 1973.

The political sophistication which surrounded the handling of the oil embargo by the Saudis, and their ever-present willingness to give serious consideration to moderate political solutions, brought about a much sought American recognition of their leadership. In its zeal to recognise the Saudi importance to any political solution of the Arab-Israeli conflict, however, Washington failed to recognise that while Saudi Arabia aspires to be one of the leaders of the Arab world, this leadership has been essentially quite conservative and also overly committed to prudence. It was only in the wake of a sustained Saudi refusal to get involved in the Camp David peace process that Washington realised that Saudi Arabia almost invariably prefers to *follow* a political consensus. This idiosyncrasy prevents that country from opting for bold measures of a political or military nature, an essential characteristic for a country that aspires to dominate the Gulf. Bold political and military steps have been two strong characteristics of Iran both as a monachy and as a republic.

The Iranian ambition to militarily dominate the region might have been viewed in a competitive spirit or it might have even been a source of envy. But the Iranian military manoeuvres under the Shah did not create security-related fears in Saudi Arabia. An important aspect of Iranian involvement was aimed at discouraging the nurturing of communist insurgencies in the region, and Saudi Arabia shared this strategic objective with the imperial Iran.

The political revolution in Iran was a source of concern to all monarchies of the Arabian Peninsula. There prevailed too many politico-economic similarities between the imperial Iran and the Gulf monarchies that would have made possible a potential emulation of the Khomeini-style revolution in any of them. To begin with, all of these states were (and still are) under monarchical rule. Second, as monarchies, none of them have either allowed channels of venting political dissent or permitted avenues of popular participation. Finally, all Gulf monarchies experienced an inflow of a massive amount of petrodollars and introduced massive and rather haphazard modernisation endeavours.

If the establishment of an Islamic republic in Iran *per se* did not result in much heightening of the security-related fears among the Gulf monarchies, the exportability principle of the Khomeini regime, as discussed in an earlier chapter, convinced them that Iran is indeed determined to alter the political status quo in the Gulf in its own image.

The Iranian revolution was viewed both as a source of promise and problem by Saudi Arabia. The promising aspect of this revolution was that it provided a definite opportunity for the Saudis to exercise their leadership, and the latter aspect was its possible export to the neighbouring states. That country properly utilised this opportunity by becoming one of the chief protagonists for the creation of the Gulf Cooperation Council (GCC). Now Saudi Arabia, along with its allies of the GCC, was viewing Iran as one of the chief threats to the political status quo in the Gulf, the Soviet Union being perceived as the foremost destabilising threat to the region.

One of the most significant differences between the Saudi and Iranian aspirations to dominate the region is that Saudi Arabia has always been aware of the fact that its dominance over the region may only be established with the support and active cooperation of the United States. Iran under Khomeini, on the contrary, is determined to eliminate the influence of both superpowers. This Iranian predeliction is likely to produce mixed results for that country. Since it wants to minimise (or eliminate) the strategic influence of both super-powers, either of these actors, may manoeuvre to undermine the Iranian aspirations perceived of as potentially detrimental to the prospects of their own strategic dominance of the Gulf. The chief advantage to Iran is that neither superpower may take overt measures aimed at overthrowing the Khomeini regime lest it create a retaliatory response from the other. This reality has been quite frustrating from the perspective of the Saudi leadership.

As Iran prolonged its war with Iraq, the GCC states became more and more involved by providing political and material support for the latter belligerent. The traditional competitive nature of the Saudi-Iraqi and Iraqi-Kuwaiti rivalries were set aside because of a larger threat stemming from the exportability principle of the Khomeini regime. Even in supporting Iraq, the GCC states under the Saudi leadership maintained their position of non-reliance on a superpower except under a condition of extreme emergency. For instance, Saudi Arabia in June 1984 shot down an Iranian aircraft that penetrated its airspace, and in September of the same year a Saudi merchant vessel was damaged by mines that were allegedly planted in the Red Sea by a fundamentalist group, al Jihad (the Holy War). In view of these events, when the United States and other Western states offered to intervene to help Saudi Arabia, if necessary, that country maintained that it will take offensive measures when there is an attack on its territory or there is an attempt to close the Strait of Hormuz, its major export outlet. It also expressed its willingness to grant the United States access to onshore military facilities in the event of a major escalation of war.

Until the summer of 1987, the Saudi leadership remained unflinched in opting for self-reliance, choosing an improvement of its defence system and those of its GCC allies. In fact, the Saudi quest for the purchase of the Airborne Warning and Control System (AWACS) from the US in 1981 and the GCC's decision in October 1985 to establish a rapid deployment force – emulating the USCENT-COM – were prime examples of its policy of self-reliance.

In a previous chapter, it has been argued that this policy of maintaining a distance with the United States was an example of a policy of appeasement of Iran by the Gulf states. At this point it will be argued that this appeasement policy in tandem with the policy of self-reliance was quite complementary to the long-cherished Saudi objectives of emerging as a major military force in the Gulf.

The possession of military capability by itself does not make a nation-state a dominant regional actor, however. A related, and an extremely vital condition, is the *willingness* to use this power when circumstances deem it necessary. On this point alone Saudi Arabia has maintained a consistently poor record, especially since the summer of 1987.

Since the summer of 1987, Kuwait, whose historical preference for sustaining a balanced relationship with both superpowers, emerged as a pace-setter of the GCC states. The Kuwaiti invitation to both superpowers to provide their military shields brought an end to the 'appeasement phase' of the GCC states, as was discussed in an earlier chapter. This Kuwaiti act might also be viewed as yet another example of the Saudi inability to be actively involved in forming a new consensus. This inability, along with its pervasive refusal to take offensive measures in the Gulf are two of the biggest variables undermining the Saudi leadership in the Gulf.

THE BALANCING ACT

Since the Iranian revolution, Saudi Arabia has been investing a considerable amount of its energy on balancing its relationship with the Islamic Republic of Iran, its aspirations to be the leader of OPEC, and a dominant actor in the Gulf. Within OPEC, there is little doubt that this country is a dominant force because of a combination of such factors as the sheer weight of its proved oil reserves, its willingness to be a swing producer, and its sustained activism in looking for avenues of cooperation between OPEC and non-OPEC states for the control of production and firming up prices. In the 1980s, the leadership of OPEC has become an issue of diminished significance, but an elevation of its importance is quite likely in the 1990s under a buoyant oil market. This conflict is far from settled. In the late 1980s, the attention of Saudi Arabia and Iran have been focused on security-related issues.

If one examines the behaviour of Iran under the Khomeini regime, it seems there are two Irans: an 'economic Iran', operating inside the framework of OPEC, and a 'political Iran', operating outside OPEC. The economic Iran appears pragmatic and willing to cooperate with other oil states on matters of economic interests. Iran is still a member of OPEC, an organisation whose membership includes not only Iraq, the country with which it has been fighting a war since

September 1980, but also a number of Gulf states who have been supporting Iraq in this war.

Naturally, the war itself became one of the chief reasons underlying the heightening of acrimony among the oil states of the Gulf. Both Iran and Iraq want to be given a production quota which is at least as high as that of the other. What makes Iran bitter during the debate over the assigning of production quotas is that it finds virtually no sympathy among other oil states in the Gulf about the fact that its production has gone considerably down, as a result of deliberate policy of the Khomeini regime, from about 6 million b/d to a little over 2 million b/d. Now Iran finds itself bickering over a production quota of about 3 million b/d.

The requirements of bankrolling a war not only forced Iran to argue for higher production, but it also aggressively violated production quotas and undercut prices throughout the 1980s to fulfil its evergrowing needs for hard currency. The price and production-related aggressiveness of Iran under Khomeini has been one of the reasons underlying the inability of OPEC to successfully implement its production quotas in the 1980s. It is important to note that other oil states have also been quite active in emulating the Iranian aggressiveness. The cumulative results of these activities, along with the production escalations of non-OPEC states, emerged in the inability of OPEC to firm up prices.

The political Iran has been quite intransigent and has manifested an unwillingness to accept negotiated solutions to a number of conflicts affecting the security and stability of the Gulf and the Middle East. The Iranian posture toward the protracted war with Iraq is a glaring example of its stubbornness. The Khomeini regime has continued to insist on the removal of Saddam Hussein from the presidency of Iraq, on the branding of Iraq as the aggressor by the world community of nations, and on Iraqi payment of reparations to Iran as its non-negotiable demands to end the war.

The second example of the Iranian inflexibility is the potential exportation of Islamic revolution to the Gulf states. Iran has raised the political stakes by declaring that the policy posture of its neighbours toward both superpowers, and especially toward the United States, would be the litmus test of the Islamic character of the neighbouring states. Any state closely linked with the so-called Great Satan cannot lay claims to being faithful to Islam, and becomes a potential target of the exportability principle. Now the neighbouring states must rethink their long-standing close ties with the United

States. Militarily, they must remain at least neutral.

The third example of the uncompromising posture of Iran involves its insistence on the resolution of the Palestinian question. The Khomeini regime wants the Arab states to actively seek a solution of the Arab-Israeli conflict that fulfils the aspirations of the Palestinians. When examined collectively the Iranian position on these issues – i.e., the Iranian demands for the neutrality of the Gulf states and its insistence on the resolution of the Palestinian question – appear contradictory. From the perspective of politics, Arab states may be in a better position to influence American policy toward the Arab-Israeli conflict by being friendly, not necessarily neutral, toward the United States. The fact that the prolonged friendly ties between the moderate Arab countries and the United States failed to produce a solution desired by the Arabs does not mean that a continuation of this attitude would not produce a negotiated solution to this obdurate conflict. Moreover, the insistence of the Khomeini regime that the solution of the Palestinian question should fulfil the aspirations of the Palestinians also underscores a solution that involves the dismantlement of Israel. Needless to say, such a scenario is unthinkable under current political realities.

One can argue that on the Palestinian question the Khomeini regime has deliberately taken an extreme position and it might abandon in the future its insistence that the Gulf states stop being friendly to the United States and promote avenues for the creation of Palestine. This argument cannot be categorically rejected because Iran, especially in its arms purchase with Israel and the United States in the early 1980s, demonstrated that it is quite capable of being pragmatic. What has been creating enhanced tensions on the balancing act between Saudi Arabia and Iran, however, is a sustained manifestation of 'selective pragmatism' by the Khomeini regime. This behaviour enables Iran to act as a rational and pragmatic actor on economic matters and in its quest for arms. But in its dealings with the Gulf states, especially on the conditions to end the war with Iraq, its insistence on exporting the Islamic revolution, its demands for neutrality, and its adherence to an unrealistic solution to the Palestinian question, Iran has been consistently acting as an inflexible and strident actor and as a destabilising force.

This selective pragmatism has so enhanced its fears since the summer of 1987, that Saudi Arabia, along with other GCC states, has given a high priority to further strengthening its military ties with the United States. Thus, Iran appeared to have defeated its own purpose of forcing the neighbouring states to move away from the super-powers.

The escalation of war, the sustenance of the oil glut, and the vitriolic tone of the political rhetorics of the Khomeini regime have collectively made the Gulf a highly explosive region. What is troubling is that neither superpower can influence the course of events. In the wake of continued Iranian intransigence to either end the war or lower the level of political tensions, Saudi Arabia may not be able to sustain balance in its ties with Iran. OPEC deliberations are likely to become more acrimonious; the continued oil glut, along with growing tensions within OPEC may also bring about its dis-mantlement, a nightmarish scenario for all the member states.

Notes

1. The vital statistics on Iran and Saudi Arabia are from *The Europa Yearbook 1987* (London: Europa Publications, 1987).
2. Issues of high politics are of primary concern to top decision-makers. Low politics include those issues that are relegated to authorities at the low eschelon. See Stanley Hoffman, 'Obstinate or Obsolete?: The Fate of Nation State and the Case of Western Europe', *Daedalus*, Summer, 1966, 95, pp. 862–915.
3. M. E. Ahrari, *OPEC – the Failing Giant* (Lexington: The University Press of Kentucky, 1986), pp. 42–7.
4. For details of the Tehran agreement see ibid., p. 47.
5. For a detailed discussion of the participations agreements see ibid., pp. 99–105.
6. Ibid., p. 72.
7. 'Output Cut at OPEC is less likely', *The New York Times*, 12 March 1988.

4 Fools Rush In: American Policy and the Iraq–Iran War, 1980–88

Gregory F. Rose

> ... a war in which every principle of equity and justice was
> sacrificed to considerations of policy, and that policy so fatally false
> that its success served only to augment our danger.
>
> *John Clark Marshman*
> *on British policy in the First Afghan War*

INTRODUCTION

Marshman's devastating assessment of British policy in the First
Afghan War seems, at first, an obscure starting point for a discussion
of US policy toward the Iraq–Iran war. However, a careful examination of the history of that policy, particularly the turn it has taken
since late 1986, suggests that Marshman's assessment may yet be as
painfully true of US policy as it was of Great Britain's. Indeed, while
explicably charting the oscillations of US policy may be taxing of
social scientific theory, the implications of such a study for analysis of
US decision-making and for the future interests of the United States
in the Gulf region are deeply distressing. This chapter attempts, first,
to summarise the history of this policy and, second to venture some
preliminary generalisations from that history about the policy which
may enable explanation and prediction of that policy's future course
and consequences. If it is neither pleasant nor comforting, it has, at
least, the saving grace of being true.

A BRIEF HISTORY OF US POLICY TOWARD THE IRAQ–
IRAN WAR

From the inception of the Iraq–Iran war, US policy has meandered
through five distinct stages of development, each with its own

particular policy objectives and means. At first appearance this policy has been singularly inconsistent. However, careful scrutiny discloses some interesting underlying patterns.

Vicarious vengeance, 1980–81

While the precise extent to which the United States was the author of Iraq's decision to invade Iran in September 1980 remains uncertain, that the US government both encouraged and sought to profit from the invasion is almost certain. The pressures impinging upon an American administration, facing a difficult re-election battle in a political environment charged with constant reminders of the utter failure of that administration to obtain release of its hostages in Tehran or to inflict vengeance for the international humiliation it had thereby endured, can certainly be understood. While leading figures in the Carter Administration have denied any advance knowledge of Iraq's invasion plans, press reports of meetings between US intelligence and national security officials and representatives of Saddam Hussein's regime in the months immediately prior to the invasion, as well as the Administration's strong encouragement of Egyptian, Jordanian, Moroccan and Sudanese support for the Iraqi war effort, give these protestations an air of implausibility. In any case, once the war began and Iraqi victory – or, more properly, Iranian defeat – seemed likely, the Carter Administration ill concealed its delight at the emergence of another source of international pressure on the Iranian government. Indeed, the Carter Administration believed that the Iraqi invasion could only hasten the willingness of Iran to negotiate a settlement to the hostage crisis in hopes of obtaining military spares purchased under the Shah but embargoed by the US.[1] So long as Iraq appeared successful in the war and pressure was appropriately applied thereby to induce greater Iranian tractability in the hostage negotiations, the Carter Administration was content to oppose 'the dismemberment of Iran', in Secretary of State Edmund Muskie's phrase, and call for an end to the war, while transferring US military materiel to Egypt to replace Soviet-made Egyptian stores being donated to Iraq. It is questionable whether this American support for Iraq's aggression had any significant impact on the hostage crisis settlement. Indeed, the general lines along which a settlement was eventually negotiated were enunciated by Imam Khomeini in a speech of 12 September 1980, ten days prior to the

Iraqi invasion. None the less, the sentiment in Washington in the latter days of 1980 was that, regardless of its impact on the negotiations, the Iraqi invasion provided some well-deserved vicarious vengeance against Iran.

Malign neglect, 1981–3

Iran little interested the Reagan Administration in its first two years in office: the Administration had larger domestic and international concerns and, while the Iraqi offensive stalled by the Spring of 1981, the Administration showed little interest in the war or either of the contending parties.

SHORING UP THE DIKE, 1983–5

The successful Iranian offensives of 1982–3, liberating most of the territory Iraq had seized, including the city of Khorramshahr, the only major city to fall into enemy hands, was a fearsome testimony to the precariousness of Iraq's position and, by implication, that of the Arab principalities of the Gulf. Assistant Secretary of State for the Near East and South Asia Richard Murphy and others with close ties to the Arab monarchies impressed upon Secretary of State George Shultz the necessity for a strong US tilt toward Iraq, including open support for the Iraqi war effort if necessary. Key personnel in the Defense Department, including Secretary Caspar Weinberger, were enlisted in this effort to build support for Iraq. The chief argument put forward by these pro-Iraqi activists was the necessity of an Iraqi buffer to prevent the threat of Iranian hegemony in the Gulf from overwhelming Saudi Arabia, Kuwait, and the other Arab principalities; other arguments alleging Iranian complicity in international 'terrorism' and the threat posed to international shipping in the Gulf by the nascent 'tanker war'.[2]

As early as 1982 the US removed Iraq from the list of countries alleged to be supporters of international terrorism (and at a time when the Baghdad regime was sheltering the Abu Nidal organisation. Senior diplomatic contacts were commenced with the Iraqi regime, culminating in reestablishment of diplomatic relations in November 1984. Efforts were launched to shore up the desperately contracting Iraqi economy with nearly $2 billion in US credits and US encouragement of increasingly large loans floated by French banks and the governments of Saudi Arabia and Kuwait. The scale of US AWACS aircraft to Saudi Arabia and their operational deployment was denounced by Iran as a blatant attempt to provide US intelligence gathering support to the Iraqi armed forces. While this was denied by the administration at the time, in May 1984 Saddam Hussein publicly admitted the considerable help provided to the Iraqi war effort by the US-piloted AWACS.

While the US encouraged France and others to arm the Iraqis, it initiated an extensive diplomatic campaign aimed at dissuading foreign governments from engaging in arms sales to Iran. Great Britain, West Germany, Italy, Belgium, Argentina, Brazil, South Korea, Tawain, and the People's Republic of China were all variously cajoled or threatened by the US government for their sales of military and military-related equipment to Iran. In most cases the pressure was to little avail. Despite US silence regarding the original Iraqi invasion, the administration launched a relentless stream of diplomatic invective against each Iranian counter-offensive; Iraqi attacks on international shipping in the northern half of the Gulf were ignored, while Iranian retaliatory strikes, generally in the southern half of the Gulf were lambasted as barbaric assaults on freedom of the seas. There was, however, one catch to this shift in American policy: despite the administration's boldest efforts its erstwhile Iraqi friend appeared to be losing the war.

Sense and nonsense, 1985–6

While the Reagan Administration, with not insignificant help from the Congressional investigation committees, attempted to portray the shift in US policy toward Iran in 1985–6 as an aberration brought on by the excesses of over-zealous underlings plotting macabre scenarios in the bowels of the NSC, a careful examination of the documentary record suggests quite a different reality. The first stirrings of opposition to the pro-Iraqi policy were seen in CIA officer Graham Fuller's May 1985 estimate that Iran was dangerously close to internal collapse, a collapse which threatened to create a political vacuum in the region into which the Soviet Union threatened to loom. Fuller's memorandum was seized upon by two NSC staffers, Donald Fortier and Howard Teicher, in their draft of the 17 June 1985 National Security Decision Directive as further evidence of a grave Soviet threat to Iran and the Gulf region (*viz.*, John Tower *et al.*, *Tower Commission Report*, Bantam, 1987, pp. 112–21). This assessment lacked, as events have demonstrated, any basis in fact. Indeed, only a fevered preoccupation with a grandly over-estimated Soviet Union could have blinded professional intelligence officers to the evidence of growing stability and internal resiliency in Iran. Indeed, less than a year later the CIA was predicting an eventual Iranian victory in the war with Iraq. However, other factors as well weighed in the growing pressure from within the NSC and CIA, as well as a number of the President's political advisors, for abandonment of the pro-Iraqi tilt and a reassessment of US-Iranian relations. First among these was the increasing *realpolitik* of the Arab principalities of the Gulf. Already Bahrain had found a *modus vivendi* with the Islamic Republic, and the Saudi foreign minister's surprise visit to Tehran in May 1985 heralded a considerable warming in the hitherto frigid Saudi-Iranian relationship. These governments could tell which way the wind blew, and it blew in early 1985 toward Tehran, not Baghdad. Second, the collapse of international oil prices in late 1985 made a virtue of this *realpolitik*. As James Bill cogently argues, this development was powerfully felt in the Reagan Administration:

> Throughout much of 1986, oil prices had plummeted until they bottomed at less than ten dollars per barrel. This occurred primarily as a result of sharply increased Saudi production, production that cut severely into the revenues of the major oil-producing states. In the United States, it had badly crippled the economies of the Southwest; in Washington, the cries of the independent oil industry became loud and threatening. Influential national politicians from Texas – Vice President George Bush, Treasury Secretary James Baker, House Speaker Jim Wright, and Sens. Phil Gramm and Lloyd Bentsen – sought to defend the interests of their constituents. In the Middle East, Iran's and America's interests converged on this issue. Within the halls of OPEC, the Islamic Republic had long struggled for lower production and higher prices. The United States, meanwhile, needed prices high enough to protect the domestic oil industry but low enough to placate the consumer. The surprise Saudi-Iranian agreement on lower production in August–September 1986 achieved this goal, and prices rose steadily to the eighteen-to-twenty dollar level per barrel in 1987. (*The Eagle and the Lion: America and Iran*, Yale UP, 1988, p. 311)

Finally, the issue of the hostages in Lebanon burned in the Administration's craw and recognition among the President's senior political advisors was growing that the failure to win their release could cause not insignificant damage to the Administration's domestic political fortunes. The Administration's grandiose estimate of the degree of Iranian influence with militant Shiah groups in Lebanon contributed to the belief that a *rapprochement* with Iran was the key to obtaining the hostage's freedom. The initiatives which followed from these concerns are well known.

However ineptly executed and burdened with whatever unrealistic assumptions and expectations the Reagan Administration's opening to Iran in 1986 held real promise. As one senior Iranian diplomat admitted, 'America's willingness to recognize the permanence of our revolution and to aid our struggle against Saddam Hussein caused the leaders in Tehran to stop and think whether the US had a real change of heart and we could deal with it now. Many people thought, "if Reagan can go this far, maybe we can trust the Americans"' (private communication, 1987). The retrospective – and self-serving – admissions of Lieutenant Colonel Oliver North and others in the Administration of wholesale duplicity in their dealings with Iranian representatives – 'I lied every time I met the Iranians', as North confessed – casts doubt on the ultimate chance for success for a pro-Iranian tilt in US policy. The domestic and international uproar which ensued thrust the American government into a 180-degree change of tack and sent into careening into increasingly violent confrontation with Iran and open intervention into the war on behalf of Iraq.

The empire strikes back, 1987–8

While the Arab princes of the Gulf were prepared for some limited US-Iranian *rapprochement*, particularly on the question of oil prices, they were aghast at the extent to which the Reagan Administration was prepared to accept Iran as a regional hegemon. Bitter recriminations between Kuwait and Saudi Arabia, the chief bankrollers of Iraq's war effort, and the US ensued. Its Iran policy in shambles, the Administration faced a grave rupture in its hitherto friendly relations with the riparian Arab states. The reactions of the Kuwaiti and Saudi governments were, however, relatively mild compared to the vitriolic outcry faced by the Administration on the domestic front. Any sensible explanations of national interest were abandoned immediately by the President and his advisors, who proceeded to dig themselves in deeper still with protestations about negotiations with non-existent 'moderates' to secure an American influence in post-Khomeini Iran.[3] A deeply embarrassed Reagan Administration abjectly fled from any policy which hinted of *rapprochement* with Iran. Once again, the pro-Iraqi group around Secretary of State Shultz was ascendant and policies most like those of 1983–5 were again adopted, albeit with rather less success, as those nations engaged in military sales to Iran were little inclined to take instruction from the United States after its arms sales.

The US embrace of Iraq was dazzlingly total. Indeed, when an Iraqi aircraft attacked the USS Stark on 17 May 1987, killing thirty-seven Americans, the Administration responded, astoundingly, by warning Iran not to be provocative. Repeated use of chemical weapons by Iraq – including attacks on civilian populations in Kurdistan which killed thousands – went unchallenged by an Administration which seemed to justify these desperate Iraqi measures on the grounds that Iran's refusal to negotiate an end to the war provoked them. Diplomatic initiatives were mounted at the United Nations to impose an international arms embargo on Iran, but these were thwarted by Soviet and Chinese reluctance to proceed against Iran alone.[4] However, these measures were exceeded by an order of magnitude in the early summer of 1987, when the United States militarily intervened in the Gulf.

The decision to reflag Kuwaiti oil tankers and deploy US naval vessels for their escort was presented to Congress and the American people as a defence of freedom of the seas. The truth of the matter was rather more sordid. Certainly Iran had attacked vessels en route to Kuwaiti and Saudi terminals and, international military sources suggest, had laid mines in the Gulf. However, Iran regarded these attacks and the mine-laying as retaliation against the vastly more numerous Iraqi attacks on international shipping destined for Iran and as a means of interdicting the flow of contraband to a belligerent through 'neutral' ports. Specifically, Kuwaiti and Saudi neutrality in the war had been a facade behind which both nations had funded the Iraqi war effort with loans and grants (indeed, to such an extent that without such aid Iraq would likely have lost the war outright by 1983), had provided facilities for transshipment of military materiel off-loaded at their ports destined for Iraq, and had shared vital intelligence, provided by US AWACS aircraft, with the Iraqi armed forces. The attempted *rapprochement* with Saudi Arabia, which collapsed in the aftermath of public disclosure of the US negotiations with Iran, had failed to provide Iran with relief from the effects of Kuwaiti and Saudi aid to the Iraqi war effort. Iran resolved to make these states pay for their not-so-clandestine belligerence.[5] It was in this environment that the Amir of Kuwait first requested the American reflagging of Kuwaiti tankers. The first request was politely declined by an administration reluctant, regardless of its support for Iraq, to militarily intervene in the Gulf. However, a threat to similarily invite a Soviet reflagging proved sufficient to bring the Reagan Administration to heel. No doubt domestic political concerns – in particular the desire to project an image of anti-Iranian commitment at a time when the Administration's Iran initiatives were undergoing daily televised *auto-da-fé* at the hands of Congress – played a role in the American decision to intervene. However, despite this intervention, the Islamic Republic remained open to reaching a *modus vivendi* with the US government, a project which Iranian President Ali Khamene'i had hope to advance during his September 1987 visit to the United Nations General Assembly. Whether the attack on the eve of Khamene'i's visit on an Iranian vessel allegedly laying mines was a result of factional disagreement within the Administration over the Iranian initiative or a concerted demonstration by the Administration of its uninterest in such overtures is, as yet, unknown. However, the attack, and the consequent destruction of Iranian oil platforms in the Gulf a few weeks later, sealed any chance of improvement in US–Iranian relations and convinced many in Iran that the US planned to directly intervene on Iraq's behalf in the war. There were, however, voices in Tehran which counselled moderation and restraint in the face of these provocations and these voices prevailed. Similar moderation did not prevail in Washington.

The 18 April 1988 US attacks on Iranian oil platforms and the Iranian navy marked a vast escalation in the American intervention in the Gulf. Coinciding with an Iraqi offensive on the Fav Peninsula (an offensive which involved extensive chemical attacks), the US strikes, allegedly in retaliation for a mine which damaged a few days earlier the USS Roberts, cemented the conviction in Iran that the US was waging war against the Islamic Republic. That the voices of restraint in Tehran will prevail in the face of such a fact is increasingly unlikely. Indeed, the Reagan Administration seemed incredulous that Iran chose to defend itself against these strikes. 'I'm not sure it's explainable in terms of Western logic', Secretary of Defense Frank Carlucci opined regarding the Iranian attempt to defend its oil platforms and naval vessels against American attack. It takes, however, no exercise in esoteric logic to understand why any government could not stand by, regardless of the odds against it, in the face of repeated attacks on its installations by a hostile foreign power: Iran fought back because the US navy gave it no choice. The precedent should have been sobering to US policy-makers: they were dealing with no prostrate Grenada, incapable of self-defence. However, the Administration's public posture in the aftermath of its attacks suggested that the lesson had not been learned. If the avowed intention of the United States had been to wage war on the Islamic Republic of Iran, it could not have more efficiently achieved its aim.

EXPLAINING THE INSCRUTABLE

The wild oscillations of US policy toward the Iran–Iraq war are a daunting subject for systematic explanation. In the absence of such a general explanation, we venture four generalisations bout US policy toward the Iran–Iraq war.

1. American policy toward the Iraq–Iran war seems less driven by a systematic assessment of US interests in the region than the exogenous buffeting of the course of international, regional, and domestic events. It is likely that we are less dealing here with systematic decision-making than *ad hoc* crisis management.
2. The Soviet centricity of American policy thoroughgoingly colours US perceptions of political, military, and economic realities in the Gulf. Both the original CIA assessment and National Security Decision Directive which initiated the US *rapprochement* with Iran and the decision to militarily intervene in the Gulf were largely determined by an over-arching preoccupation with Soviet intentions and capabilities which had the effect of vastly inflating estimates of Soviet involvement and deflating estimates of regional causes of conflict.
3. The exigencies of US domestic politics play a considerable role in driving US policy toward the war. The virulence of anti-Iranian sentiment in American domestic politics is well known and the Reagan Administration's desire not to provide potent ammunition to domestic political opponents accounts for much of the vigorous back-pedalling after disclosure of the 1985–6 overtures to Iran.

4. Concern with America's international reputation for efficacy and tenacity has become a focal point for the Reagan Administration in its dealings with the Gulf region. It if is true that the US is a declining hegemon (*viz.*, Robert Keohean, *After Hegemony: Cooperation as Discord in the World Political Economy*, Princeton UP, 1984), then, as American political and economic resources decline, so also does its ability to unilaterally impose international outcomes. In such an increasingly difficult environment reputation becomes the international coin of the realm for the declining hegemon. The selection of salient targets against which reputation can be accrued becomes increasingly important.[6] However, exercises in reputational enhancement conducted against targets which can respond and protract the conflict can quickly become exercises in reputational diminishment. In such circumstances the impulse to escalate, to make an end of the encounter by fiat, is a highly potent one.[7] US policy toward Iran since 1987 seems to fit precisely such a pattern.

UNSETTLING PREDICTIONS

Examining the four generalisations set forward regarding US policy toward the Iraq–Iran war, there are few hopeful signs. Indeed, the only hope one can draw from these generalisations is the recognition that real constraints exist on the extent to which the US can effectively intervene on Iraq's behalf in the war. First, while naval and air strikes remain available to the US – and, indeed, remain almost costless to the extent that Kuwait is prepared to foot the bill for the US naval deployment[8] – such sorties will, by their nature, remain limited. Second, it is unlikely that the Congress would countenance commitment of US ground forces. Third, should the possibility of any significant costs in lives and equipment arise, it is unlikely that the Reagan Administration would continue such intervention in the midst of a presidential election campaign. To be sure, jingoistic popular responses routinely follow such operations, but the prospect of protracted conflict and its concomitant delivery of coffins to the bereaved next of kin of US servicemen in the glare of television news coverage during an election campaign seems a reasonable constraint to assume. However, even given these constraints, we cannot underestimate the potential for catastrophe to which American policy in the Gulf has been brought. The Reagan Administration has effectively chosen to wage war on the Islamic Republic of Iran. The first consequence of this decision has been to poison any hope of a *modus vivendi* between Iran and the US for the foreseeable future. The regional consequences within the Muslim world have not yet begun to appear clearly. It should be, however, sobering to recognise that Iran, in all its apparent weakness *vis-à-vis* the United States, still has the weapons of the weak and history suggests that such weapons can be as effective as carrier-based air strikes. One can only pray that Ronald Reagan's bringing of war to Iran has not brought that war home.

Notes

1. Gary Sick, Zbigniew Brzezinski's action officer for Iran at the NSC, recounts discussions between Deputy Secretary of State Warren Christopher and Sadegh Tabataba'i, representing the Iranian government, in Bonn in mid-September 1980 in which Tabataba'i expressed interest in military equipment as a trade-off for release of the hostages; Christopher indicated that approximately $50 million in spares 'could be made available to Iran once all other aspects of the dispute were resolved (Gary Sick, *All Fall Down: America's Tragic Encounter with Iran*, Random House, 1986, p. 368). State department officials privately suggest that Brzezinski saw the Iraqi invasion as 'sweetening' the deal by increasing Iran's eagerness to trade the hostages for such equipment. Throughout these negotiations, however, the US sought to deceive the Iranians as to how much material purchased by the Shah had been embargoed in order to keep the price-tag as low as possible and to limit any military benefit which might accrue to Iran from such a trade-off. As Sick suggests, 'part of the negotiating strategy was to keep the Iranian side as unenlightened as possible on this issue' (p. 368). Former Assistant Secretary of State for the Near East and South Asia Harold Saunders has contextualised the Iraqi invasion in the following way:

    > In the slightly longer term, [as a result of the war] Iran's leaders became acutely aware in concrete ways of the consequences of Iran's diplomatic isolation, their inability to resupply Iran's military forces, the impact of further reductions in oil sales on dwindling financial reserves, and the economic sanctions which had begun to make themselves felt. (in Warren Christopher *et al.*, *American Hostages in Iran*, Yale UP, p. 290)

    Roberts B. Owen, former Legal Advisor to the Secretary of State, expressed the view more callously:

    > . . . we took what comfort we could from the realization that, with a war on its hand, Iran would be feeling the pinch of the sanctions more than ever and would thus be forcefully reminded, on a daily basis, of the harm that the

detention of the hostages was doing to Iranian national interests. (in Christopher, 1985, p. 306)

A former CIA official, commenting later on the situation, put the matter somewhat more bluntly still: 'the Iraqis had Iran by the b---s, and that permitted us to gently squeeze'.

2.   The particular shamelessness of this latter allegation is highlighted by the fact that, at the time it was made, only Iraq had engaged in attacks on Gulf shipping; indeed, up to the present Iraqi attacks on international shipping have considerably outnumbered Iranian attacks. Nor has the Administration, to this date, made public any evidence for its claims of Iranian complicity in the bombings of the US embassy in Beirut or the US Marine Amphibious Landing Group compound; this has led some observers to wonder whether such evidence, in fact, exists.

3.   The derision with which these protestations was met is suggested by a colleague of the author who observed, 'the poor bugger I wouldn't want to be is the one who has to explain to Ayatollah Khomeini just what moderates they were dealing with in Washington'.

4.   To be sure, revenue from a lucrative arms trade with Iran via North Korea also played a role in the Chinese opposition, as did the desire to use the embargo as a bargaining chip in a grander strategic setting in the Soviet case.

5.   Some observers have argued that the massacre of Iranian pilgrims in Mecca on 31 July 1987, was a result of Saudi determination to retaliate for Iranian attacks on Saudi-destined shipping. This explanation, however, seems far fetched. The virulently anti-Shiah character of the Saudi regime and its not unjustified paranoia about Islamic revolutionary sentiments in the Muslim world seem more likely the basis for this atrocity.

6.   It is useful to regard the invasion of Grenada, the bombing of Libya, and US aid to the Nicaraguan contras in this context.

7.   Indeed, much of the US policy during the Vietnam war may well be exemplary of this pattern.

8.   Defense Department officials openly admit that Kuwait is providing the deployment's fuel requirements; they privately admit that additional Kuwaiti subsidies for the operations are forthcoming.

5 Security Concerns in the Arabian Peninsula

J. E. Peterson

The Arab states of the Gulf have taken a variety of steps to enhance their security. First, they have banded together in the Gulf Cooperation Council (GCC), a sensible move that not only provides a little more bulk, manpower of financial resources for defence purposes, but also makes considerable sense economically and culturally. Led by Saudi Arabia's predominant size and financial resources, the GCC states have embarked on ambitious military modernisation programmes. These cannot overcome obvious constraints of small size and manpower problems but nevertheless will help these countries to meet a myriad of lesser security threats. They have worked toward accommodation with more powerful and radical neighbours in the Gulf, as well as elsewhere in the Arabian Peninsula and the Middle East. They have also sought friendship and economic and political cooperation with the United States and the West. But, mindful of the lessons of the past, they have insisted that military cooperation remain limited to an 'over-the-horizon' role.

THE SECURITY ENVIRONMENT OF THE ARAB GULF STATES

The six Arab monarchies of the Gulf have much in common. Their small indigenous populations are predominantly Arab and Sunni Muslim. They are still tribal societies, strongly traditional with emphasis on the family. Most of the ruling families emerged around the eighteenth century out of the tribal environment, and their leadership continues to be highly legitimate in the eyes of nearly all nationals (see Table 5.1). Independence came in 1961 for Kuwait and in 1971 for Bahrain, Qatar, and the United Arab Emirates. While the modern Kingdom of Saudi Arabia dates only from 1934 under that name, its Al Sa'ud roots extend back several centuries. Oman always has been technically independent.

These countries share a common legacy of traditional economies based on pastoralism, pearling, and some fishing. Before oil, the decline of pearling and onset of the world depression had rendered them poverty stricken. The discovery of oil in the decades between 1930 and 1970 was fortuitous, and their economies remain dependent on oil revenues, as well as some oil-based or oil-fuelled industries. There are few resources apart from oil: the land is generally unproductive, water is scarce, there are few exploitable minerals and the populations are small. The period of oil boom and economic development has produced a flood of expatriates, who fill positions ranging from those with considerable skill to common labour.

Table 5.1   The member states of the Gulf Cooperation Council (GCC)

Country	Ruler (and title)	Ruling family	Total population[1]	Percentage of citizens[1]
Bahrain	'Isa bin Salman (Amir)	Al Khalifa	410 000	66
Kuwait	Jabir Al Ahmad (Amir)	Al Sabah	1 700 000	40
Qatar	Khalifa bin Hamad (Amir)	Al Thani	270 000	25
Oman	Qabus bin Sa'id (Sultan)	Al Bu Sa'id	1 300 000	78
Saudi Arabia	Fahd bin 'Abd al-'Aziz (King)	Al Sa'ud	11 000 000	60
United Arab Emirates	Zayid bin Sultan (President)[2]	Al Nahyan[2]	1 600 000	20
Total population			16 280 000	55

Notes:
1. Population figures are author's estimates, extrapolating from recent editions of each country's statistical yearbook or other sources.
2. Shaykh Zayid, the ruler of Abu Dhabi, has served as the only president of the seven-member United Arab Emirates (UAE) since independence in 1971, and was elected by his fellow rulers to a fourth five-year term in 1986. Similarly, Shaykh Rashid bin Sa'id, the ruler of Dubai, has served as the UAE's only Vice-president.

These states face a number of potential threats to internal security, including concerns over (1) sectarian and ethnic minorities, (2) the sheer size of the expatriate population, (3) possible discontent arising from the process of development and the economic recession of the 1980s, and (4) the possibility of organised and subversive opposition groups from either the secular left or the Islamic right.

Sectarian and ethnic minorities

The presence of sectarian and ethnic minorities poses more of a potential security threat than an actual one. The Shiah population is frequently cited in this regard although it is misleading to regard the Shiah of the Arab littoral as a monolithic and subversive bloc. Ethnically, they embrace Arabs, Iranians and Indians, with further subdivisions. The Arab Shiah include Basrawis from Iraq, Hasawis from Saudi Arabia, *hawala* who have migrated to the Iranian coast and back again, and the Baharna who are probably descended from the original inhabitants. Not all Iranians living in Arab states are Shiah. Some Shiah from India are recent arrivals; others, such as the Liwatiya, have resided in the Gulf for hundreds of years.

Some of the most respected and wealthiest merchant families are Shiah, politically conservative and among their governments' staunchest supporters. Others have migrated to these countries because of the oil boom and do not hold citizenship. Ideology, education, generational differences and varying degrees of secularisation add to the multiplicity in Shiah attitudes. While the Iranian revolution stirred passions in 1979 and 1980, suggesting a way for ordinary Shiah (and Sunnis as well) to gain attention and redress their grievances, few apparently saw the Ayatollah Khomeini as their guiding light. The excesses of the Islamic Republic of Iran and the course of the war have further diminished the appeal from the other side of the Gulf except for a few extremists.

Expatriates

While the education and training of citizens and the end of the construction boom may decrease the demand for some expatriates, there will always be a need for a large non-national workforce. Expatriates come from most parts of the world. Arab immigrants, particularly Egyptians, Jordanians and Palestinians, form the oldest and most entrenched communities. The second largest grouping comes from the Indian subcontinent. In recent years, the numbers of Southeast Asians, particularly from the Philippines and South Korea, have increased and there is also a sizeable contingent of Westerners.

The majority of expatriates stay only a few years before returning home with their savings. Consequently, most have little interest in local politics. Non-national Arabs pose a particular problem, as they melt more easily into the environment, tend to stay longer, and may be involved in Arab political causes. Most Gulf states have hosted a permanently resident Palestinian community since the creation of Israel and over half of the 500 000 or more Palestinians in the Gulf were born there. They are not citizens, however, and do not receive the same benefits as nationals. The presence of so many outsiders not only introduces a potential security risk but is perceived by the citizenry as diluting their culture and eroding their national identity.[1]

Impact of development and the economic recession

Despite the attempts to preserve traditional societies, economic development has had far-reaching social and even political impact. Any economic development necessarily involves social change, no matter how carefully considered or resisted. Development in the Gulf has produced, *inter alia*, near-total sedentarisation of the formerly large populations of bedouin, changes in the occupations and life-styles of the majority of the people, a rising dominance of Western or Western-style education, and significant alterations to family structure (as demonstrated in the change from housing based on the extended family to homes designed for use by only the nuclear family).

Increasing numbers of nationals receive primary, secondary, and then higher education, either at home or abroad. Geographic mobility is increasing and many nationals have established private businesses or entered government service. Their perceptions of society and expectations of the government inevitably have been transformed. The impact of the economic recession has been to force government cutbacks in government spending and some increases in charges for public services. Incomes, particularly for businessmen and property speculators, have fallen but few nationals seem to have been truly hurt economically. The possibility of widespread discontent seems to be muted by expectations of a new oil boom in a few years.

Political opposition

Western conceptions of these monarchies as being absolutist, anachronistic, and/or repressive are inaccurate. While the regimes have been very responsive to the needs and demands of their citizenry, and many nationals play important roles in the shaping of decisions and policies through government positions, the possibility remains that future generations will expect greater means of formal political participation. Elected national assemblies have existed in Kuwait and Bahrain but presently are suspended. Consultative councils exist in Qatar, the UAE and Oman; Saudi Arabia has promised a similar council on numerous occasions but has never implemented the proposal.[2]

The heyday of opposition from the secular left would seem to have been the 1960s, with the widespread appeal of pan-Arab socialist ideologies, including Nasirism, Ba'athism, and even Marxism. Since then, there seems to have been little significant support for opposition along these lines. Concern over the Islamic right has multiplied since the Iranian revolution. The seizure of the Great Mosque of Mecca in November 1979 by a small number of Sunni Islamic extremists (mostly Saudis but also including Yemenis, Kuwaitis and Egyptians) shocked the Saudi government. Some observers perceive a growing gulf between establishment Islam and populist Islam, with a feeling that popular sentiment is growing against the perceived misdirection of development and modernisation with its strong overtones of Westernisation and materialism. They fear a grassroots Islamic backlash, much as happened in imperial Iran, against the Gulf regimes for their allegedly un-Islamic nature.[3]

It is undeniable that Gulf societies are becoming more conservative, that many individuals seek to be better Muslims, that arch-conservative Sunni and Shiah movements have displayed considerable strength, and that the Islamic Republic of Iran continues to provide support for subversive Islamic organisations in the Peninsula. Nevertheless, there is little evidence that the majority of the population is sufficiently alienated to actively subvert still-legitimate political systems. This does not rule out the possibility of isolated terrorist acts and sabotage against vulnerable oil installations. To date, however, incidents have been remarkably rare, with the exception of Kuwait.

STATE SECURITY PERCEPTIONS

Saudi Arabia is the largest of these states, both in territory and population. While no census has ever been made public, the Saudi government claims that Saudi nationals number some 9 million out of a total population of 12 million; most independent estimates are considerably lower. Given its recent consolidation, the kingdom still consists of a number of discrete regions linked together principally by oil income (generated exclusively in the Eastern Province) and the leadership of the Al Sa'ud (whose home is Riyadh in the Najdi interior).

Most Saudis are Muwahhidun (Wahhabis), a conservative and ascetic movement within Sunni Islam, but several hundred thousand Shiah live in the agricultural oases of the Eastern Province. To some extent, the satisfaction of Shiah demands has importance far beyond their numbers, as they comprise a majority of the ARAMCO labour force. Demonstrations by Shiah youth, who regard themselves as less middle class and less beholden to ARAMCO than their elders, occurred in al-Qatif and al-Hasa in 1979 and 1980. These developments prompted the government to replace the provincial governor and to provide promises of better living and working conditions and additional development assistance for the region.

Saudi Arabia's possession of one-quarter of the world's total proved crude oil reserves gives it more standing and relatively more power than its size would otherwise indicate. Beginning with the reign of King Faysal (r. 1961–75), Saudi Arabia has sought to exercise greater influence and visibility in matters outside its immediate periphery. In large part, the ruling Al Sa'ud family sees these measures as defensive, believing the kingdom to be encircled by potential or actual enemies. They see potential sources of threats as including Iran, Israel, the Yemens (especially Marxist South Yemen), Ethiopia, Afghanistan, the Soviet Union, Libya, and possibly Syria or even Iraq under changed circumstances.

The kingdom has sought to counteract these threats by a number of strategies. It has embarked on a sustained build-up of its armed forces and has forged strong military ties with the United States. Riyadh has sought to play a mediating role in pan-Arab affairs and has advanced its own version of an Arab-Israeli peace plan for Arab approval. At the height of the oil boom, Saudi Arabia provided more foreign aid than the United States, and it covertly subsidises friendly governments and movements against hostile and communist forces around the globe.[4] While staunchly conservative and pro-Western, the kingdom has taken the first tentative steps toward a renewal of relations, broken off a half-century ago, with the Soviet Union.

Saudi Arabia has given its fullest support to Iraq in its war with

Iran, including the provision of loans and crude oil, allowing Iraq to tie into the oil pipeline that carries part of the kingdom's production across the Arabian Peninsula to the Red Sea, and giving Iraq permission to build its own pipeline across the kingdom. Generally, it has backed away from direct confrontation with Iran, although provoked by harsh Iranian rhetoric, attacks on Saudi oil tankers, and agitation by Iranian pilgrims on the *hajj* (Islamic pilgrimage). In the summer of 1984, Iran went too far and the Saudi air-force shot down an Iranian fighter intruding into Saudi air space.

Relations between the two countries worsened markedly after an Iranian demonstration during the 1987 hajj erupted into violence after Saudi police prevented the demonstrators from marching on the Great Mosque of Mecca. In the ensuing mêlée between stick- and knife-wielding Iranians and Saudi security, 275 Iranians, 85 Saudis, and 42 other nationalities were killed, and an additional 649 were injured.[5] Iranian mobs occupied the Kuwaiti and Saudi embassies in Tehran and a Saudi diplomat died three weeks later, allegedly from injuries received during the takeover. The Saudi government subsequently mounted a campaign for the rupture of diplomatic relations between Iran and all Arab countries, but with only partial success.[6]

Under present circumstances, Kuwait has even more reason to feel encircled. Kuwaitis form a minority of some 40 per cent in their own country. While most of Kuwait's expatriates are only temporary residents, the 300 000–400 000 Palestinians pose a potential threat because of simmering grievances over their treatment as outsiders despite their long residence and manifold contributions to the country's development.

Externally, Kuwait has long sought to safeguard its precarious position by espousing neutrality. Financial aid to both friendly and hostile states, based on strictly economic criteria, has been a principal component of the amirate's foreign policy, as has a sort of official even-handedness between the superpowers. Even though Saudi Arabia is a principal ally (particularly in the the perceptions of the ruling Al Sabah family), many Kuwaitis are uneasy about too close a relationship with their much larger neighbour. Iraq asserted its claim to all of Kuwait upon Kuwaiti independence in 1961 and continues to voice its claims to several islands, despite fullsome Kuwaiti war loans, the provision of oil, and Kuwait's role as the major transshipment port for Iraqi arms and other war supplies.

The amirate's exposed position, well within missile range of the fighting, has forced it to be Iraq's most ardent supporter within the

GCC. This makes Kuwait a principal target of Iran and its militant Iraqi and Lebanese Shiah allies. Already the amirate has suffered 'accidental' Iranian air raids, multiple Iranian attacks on Kuwaiti tankers plying the Gulf, the bombing of government buildings and the US and French embassies, the hijacking of a Kuwaiti airliner to Tehran, an assassination attempt on the ruler, bloody attacks on two seaside cafes, explosives set off at its main oil installations, and Silkworm missle attacks on its main oil terminal (see Table 5.2). Other would-be perpetrators have been captured before they could act.

But Kuwait has remained defiant in the face of these threats. It continues to provide Iraq with moral, financial and material assistance. It steadfastly refuses to release the seventeen saboteurs convicted for the 1983 embassy bombings. The modest armed forces have been upgraded and the security forces strengthened with American (as well as some Soviet) assistance. Kuwaiti oil tankers have been re-registered under the American and British flags and other tankers leased from the Soviet Union.

The amirate has found that there is a price to pay for principle. Internal tensions are appearing for the first time between the dominant Sunnis and the Shiah (who comprise some 30–40 per cent of the population). Security needs have forced the deportation of more than 50 000 non-Kuwaitis. The vigorous and vociferous Kuwaiti parliament, the freest in the Arab world, was suspended in July 1986 for the second time in its history.

Bahrain was the first Arab Gulf state to benefit from oil and it is the first to experience a post-oil economy. Most Bahrainis are less prosperous than Saudis or Kuwaitis and economic grievances underlie the relationship between the large Al Khalifa ruling family and rest of the citizenry. The situation is exacerbated by the status of the Shiah majority (55–70 per cent of the total population), who tended to be poorer, less educated and less represented in the government. There is a long history of dissident activity in Bahrain and a Shiah coup attempt was discovered in its early stages in 1981. The government has developed a solidly entrenched internal security network but has very little capability to deal with larger threats. As a consequence, it must rely on a quick Saudi response to any major threat situation.

Qatar is the smallest of the Arab Gulf states, as well as arguably the quietest. The high degree of homogeneity of its people, common tribal consciousness and a favourable ratio of abundant oil income to

Table 5.2   Kuwaiti security incidents since the Iranian Revolution

---

1979

Nov. 30   Several thousand Kuwaitis and Iranians demonstrate at the US Embassy before being dispersed.

1980

Apr. 29   Assassination attempt is made on visiting Iranian Foreign Minister Sadeq Qotbzadeh, who escapes unharmed.

May 1   A Kuwaiti diplomat is shot and wounded in Tehran.

May 26   Two bombs explode in front of Iranian airlines office in Kuwait.

Jun. 1   A bomb explodes at London office of Kuwait Oil Company.

Jun. 4   A bomb explodes at Iranian embassy in Kuwait.

Jul. 1   Electricity is cut in Kuwait for three days; sabotage is suspected.

Jul. 12   Two explosions at offices of Kuwait daily *al-Ra'i al-'Amm* kill at least one.

Jul. 24   Two Jordanians hijack a Kuwait Airways plane but surrender in Kuwait the next day.

Aug. 15   Border police capture several infiltrators allegedly intending to attack government installations and spark revolution.

Nov.   Iranian aircraft make two attacks on Kuwaiti customs post along Iraqi border.

1981

Jun. 13   Three Iranian aircraft violate Kuwaiti airspace.

Oct. 1   Three Iranian aircraft attack a Kuwaiti oil installation at Umm al-'Aysh, setting it on fire.

1982

Aug. 23   The UAE charge d'affaires is shot and wounded.

Sep. 15   A Palestinian gunman kills a Kuwaiti diplomat in Madrid and another Kuwaiti diplomat is wounded in Karachi.

Oct. 28   Iran's ambassador protests action of Kuwaiti police in dispersing Shiah religious procession.

1983

Dec. 12   Six people are killed and 86 injured in a series of bomb attacks against the US and French embassies, the airport control tower, the control centre of the Ministry of Electricity and Water, the Shu'ayba industrial area offices, the passport control office, the Raytheon Corporation headquarters (engaged in installing a Hawk missile system), and an apartment house occupied by Raytheon employees.

1984

Aug. 5   The editor of Kuwaiti daily *al-Anba'* is shot at in Spain.

Jun. 7   Explosives are discovered in the possession of four Iranians arrested in Kuwait on charges of sabotage; another Iranian and a Kuwaiti are arrested later.

Table 5.2 – continued

Dec. 4	Five men hijack a Kuwait Airways flight and land in Tehran. Two American passengers are killed and two Kuwaitis are wounded before Iranian security forces storm the plane and overpower the hijackers on Dec. 9.

1985

Feb. 28	An Iraqi diplomat and his son are killed at his home in Kuwait.
Apr. 23	The editor of Kuwaiti daily *al-Siyasa* is wounded in an assassination attempt.
May 25	An assassination attempt is made on the Amir of Kuwait; the Amir is wounded slightly while two bodyguards and a passing pedestrian are killed and eleven others are injured.
Jul. 11	Two seaside cafes are bombed; ten are killed and 90 injured.
Dec. 30	Three Lebanese and a Syrian are arrested for plotting to blow up Doha desalination plant and power stations.

1986

Feb. 22	Kuwait protests harassment of one of its naval vessels by two Iranian helicopters while in Kuwaiti territorial waters.
Jun. 17	Sabotage causes explosions and fires at Mina al-Ahmadi oil terminal and a nearby oilfield, nearly bringing oil exports to a standstill.
Oct. 25	Two missiles are fired unsuccessfully at plane over Kuwait's Kubbar Island.
Dec. 14	Two infiltrators are killed and twenty arrested when a Kuwaiti patrol boat intercepts their boat in Kuwaiti territorial waters.

1987

Jan. 19	Bombs set off fires at Sea Island oil terminal and several inland oil installations a week before Islamic summit conference convenes in Kuwait.
Jan. 21	Kuwait's Faylaka Island is struck by an artillery shell.
Jan. 24	A car bomb explodes near al-Salhiya commercial complex in downtown Kuwait but no casualties are reported; for the first time, nearly all those accused of responsibility are Kuwaiti Shiah.
Jan. 30	Mob attacks Kuwaiti police while attempting to make arrests in connection with January 1987 bombings.
Apr. 26	A car bomb explodes outside offices of Kuwait Oil Company in al-Ahmadi.
May 11	A bomb is set off in front of travel agency in downtown Kuwait on eve of arrival of US envoy, killing one.
May 22	A Kuwaiti national is killed in act of setting off an explosion and fire at al-Ahmadi oil complex.
Jun. 16	Tehran claims Kuwaiti security forces raided a Shiah mosque.
Jul. 15	Two saboteurs are killed while planting a car bomb near al-Salhiya commercial complex in downtown Kuwait.
Aug. 1	Iranian demonstrators, protesting deaths of Iranian pilgrims in Saudi Arabia, seize Kuwaiti embassy in Tehran.

Table 5.2 – continued

Sep. 4	Third Iranian Silkworm missile fired at Kuwait in four days strikes southern coast of Kuwait.
Sep. 5	In response to a second missile hitting Kuwait, five out of the seven Iranian diplomats in Kuwait are declared personae non gratae and given one week to leave the country.
Oct. 15	An Iranian missile strikes a US-owned oil tanker off Mina al-Ahmadi oil terminal.
Oct. 16	One of the eleven Kuwaiti tankers re-registered under the US flag is struck by an Iranian missile as it entered Mina al-Ahmadi oil terminal.
Oct. 20	Artillery shells fired into Kuwait's northern desert, in reprise of similar incident earlier in 1987.
Oct. 21	The main Sea Island oil terminal is put on fire and seriously damaged when hit by an Iranian Silkworm missile.
Oct. 24	A bomb explodes at office of Pan American Airways agent.

Note: This chronology does not include Iranian attacks on Kuwaiti shipping elsewhere in the Gulf. Not all incidents can be related to Iran or its agents.

Sources: Quarterly chronologies of the *Middle East Journal* and other sources.

tiny population has protected Qatar from the socio-political tensions of Bahrain and Kuwait. The social homogeneity is reinforced by a common conservative outlook, since most Qataris are Muwahhidun (Wahhabis) and the socio-economic change set in train by oil came late to the amirate. Nevertheless, Qatar exhibits an extreme dependence on expatriates, who form at least 75 per cent of the population. The war has come close to Qatari shores with waters off the northern tip of the Qatar Peninsula serving as a frequent location of Iranian attacks on oil tankers. Possessing only a tiny armed force, Qatar's external security is highy dependent on the Saudi umbrella.

The United Arab Emirates (UAE) is a federation of seven small amirates formed at independence in 1971. The persistence of long-standing internal rivalries and an unequal and resented contrast between the richer amirates and the proud-but-poor smaller ones perpetuates the tension between the opposing forces of increasing federalisation and the preservation of amirate sovereignty. While the federal government has assumed greater jurisdiction in such fields as foreign affairs, education, communications and development planning, the member states retain full sovereignty in such vital areas as oil production, finances and defence.

Since its birth the federation has been dominated by Abu Dhabi, the most populous and richest member, while Dubai, the second most important amirate, has been a leader of resistance to federal authority. The smaller amirates have vacillated between accepting Abu Dhabi's financial aid and fulminating against that amirate's domination of the UAE. Abu Dhabi's influence has waned in recent years as the fall in oil income has forced the amirate to cut back its aid and the leading proponents of federalisation have suffered burn-out. Simultaneously, Dubai's influence has risen slightly and the discovery and export of modest amounts of oil condensate have provided Sharjah and Ra's al-Khayma with a greater measure of independence.

In addition to these internal divisions, the UAE faces an imminent crisis in leadership, as Abu Dhabi's ruler is virtually retired, Dubai's ruler hovers near death, and questions revolve around the leadership capabilities of their heirs apparent. The economic recession has hit the smaller amirates hard and the federal government has yet to come to terms with the overwhelming expatriate presence.[7] The UAE's distance from the battlefront and Dubai's large Iranian community and strong trading ties with Iran has led the UAE to adopt a conciliatory stance *vis-à-vis* the Islamic Republic, but this has not protected it from increasing Iranian attacks on shipping just off its shores.

Oman was the last of the Gulf states to eschew its traditional isolation and the Omani government is still chary of too close an embrace with its Gulf neighbours. Even though Sunnis form a narrow majority of the population, the small Ibadi sect has provided the traditional form of government. The mountainous interior is solidly Arab but sizeable concentrations of Baluch and Indians are found along the coast. The southern province of Dhufar, culturally closer to the Yemens, was added to the Omani dominions only in the nineteenth century.

Almost completely isolated from the outside world until recently, the Sultanate of Oman has undergone an amazing renaissance. Sultan Qabus bin Sa'id, who overthrew his father in a palace coup in 1970, has realised two major accomplishments. The country has been opened up to socio-economic development and the long and dangerous rebellion in the southern province of Dhufar was put to an end. Beginning as a nationalist uprising against the old reactionary sultan, the Dhufari rebellion gradually acquired a Marxist cast and the revolutionaries were supported first by China and then the Soviet Union. It took considerable assistance from Britain, Iran and Jordan, as well as an extensive development programme in the isolated mountains, before the sultanate was able to clear the province of rebels in late 1975. Relations with neighbouring South Yemen, which nearly reached blows during the rebellion, have improved dramatically in recent years.

But Oman is prey to many of the same problems afflicting its neighbours. The competitive desire for prestige projects has resulted in a waste of money, now sorely missed. Revenues are highly dependent on oil and there is a scarcity of other resources. Unlike the other states, Oman possesses a highly developed traditional agriculture but the development process has encouraged many Omanis to desert the countryside for better-paying jobs in the capital. While the internal security threat has diminished in recent years, Oman still perceives itself as being in an extremely precarious position. The shipping lanes through the Strait of Hormuz, the only waterway out of the Gulf, lie in Omani territory.

FRICTIONS BETWEEN THE ARAB GULF STATES

The six monarchies exhibit close similarities and warm ties but areas of friction still remain. A number of borders (both onshore and offshore) are still undemarcated or disputed. Borders are a relatively new concept in the Gulf as there was no real need for precise demarcation of frontiers before oil. But definition of territorial limits became a primary requirement for granting oil concessions to competing Western companies.

The problem was well illustrated in the 1950s when Saudi Arabia backed up its longstanding claim to the Buraimi oasis with an armed occupation of one of its villages. Recognition of this claim would have extended Saudi boundaries far to the east and increased the potential value of its oil concession, then in the hands of the American company ARAMCO. The Saudi claim was rejected by Abu Dhabi and Oman, which had long administered the villages of the oasis.

The latter states were supported by Great Britain, bound to Abu Dhabi by a treaty of protection and to Oman by its predominant political influence in Muscat. British stakes were also economic, as the Abu Dhabi and Omani oil concessions were held by the principally British-owned Iraq Petroleum Company. Both sides prepared memorials and the issue was submitted to an international tribunal at The Hague. Three years later, with no decision in sight, British-officered troops forcibly ejected the Saudis from the oasis and control has remained in the hands of Abu Dhabi and Oman ever since. The status quo was recognised by a still-secret border agreement between Abu Dhabi and Riyadh in 1974, although Oman and Saudi Arabia have yet to formally demarcate their common border.

Few of the existing border disagreements escalate into active disputes any more. Many are settled on practical terms or remain on the back burner. The potentially thorny dispute over the Saudi-Kuwaiti Neutral Zone was settled by dividing the territory in two and agreeing to split evenly all oil revenues from the old zone. The question of several small islands opposite the zone was more vexing but Kuwait has apparently acquiesced in Saudi occupation and *de facto* sovereignty. Since the formation of the UAE, territorial disputes between its members frequently have been settled amicably and through mediation by other members. The Iranian occupation of the UAE-held islands of Abu Musa and the Tumbs in 1971 has become tacitly accepted. While Bahrain maintains its right to the Zubara enclave on the Qatar Peninsula, it has no realistic hope of ever realising its claim.

But other territorial claims disputed by Bahrain and Qatar indicate the continuing possibility of violent clashes. The Hawar Islands, just off Qatar's western shore, are a matter of national pride to both countries, despite a British award to Bahrain in 1939. Occasional Bahraini actions, such as the naming of a patrol craft after the islands in 1983, provoke heated Qatari rhetoric and objections. The claim has prolonged settlement of the amirates' offshore boundary and helped to provoke Qatar's seizure of the tiny islet of Fasht al-Dibal in April 1986. Qatari forces detained the workers constructing a Bahraini coast-guard station on the islet and the amirate built up its forces opposite the Hawar Islands. Quick mediation by neighbouring states was necessary to prevent the clash from escalating.

There are other sources of potential friction, as well. Until recently, much of the Arab littoral regarded the Al Sa'ud as a threat to its independence. The recrudescence of Saudi power in the early twentieth century under the leadership of 'Abd al-'Aziz (Ibn Sa'ud) brought fears of a renewed cycle of Saudi expansionism along the Gulf shores. These fears were given expression by Ikhwan raids into Iraq and Kuwait in the 1920s, a trade blockade of Kuwait in the 1920s and 1930s, and the Buraimi incident and Saudi intrigues in the Omani interior in the 1950s. While the British presence kept the small amirates out of Saudi hands, the disparity in size between Saudi Arabia and its Gulf neighbours still gives substance to lingering suspicions of Saudi hegemony and provokes an occasional ambivalence in cooperation with the kingdom.

Economic issues also provide occasional friction. The comparative advantage of all six states lies in crude oil, oil products, and oil services, making them all very real economic rivals. In a period of prolonged oil glut, there is considerable concern about maintaining market shares, even if it means violating OPEC quotas. When the Organisation of Arab Petroleum Exporting Countries (OAPEC) chose Bahrain as the site of an aluminium smelter and a dry-dock in the 1970s, Dubai went ahead with construction of its own competing smelter and dry-dock. The resultant competition rendered both ventures unprofitable. Despite recent moves toward economic cooperation, Oman has maintained import barriers erected against its neighbours in order to protect infant industries. Bahraini merchants rued the 1987 opening of the causeway to Saudi Arabia for fear of losing their market to cheaper Saudi competition. In the final analysis, however, political and economic differences are far outweighed by the need and desire for cooperation.

COOPERATION WITHIN THE GCC

The desire for a Gulf security pact dates back to British withdrawal in 1971. The December 1976 Gulf foreign ministers' conference in Muscat ended predictably without agreement, due to the incompatibility of Iran and Iraq with the six smaller states. The Arab states had long mistrusted Iran (which had even claimed sovereignty over Bahrain until 1971) and the Shah was strongly suspected of harbouring hegemonic designs. At the time, Iraq was the only revolutionary state in the region and in times past had actively sought to subvert its conservative neighbours. Ironically, it took the outbreak of a principal threat to Gulf security, the Iran–Iraq war, to provide the conditions for the remaining six Gulf states to form a security organisation.

The six Arab monarchies had much in common, including a basic similarity in their political, economic and social systems. Most had maintained close ties for many years, and bilateral relations were close with Britain and the United States. With the temporary removal of Iraq and Iran from inclusion, agreement on cooperation was assured. The outlines of an organisation were drawn up by the six foreign ministers in February 1981 and the charter was ratified at a summit of the heads of state in Abu Dhabi in May 1981. Thus, the

Cooperation Council of the Arab States of the Gulf, more commonly known as the Gulf Cooperation Council (GCC), came into existence.[8]

The GCC's highest authority is the Supreme Council, composed of the six heads of state, with the presidency rotating among the members on an annual basis. The six foreign ministers, as the Ministerial Council, provide the working basis of cooperation and prepare studies and options for the Supreme Council's approval. A small secretariat based in Riyadh is headed by a Secretary-General; Kuwaiti diplomat 'Abdulla al-Bishara has been the only holder of this position to date.

While security concerns were a principal impetus for the council's creation, they have not been the sole focus. From the beginning, the GCC stated its intention to seek cooperation and standardisation in economic and financial affairs; commerce, customs, and communications; education and culture; social and health affairs; media and tourism; and legislative and administrative affairs.

A primary, if unstated goal, has been a continuation of the process of political harmonisation that has grown stronger since British withdrawal in 1971. On the positive side, the GCC states often speak with a single voice on a variety of domestic and foreign matters, reflecting their genuinely common outlook. On the negative side, it may mean bowing to Saudi wishes, as in allegations of Saudi pressure for the banning of alcohol in various amirates and the suspension of the vocal National Assembly in Kuwait in July 1986. Disputes between GCC members have been settled by GCC mediation, as in the case of the Bahraini-Qatari contretemps over Fasht al-Dibal and the internal allocation of oil production levels between Abu Dhabi and Dubai in early 1987 in order to meet the UAE's OPEC quota. The GCC also has sought to serve as a disinterested mediator in various regional disputes, including the Iran–Iraq war.

Economic cooperation has been emphasised as well, especially through the partial implementation of a 'Unified Economic Agreement' in 1983. The agreement eliminated customs duties between GCC states and established a common external tariff. It also provided for the free movement of labour and capital between member states, for the coordination of oil policies, for the standardisation of industrial laws, and for the establishment of a unified investment strategy. Toward this end, the Gulf Investment Corporation was created in 1982 with $2.1 billion in capital for investment in regional projects and on the international level.

Not surprisingly, security has been a major priority. While the Iran–Iraq war permitted the creation of the GCC, the takeover of the Great Mosque in Mecca by Islamic extremists in late 1979 illustrated the need for better cooperation on internal security matters and spurred some planning along these lines. By 1982, two initiatives firmly implanted security as an aspect of GCC concerns. Recognition of the need for military cooperation was first prompted by the threat to Oman posed by South Yemen. The November 1981 GCC summit ordered a military mission to Oman to determine the sultanate's situation and, as a consequence, the six defence ministers met for the first time in January 1982 to discuss the mission's report and military cooperation. The second initiative involved internal security coordination. It was prompted by the capture of dissidents in Bahrain in December 1981 and resulted in the first meeting of the GCC's interior ministers in February 1982.[9]

Since the discovery of the Bahrain plotters, the GCC states regularly exchange intelligence and all but Kuwait signed bilateral security agreements with Saudi Arabia in early 1982. The Saudi internal security umbrella holds the greatest relevance for tiny Bahrain and Qatar, and the principal impetus for the Saudi-Bahraini causeway (paid for by Riyadh) was its value in quickly rushing troops to the island state when needed. A small 'Peninsula Shield' force, comprised mainly of Saudi and Kuwaiti brigades with token contributions for the other states, has been established at the Hafr al-Batin military base in northeastern Saudi Arabia, for dispatch to any member state requesting security assistance.

Military coordination to meet an external threat is more difficult to achieve. Even in combination, the GCC states are far smaller in total population, armed forces, and industrial base than Iran, Iraq, or Israel. The combined number of GCC military personnel is less than 150 000. In contrast, Iraq has 600 000 men under arms (1.25 million if the Popular Army is included) while Iran totals over a half million regular troops and Pasdaran, with an additional several million paramilitary forces. Even Israel maintains a standing army of 142 000, with an additional 370 000 reservists.[10] More importantly, GCC military establishments are new and untested. Arms acquisitions have skyrocketed in the last decade but trained indigenous personnel to operate them are in short supply.

Due to its expansive physical size, Saudi Arabia has placed emphasis on the development of its air-force while ground forces are split between the army and the national guard. Oman's armed forces, battle-tested in Dhufar, nevertheless are basically a light-infantry force with a small air-force that can offer little assistance outside the sultanate. Kuwait's military is even smaller, its tiny air-force is dependent on ageing aircraft, and many of its personnel are stateless Bedouin. In keeping with its fragmented politics, the UAE armed foces are split into a number of commands directly and solely under the control of the individual amirates; the Minister of Defence and the Deputy Commander-in-Chief (there is no Commander-in-Chief) come from rival ruling families and have minimal contact. Bahrain and Qatar are only now beginning to upgrade minuscule internal security forces.

Serious efforts have been made to implement a collective air-defence system, based on Saudi Arabia's AWACS radar and C3I capabilities, linked to anti-aircraft missiles and interceptor aircraft. Joint military manoeuvres, largely bilateral in nature, have become commonplace, and a GCC-wide exercise takes place nearly every year. At the very least, these efforts provide a basis for communication between military commanders in the various states. Nevertheless, the absorption of large numbers of highly sophisticated weapons, the complex mix of various types of weapons from a wide variety of suppliers, the small base of indigenous manpower and serious training problems, the intensive competition for skilled manpower and the lack of combat experience, as well as differences in outlooks and policy goals among the defence institutions of the six member states, continue to hinder GCC attempts at self-defence.

THE GCC AND THE YEMENS

The only potential security threat to the GCC from within the Arabian Peninsula comes from the two Yemens. The southern corner of the Peninsula and its relationship to Gulf security is frequently and mistakenly overlooked by observers. The Yemeni threat is posed by their relatively larger populations (more than the GCC states combined), the number of Yemenis working in the GCC states (as many as 750 000 during the height of the oil boom), and their poverty and industriousness.

North Yemen (the Yemen Arab Republic; YAR) was transformed from a traditional monarchy into a republic as the result of a Nasirist revolution in 1962. Eight years of internecine fighting between royalist and republican forces ended with the Yemen Arab Republic intact but too weak to deal effectively with an extremely conservative and tribally dominated countryside. In 1974, the military once again took control but two successive heads of state were the victims of assassination. Army officer Ali 'Abdullah Salih was well placed to assume the presidency in 1978 and, rather surprisingly, he has remained at the helm ever since.

Before independence in 1967, South Yemen consisted of the British colony of Aden and a British protectorate in the hinterland. Four years of bloody fighting against the British left the radical National Liberation Front in position to take charge upon British withdrawal. Given the radical ideological nature of the new regime and the hostility it perceived from the Gulf States and the West, the new People's Democratic Republic of Yemen (PDRY) turned to the Soviet Union, Cuba, East Germany and Marxist Ethiopia for support and assistance. The PDRY's support of the Dhufari rebels put it on the verge of war with Oman and hardline policies among Aden's leaders provoked border wars with North Yemen in 1972 and 1979. The emotional call of unity between North and South Yemen has been affirmed by successive governments in both Aden and Sanaa but ideological differences make implementation impractical.

The continuing struggle between Marxist ideological purity and pragmatism based on the need for development and foreign aid have helped to provoke a series of violent struggles for power over the years within the Yemeni Socialist Party, the successor organisation to the National Liberation Front. The latest occurred in January 1986 when the head of the party (and head of state) precipitated a failed attack on his radical enemies and was forced into exile, but not before thousands of South Yemenis were killed. The resultant coalition of radicals, ideological pragmatists and apolitical technocrats has produced a relatively moderate regime that appears to seek closer relations with the GCC.

Saudi Arabia is the only GCC state bordering both Yemens, and a major focus of Saudi security concerns has centred on threats from this corner of the Arabian Peninsula since Egypt became involved in the North Yemen civil war of the 1960s. Following the resolution of that conflict, Riyadh has attempted to play a predominant influence in North Yemeni politics by providing budgetary, development and military aid, while also subsidising the semi-autonomous tribes and sundry politicians and army officers. Relations between the two countries are close on the surface but the great majority of Yemenis are hostile toward the Saudis for their sometimes arrogant behaviour in Yemen and naked manipulation of the Sanaa government, for the treatment of Yemeni workers in the kingdom, and for the absorption into Saudi Arabia of three provinces still held to be Yemeni. Past and present YAR leaders have been fully occupied in maintaining a precarious balancing act between conservative Saudi Arabia to the north and Marxist PDRY to the south.

Saudi relations with South Yemen generally have been characterised by confrontation. Aden's extreme poverty has led it to seek *rapprochement* with Riyadh on several occasions since the late 1970s but the results have been meagre. It has been left to Kuwait to keep open communications, particularly through the provision of project aid, and Kuwaiti and UAE mediation was responsible for the establishment of a dialogue with Oman in 1982, culminating in diplomatic relations in 1984. The virtual disappearance of the radical faction from the scene in Aden, combined with a burgeoning Soviet-GCC honeymoon (diplomatic relations between Moscow and both Muscat and Abu Dhabi were announced in 1985), indicates that the Yemeni threat has receded for the foreseeable future.

GCC STRATEGIES AND EXTERNAL ALLIANCES

Ever since British withdrawal from the Gulf in 1971, the Arab Gulf states have been frequently portrayed as unstable anachronisms awash in a sea of turbulence and unlikely to outlast 'the decade' (first defined as the 1970s and then as the 1980s). One writer opined in 1975 that the only survivable monarchy in the region was Pahlavi Iran. Another pseudonymous author devised a 'stability index' in 1980 which rated the UAE's chances of survival as 20 per cent through 1985 and only 5 per cent through 1990; Saudi Arabia fares the best of the Peninsula states, with survivability estimated at 65 per cent through 1985 and 25 per cent through 1990. A 1982 book on territorial disputes and internal social composition was entitled *The Unstable Gulf*.[11]

Despite these opinions, the GCC states are not as fragile and domestically vulnerable as many still think. In fact, the profusion of published materials on the Gulf in the last decade or so is notable for its astonishingly superficial analysis of the region's countries. Certainly, internal security threats are real, but they are manageable. One need only look at what Kuwait has undergone in recent years without changing its policies or collapsing. Far from being anachronisms, the

GCC governments are legitimate, responsive to their citizenry and fully capable of necessary adaptions to changing circumstances.

Obviously, the GCC states cannot be expected to cope adequately with the entire range of security threats from the outside. They have taken significant steps to acquire the ability to buy time until outside help arrives and they have done very well in protecting themselves from more likely, if more limited, internal and regional threats. Some additional protection may come from fellow Arab states, such as Iraq, Egypt or Jordan, but Gulf security essentially depends on a partnership between the GCC and the West, principally the United States. Clearly, the US or Western role is one of 'backup', to be invited in when the GCC states cannot handle a threat on their own. In military terms, an 'over-the-horizon' partnership is less than ideal, but it is workable. More importantly, it is the only type of partnership that the GCC states can countenance. For the United States, reassurance of its friends in the GCC is just as important as deterrence of the Soviet Union and regional threats.

The uncertain partnership between the Gulf states and the West was well illustrated in the 'reflagging' crisis of mid-1987. The Iran–Iraq war had long come to a virtual stalemate. The last successful Iranian push was the capture of Iraq's al-Faw peninsula in early 1986. Another prolonged 'final offensive' in early 1987 put tremendous pressure on the Iraqi forces defending Basra, the country's second-largest city, but the defences held. Once again, it became clear that Iran, while clearly the stronger belligerent, did not have the resources immediately available to defeat Iraq. Nevertheless, any continuing no-win situation would seem to favour much larger Iran.

Iran also stepped up its attacks on seaborne shipping bound for Kuwaiti and Saudi ports. Vessels plying the Gulf were forced to hug the Arab shore, but even that was no guarantee of safety. By the end of 1986, more than a dozen Kuwaiti ships had been struck and the Iranian navy was increasingly boarding Kuwaiti ships passing through the Strait of Hormuz. In response, Kuwait, pushed to the limit by escalating Iranian attacks on its commercial vessels and by Iranian-inspired incidents of sabotage, reversed its traditional position opposing superpower involvement in the Gulf and called on the superpowers in December 1986 to help protect its shipping (see Table 5.3).[12]

Requests by the Kuwait Oil Tanker Corporation to re-register some of its fleet went unanswered until March 1987, when Washington learned that the Soviet Union had agreed to protect the tankers and was preparing to lease three of its own tankers to Kuwait.

Table 5.3   The tanker 'reflagging' crisis of 1987: a chronology

1986	
Nov. 1	Kuwait informs fellow GCC members that it will seek international protection for its ships.
Dec. 10	Kuwait Oil Tanker Company first queries the US Coast Guard about procedures for re-registering its tankers under the US flag ('reflagging').
1987	
Jan. 13	Kuwait asks the US embassy if Kuwait vessels operating under US flags would receive US naval protection; the Kuwaiti request first receives serious attention when the US learns that the Soviet Union has offered Kuwait protection for its tankers.
Jan. 23	President Reagan restates the US commitment to the free flow of oil through the Strait of Hormuz.
Jan. 29	The Reagan Administration, replying to the Kuwaiti inquiry on naval protection, repeats its policy commitment to Gulf and says Kuwait can re-register its vessels if they meet US requirements.
Feb. 6	Washington affirms to Kuwait that the US Navy would protect all US flag ships to the degree possible with available assets.
Late Feb.	Iran test-fires a Silkworm anti-ship missile at Qishm Island in the Strait of Hormuz; the US learns of the Soviet agreement to protect Kuwaiti tankers.
Feb. 25	President Reagan declares that 'We remain strongly committed to supporting the self-defense of our friends in the region, and have recently moved naval forces in the Persian Gulf to underpin that commitment'.
Mar. 2	The Kuwaiti tanker company asks to put six vessels under US flag.
Mar. 7	US offers to protect eleven Kuwaiti tankers.
Mar. 10	Kuwait indicates it will accept the US offer to protect its tankers.
Mar. 12	The State Department notifies the House and Senate foreign affairs committees of the US offer to Kuwait.
Apr. 2	Kuwait formally accepts the US offer, applying to re-register eleven tankers and limiting the Soviet role to chartering three Soviet tankers.
Early May	Soviet charters begin.
May 17	The US Navy frigate USS *Stark* is struck by two Exocet missiles fired by an Iraqi fighter, and 37 American sailors are killed.
Jul. 1	Moored mines are discovered off Kuwait.
Jul. 20	UN Security Council Resolution 598, calling for a cease-fire in the Iran–Iraq war, is passed.
Jul. 22	The first convoy of US warships and re-registered Kuwaiti tankers enters the Gulf.
Jul. 24	The Kuwaiti supertanker *Bridgeton*, steaming under the US flag, strikes a mine while under US naval escort.

Table 5.3 – continued

Aug. 8	The second US-escorted convoy of Kuwaiti tankers enters the Gulf on the day after Iran finishes four days of naval manoeuvres.
Aug. 8–9	A US Navy F–14 Tomcat is reported to have fired two missiles at an Iran F–4 that was said to be approaching P–3 Orion surveillance aircraft keeping watch over the convoy; the missiles miss.
Aug. 11	Mines are discovered off al-Fujayra (UAE); Britain and France announce plans to send minesweepers to the area.
Aug. 24	The destroyer USS *Kidd* fires machine-gun bursts across the bows of two small unidentified boats after they ignore radio warnings and draw too close.
Sep. 21	A US Navy helicopter fires on Iranian vessel *Iran Air*, which the Reagan Administration says was laying underwater mines 50 miles from Bahrain; three Iranian crew members are killed and two are lost at sea; the ship is destroyed several days later after twenty-six surviving crewmen are picked up and returned to Iran.
Oct. 8	US military helicopters sink three Iranian patrol boats off Farsi Island in northern end of Gulf, after at least one Iran vessel reportedly opens fire on a helicopter.
Oct. 16	An Iranian Silkworm missile, fired from al-Faw (Iranian-occupied Iraq) strikes a US-registered tanker in Kuwaiti territorial waters.
Oct. 19	Four US Navy destroyers shell and set ablaze an Iranian oil platform at Rashadat (east of Bahrain and Qatar), containing radar and communications facilities; the US Navy later dispatch SEAL explosive teams to blow up remaining section of platform and another platform nearby.

Changes in White House staff after the Iran–contra affair and a perceived need to mend fences with the conservative Gulf states also seemed to play a part in the American decision to cooperate, and American concern was intensified further by the discovery of Iran's acquisition of Chinese Silkworm anti-ship missiles.

The GCC states found themselves caught in the middle. Their governments recognised the need for American assistance but were wary of cooperating too closely, since they realised that sooner or later the American ships would depart and they would be left to face the wrath of the Islamic Republic. GCC members like Oman and the United Arab Emirates were clearly discomfited by the Kuwaiti decision to call in the Americans, since they had taken great pains to remain on correct terms with Tehran.

By the beginning of October, the Western armada of ships

patrolling the Gulf had risen to more than 70. But Iran did not back down. Since 1984 and the beginning of the 'tanker war', Iran and Iraq have carried on a 'tit-for-tat' war away from the main battlefront. The 1987 naval build-up had no effect on this secondary war: Iranian assaults on shipping continued to match those of Iraq and both sides traded aerial and missile barrages on oil, industrial and civilian targets inland. Instead, the naval build-up brought the United States squarely into the zone of fire and seemed to embroil Washington in its own 'tit-for-tat' war with Tehran. The vastly enlarged Western naval presence in the Gulf may have provided a bit more security for civilian vessels, but it solved no problems and looked uncomfortably like a permanent necessity.

CONCLUSIONS

The Gulf states have pursued a multi-layered strategy for self-defence, of which military capability is only one aspect. They have used oil income and quiet moral persuasion to encourage moderation among regional actors and to seek consensus in pan-Arab affairs. They have sought to reconcile enemies and to contain hostilities. The challenges of oil wealth have been met by extensive policies of income distribution and evolving, albeit often reluctant, adaptation to necessary social and political transformation. Chances are that preparations made in non-military fields will be more important to the continued survival and security of the Arab Gulf states than the prowess and performance of their armed forces or alliances with external protectors.

Notes

1. There has been considerable debate recently on whether expatriates are leaving the Gulf in large numbers or whether the numbers have remained relatively stable, with expatriate workers either extending their contracts for less pay or being replaced by other, lower paid expatriates. Recent representative contributions include Roger Owen, *Migrant Workers in the Gulf* (London: Minority Rights Group, September 1985; Report no. 68); Rob Franklin, 'Migrant Labor and the Politics of Development in Bahrain', MERIP Reports, vol. 15, no. 4 (May 1985), pp. 7–13, 32; Abdulrasool A. Al-Moosa, 'Stability of the Foreign Labour Force in Kuwait', *Arab Gulf Journal*, vol. 6, no. 1

(April 1986), pp. 53–6; Elisabeth Longuenesse, 'Migrations et société dans les pays du Golfe', *Maghreb-Machrek*, no. 112 (April–June 1986), pp. 8–21; and Ian J. Seccombe, 'Economic Recession and International Labour Migration in the Arab Gulf', *Arab Gulf Journal*, vol. 6, no. 1 (April 1986), pp. 43–52.

2. For further information, see J. E. Peterson, *The Arab Gulf States: Steps Toward Political Participation*. (New York: Praeger, for the Center for Strategic and International Studies, 1988, Washington Paper, no. 131).

3. James A. Bill, 'Resurgent Islam in the Persian Gulf', *Foreign Affairs*, vol. 63, no. 1 (Fall 1984), pp. 108–27.

4. Some of these activities, including aid to Afghani rebels and the Nicaraguan anti-Sandinista forces, were revealed as a result of the Iran–contra affair.

5. The full facts of what happened on 31 July 1987 will probably never be known. Saudi Arabia vehemently denied subsequent Iranian claims that 600 of its pilgrims died or disappeared during and after the fighting. Saudi authorities also denied using firearms during the fighting. Reports of bodies with bullet holes and empty cartridges were widespread, however, as were contentions that Iranian militants had beheaded one or more Saudi policemen in the initial stages of the confrontation. Detailed reports on the incident are contained in *The Economist*, 8 August 1987; the *Sunday Times* (London), 9 August 1987; and the *New York Times*, 6 September 1987. The Saudis defended themselves in an unusual interview and press conference by Interior Minister, Prince Nayif bin 'Abd al-'Aziz Al Sa'ud, who revealed that Iranian pilgrims had attempted to smuggle in 60 bags of explosives during the 1986 hajj. The interview was published in al-Siyasa, 22 August 1987 (Foreign Broadcast Information Service [FBIS], Middle East and South Asia [MESA], 25 August 1987); and the text of the press conference was broadcast by the Saudi Press Agency (Riyadh) on 25 August 1987 (FBIS/MESA, 27 August 1987).

6. It was reported that, on 3 October 1987, Iran launched a speedboat attack on Saudi Arabia's Khafji offshore oilfield, resulting in full mobilisation of the Saudi armed forces and the dispatch of fighters and frigates to turn the speedboats back. The Saudis denied any attack had taken place.

7. Sharjah's indebtedness was a principal reason cited for the attempted coup by Shaykh 'Abd al-'Aziz bin Muhammad al-Qasimi, the brother of the ruler, in June 1987. Strong support for the ruler, Shaykh Sultan bin Muhammad al-Qasimi, by the ruling family of nearby Dubai forced the UAE's governing Council of Rulers to force a compromise whereby Shaykh Sultan retained his throne and Shaykh 'Abd al-'Aziz was confirmed as heir apparent, as well as deputy ruler and head of Sharjah's National Guard. For more on this incident and the situation in the UAE, see J. E. Peterson, 'The Future of Federalism in the United Arab Emirates', in H. Richard Sindelar III and J. E. Peterson (eds) *Crosscurrents in the Gulf: Arab, Regional and Global Interests* (London: Routledge, 1988).

8. Recent works on the GCC include: Abdullah Fahd al-Nafisi, *Majlis al-Ta'awun al-Khaliji: al-itar al-siyasi wal-istratiji* (London: Taha Publishers, 1982); Shireen Hunter (ed.), Gulf Cooperation Council: Problems and Prospects (Washington, DC: Georgetown University Center for Strategic and International Studies, 1984); Joseph A. Kechichian, 'The Gulf Cooperation Council: Search for Security', *Third World Quarterly*, vol. 7, no. 4 (October 1985); Emile A. Nakhleh, *The Gulf Cooperation Council: Policies, Problems and Prospects* (New York: Praeger, 1986); John A. Sandwick (ed.), *The Gulf Cooperation Council: Moderation and Stability in an Interdependent World* (Boulder, CO: Westview Press; Washington, DC: American-Arab Affairs Council, 1987); and John Duke Anthony, 'The Gulf Cooperation Council: A New Framework for Policy Coordination', in Richard Snider III and J. E. Peterson (eds), *Crosscurrents in the Gulf: Arab, Regional, and Global Interests* (London: Routledge, 1988).

9. On the military capabilities of GCC members and GCC security coordination, see Anthony H. Cordesman, *The Gulf and the Search for Strategic Stability* (Boulder, CO: Westview Press, 1984); Thomas L. McNaugher, *Arms and Oil: US Military Strategy and the Persian Gulf* (Washington, DC: Brookings Institution, 1985); Mazher A. Hameed, *Arabia Imperilled: The Security Imperatives of the Arab Gulf States* (Washington, DC: Middle East Assessments Groups, 1986); J. E. Peterson, *Defending Arabia* (London: Croom Helm; New York, NY: St Martin's Press, 1986); and *idem*, 'The GCC and Regional Security', in John A. Sandwick (ed.), *The Gulf Cooperation Council* (Boulder, CO: Westview Press), pp. 169–203.

10. *The Military Balance, 1985–1986* (London: International Institute for Strategic Studies, 1985), pp. 69–88.

11. These examples are derived from, respectively, Alvin J. Cottrell, 'The Political–Military Balance in the Persian Gulf Region', in Joseph S. Szyliowicz and Bard E. O'Neill (eds), *The Energy Crisis and US Foreign Policy* (New York, NY: Praeger, 1975), pp. 125–38; Abdul Kasim Mansur, 'The Military Balance in the Persian Gulf: Who Will Guard the Gulf States from Their Guardians?' *Armed Forces Journal International*, vol. 118, no. 3 (November 1980), pp. 44–86; and Lenore G. Martin, *The Unstable Gulf: Threats From Within* (Lexington, MA: D. C. Heath/Lexington Books, 1984).

12. Some observers have speculated that Iraq pressed Kuwait to ask for help as a way of drawing the superpowers into the Iran–Iraq war and thereby forcing them to put an end to it.

6 American Perceptions of Iranian Threats to Gulf Security

James Noyes

INTRODUCTION

Even with reliable data about Gulf countries any analytical task would be daunting. Iran's revolution is still in process. An internal power struggle is barely contained with basic social and economic issues remaining unresolved. Over seven years of war have worn not only at the social and economic fabric of the combatant countries, but added stress throughout the region. Soviet occupation of Afghanistan has complicated the equation. So has Lebanon. So has the collapse of the Gulf oil boom. Changes are so profuse that analysts of the Gulf are like physicians asked to prescribe for patients they hardly know. And instead of lab reports these physicians must depend heavily on hearsay and official releases.

Were that not bad enough, moreover, much of the analytical task ultimately involves predicting the behaviour of societies at war – historically shown to be a rich source of error. Both Saddam Hussein and the Ayatollah Khomeini should qualify as area experts. But how poor their assessments have been. Hussein's expectation that the Arabs of Iran's Khuzistan province would welcome his invading army was as flawed as the Ayatollah's expectation that the Shiah Arabs of southern Iraq would embrace *his* advancing forces. Our own readings of the relative pulls of nationalism, religion, and ethnicity in Gulf societies must be more measured and cautious.

Apart from these obstacles public understanding of the Gulf is burdened by the overlay of distorted images that much of the media substitutes for responsible analysis of the Middle East. Edward Said is certainly correct in saying that the Middle East picture presented in the US is 'deeply flawed, deeply antagonistic, deeply uninformed and uninforming'.[1] The Arabs of the Gulf are generally caricatured by wealth and weakness. And of course Iran projects the entire Tehran embassy hostage crisis as an overlay to its image. While American outrage over those events is amply justified, the image alone can hardly serve as a basis for understanding Iran's revolution. US political rhetoric at the time dwelled on who 'lost Iran' and on the barbarism of the captors. The revolution was portrayed as an event the US should have prevented, and as a kind of insult in which American feelings were the dominant factor. The hostage humiliation came to be viewed almost exclusively as a perversely anti-American exercise rather than a calculated part of revolutionary activity. The American public learned little from these events; old images of Islamic fanaticism and purposeless violence were merely reinforced. Absent was a calm analysis of the revolution's causes, any measuring of US contributory actions, or, on the other hand, a full assessment of valuable US contributions to Iran's post-Second World War development. Loud voices at the spectrum's edges dominated the debate: 'involvement in countries like Iran creates unacceptable political, cultural, and military entanglement', versus 'we can and should tip the balance by military or other means when a friendly government is threatened internally regardless of how deeply its support base is eroded'. These loud voices would reduce policy options to, 'the US should stay home and do nothing', or 'The US must manage events everywhere'.

Ironically, aspects of the American official as well as public views of Iran during the Shah's rule helped create the environment now inhibiting cool analysis and a dispassionate US policy. The post-British era of US Gulf policy was originally designed for careful tandem encouragement of economic and military development on both sides of the Gulf. But as Vietnam wore at all US capabilities, and confidence diminished, foreign friends often came to assume exaggerated world roles as a measure of compensation for loss of US power. Richard Nixon's and Henry Kissinger's eventual virtual mesmerisation with the Shah served to remove the balance in the Iran–US relationship. A sense of US dependence on Iran and an exaggeration of Iran's world role emerged as the Shah more and more lost touch with the realities of his country. Instead of the moderating US influence that might have helped this valued ally came overly effusive encouragement from Washington. The working atmosphere between Tehran and Washington during the early 1970s was exemplified by a cable from the US ambassador asserting that 'The U.S. might as well pack up and turn the keys to Iran over to the Soviets', if the Shah's latest request for yet another weapons system were not approved by a questioning officialdom. It was an 'all or nothing at all approach' mastered well by the Shah which sapped US objectivity. Thus, the American view of Iran long contained elements of distortion and exaggerated expectation wherein the slightest US misstep would propel Iran into the Soviet camp or on the other hand, a friendly Iran could solve all US problems in the region. Despite the profound dislocations of revolution and war elements of these attitudes linger. They were quickly recognised and continue to be exploited by Iran's post-revolutionary leaders.

Like Iran's revolution, its war with Iraq presents circumstances unique in America's brief experience in the Middle East. These add to the confusion. In contrast to other Middle East wars, neither superpower has much influence over the course of the fighting. The Soviet weapons embargo against Iraq early in the war had little effect. Subsequent resumption of Soviet weapons sales has sustained Iraq's fighting ability, but French military aircraft and munitions have provided the most dramatic edge for Iraqi forces. The Soviets, like the US, have tried to straddle the conflict but have also tilted toward one adversary or another as political opportunities opened. US and Soviet long-term strategic interests in the region are of course quite different. But in tactical terms thus far neither superpower has wanted a sweeping Iranian victory. This is fortunate in reducing the risks of superpower confrontation. Because of our past tendency to exaggerate the force of the Soviet hand in Middle East conflicts, however, public understanding of the issues at stake is harder to achieve. Without our habitual 'good guy versus bad guy' scenario at hand in the Gulf conflict the politicised and opportunistic side of the US foreign policy process will likely scramble to create one. The statesmanlike side will resist. Emphasis will remain on supporting the territorial integrity of both Iran and Iraq, by confining the war in time and space.

This contest, which is so vital to how we manage our policies in the Gulf, coincides with what may become a climactic period for the war and for the resolution of Iran's post-Khomeini leadership. The concurrent impact of presidential election politics in the US hardly brightens prospects for a triumph of statesmanship, particularly with the already raw nerve of Iran in US politics inflamed further by the scandal of the aberrant Iran arms sales.

US INTERESTS IN THE GULF

Oil, from Ike to Reagan

What are the architects of a reconstructed and newly articulated US Gulf policy to say of our basic purposes? We remain vitally interested. Fortunately, when the more topical issues of hostages, the arms embargo on Iran, the existence or non-existence of moderate groups in the Iranian leadership, Israel's role and purposes, etc. are peeled away we reach a reassuringly solid bipartisan agreement of long standing. As early as 1957 President Eisenhower responded to Dillon Anderson's rejection of the use of force in retaining access to Middle East oil, 'I think you have, in the analysis presented . . . proved that should a crisis arise threatening to cut the Western world off from Mid East oil, we would *have* [Eisenhower's emphasis] to use force'.[2]

Successive presidents have said the same thing in different ways – Carter's 1980 State of the Union address noted that any outside power's attempt to gain control in the Gulf would 'be repelled by any means necessary, including military force'. The Reagan Administration has reaffirmed this position on several occasions. Congressional support for this recognition of the Gulf region as a vital interest has generally followed. The problem has arisen in obtaining congressional support for actions the executive branch considers essential to safeguard this vital interest.

While past confusion about the industrial world's oil consumption and overall world production has generated scepticism over projections, all these projections nevertheless point to the same conclusion. The Gulf states contain 55 to 65 per cent of proven world oil reserves. The future requirement for Gulf oil by the West and Japan is fundamental. This makes discussion about the intersection of production and consumption curves a matter of financial and academic interest rather than of strategic significance. With one exception the reader will be spared more detail on the oil aspect of US vital interests on the assumption of our common agreement about the linkage between US and Western European security. Those who argue that the US could manage without Gulf oil (itself a dubious long-range projection) deny this linkage.

No matter how often statistics on world oil reserves are paraded forth during discussions of Western stakes in the Gulf public understanding is inadequate. The entire proven reserves of the western hemisphere including the US and Mexico are estimated at about 118 billion barrels. Tiny Kuwait alone undoubtedly has well over 100 billion barrels and Saudi Arabia over 200 billion barrels. To make a different point it is also worth noting that Iran has proven reserves of about 48.5 billion barrels with relatively insignificant prospects (in Gulf terms) for major additional discovery. In contrast, Iraq probably has at least 65 billion barrels of proven reserves, with likely large still undiscovered resources.[3] Without jumping to conclusions about strategic implications, note that Iranian oil *per se* is not vital to Western interests. The Arab states of the Gulf are the crux, though obviously a peaceful Gulf is prerequisite to real energy security.

The magnitude of the Western world's stakes in so remote and vulnerable location of course means that the threat of denial of these resources immediately implies critically damaging military and financial consequences. Soviet ability to exert leverage on Gulf producers to serve Soviet economic and political objectives could alter the global power balance. Were the Soviets able to control Gulf oil they would be relieved of the massive investment required to develop Siberian reserves. This would allow a surge of Soviet military development coincident with a sharp cut in the oil supplies NATO would require for a sustained defence of Western Europe. Increased Soviet resources available throughout the third world, moreover, could be dedicated to undermining the West's interests.

Beyond oil

Beyond oil there are Soviet interests in the Gulf that raise the stakes for Western security. Soviet military and trade logistics would be greatly simplified were they to break the landlock between their Black Sea and Far East ports. Although Soviet pacification of Afghanistan may yet be generations away, its achievement would leave only ethnically troubled areas of Iran and Pakistan blocking access to the Indian Ocea. These Soviet interests are much described and often the feasibility of their pursuit by Moscow is exaggerated. In fact, a major frustration of this entire subject arises because, (1) Soviet interests are so strong and historically rooted, and yet, (2) a Western policy dominated by the Soviet threat at the expense of successful cooperation with the Gulf states themselves would be self destructive. US influence in the region hinges on bolstering the prestige and effectiveness of the indigenous leaders. The US military presence, therefore, is an essential component in the relationship, but must be employed as an instrument responsive to GCC-defined security requirements. There is a built-in tension between, (1) the need for military facilities in the region for US forces during emergencies and (2) political realities confronting the Gulf's Arab leaders who appreciate that an 'over-the-horizon' US military presence is inadequate in many circumstances, but perceive a potentially mortal political threat from over-identification with the US through the military link. The reflagging of Kuwaiti tankers and attendent US naval escort dramatised this tension at a level of danger for the Gulf at first glance sufficient to override political inhibitions. But it is precisely the specific religious and political challenge of the Khomeini revolution to the legitimacy of the rulers of the GCC states that has necessarily increased their need to appear independent of Western military support. As a consequence, the GCC states have evolved the practical compromise of publicly denying but actually providing for most of the US and European military requirements.

Saudi–US ties

Similarly, an assessment of US or Western stakes in the Gulf that is limited to Western needs for oil and various Soviet threats remains parochial. Saudi Arabia, in conjuction with the Gulf Cooperation Council (GCC) countries and subject to manifold pressures from throughout the Arab world, exerts the financial leverage of the bulk of Gulf oil income, however sharply reduced at the moment. Today most of this leverage favours Western interests. Gulf investments are integral to the industrial world's economy. Were some of Iran's radical mullahs, or the ideologues of Libya or the Peoples' Democratic Republic of South Yemen instead in charge of Gulf resources, the damage could be incalculable. Those Western observers who today expend extravagant energies trying to discredit the GCC countries would finally have tangible grounds. If Saudi Arabia and other GCC states, for instance, were supporting radical fundamentalists in Egypt and Lebanon, were helping the PDRY instead of the Yemen Arab Republic, the Marxist regime in Kabul versus the Afghan rebels, Iran's war versus Iraq's, or Libyan-type terrorist and subversive actions throughout the world Western interests would be severely damaged. Arab Gulf resources continue to be a major engine for influence in the Muslim world. While they have not always been used wisely, in the wrong hands their impact over time could be devastating.

The Saudi position in Islam as guardian of the holy places of Mecca and Medina, moreover, is important within the longer perspective of Islam as a basic ally of the West against Soviet expansion. Iranian efforts to topple the Saudi regime during the pilgrimage of 1987 by riots reveals the potential importance of these holy places in a political context. Imagine the impact of a Saudi government which instead of arresting pilgrims carrying weapons and subversive propaganda, exploited the pilgrimage institution by sending weapons and subversion back home with the million-plus Muslim visitors each year. Captured as a vehicle for subversive political purposes the pilgrimage institution potentially could alter the direction of the Muslim world.

Saudi–US ties, while not without differences, comprise a special relationship which informally commits the US to Saudi security. This commitment has evolved with explicit expressions of concern by several presidents and through long US involvement with Saudi defence modernisation. Numerous threats to Saudi security, including the Yemen civil war during the 1960s and the PDRY-backed Dhofar rebellion in Oman in the 1970s have provoked military and diplomatic reaction by the US in support of the kingdom. This tradition has continued during the Iran–Iraq war. The continuing presence of US AWACS aircraft in Saudi Arabia plus periodic carrier task groups in the Arabian Sea are high profile manifestations. For the US to fail this test of our national reliability and integrity would signal a disastrous debilitation of resolve and consistency. By virtue of the interdependence of the GCC states and the US–Oman special relationship, moreover, an implied American security umbrella spreads over the entire GCC. It was the credibility and validity of this broad US security structure that was put to the test by Kuwait's request for US reflagging and naval escort.

The challenge for US policy

The origins of this US security relationship with the Gulf states lie generally in the area of offsetting Soviet expansion and the subversive activities of regional states supported by the USSR – notably Iraq and the PDRY during the 1970s. While today's crisis bears the potential for direct Soviet aggression or subversion, the current Soviet posture leans toward containment of Iranian aggression. And yet both the GCC countries and the US have many coincident long-range geo-strategic interests with Iran in opposition to Moscow. This predica-ment illustrates the delicacy of the challenge for US policy.

DEFINING IRAN'S THREAT TO US INTERESTS IN THE GULF

Iranian victory seen as a plus

Is Iran a threat, first of all? Some think not. A Yale Law School professor's recent comments exemplify the position.[4] Representing an extreme edge of American perceptions, he holds that an Iranian victory would pose great problems for Moscow, not only in Afghanis-tan and Central Asia itself, but throughout the Middle East where for unspecified reasons he sees 'growing Soviet influence'. Most peculiar-ly, he suggests that an Iranian victory might induce the Syrians to more ready accommodation with Israel and Jordan and that overall the adjustments to Shiah fundamentalism forced on the Arab govern-ments of the Middle East need not include 'a swing away from the West'. Surely this misjudges the basic ideological message from Tehran as does his view that Jordanian and Syrian reactions to an Iranian victory would benefit Israel as the two states acted to thwart the eventually more than rhetorical 'march to Jerusalem' Iranian message. Finally, he sees a mullah-run Iran preferable to a 'people's republic', as though this were the sole alternative to the present regime.

There seems little reason for the West's welcoming an Iranian victory that would pose at least as many problems for it as for the Soviets. Middle East politics are not dominated today by a struggle between Islam and pro-Soviet movements. Soviet influence as an establishment power capable of brokering some regional problems may be growing. But Soviet ideological influence is on the decline as is Soviet ability to meet the economic needs of the region. While the Soviets surely would be shaken by a sweeping Iranian victory, their pain would be considerably eased if in fact the psychological impact of this victory replaced the generally moderate and pro-Western leaders of the GCC, Jordan, and perhaps elsewhere with virulently anti-Western regimes. In contrast to close and long-standing Western relationships (however troubled) in the region, Soviet links are with

(1) an impoverished and divided PDRY, (2) Libya with foreign and domestic policies in shambles, (3) Syria bankrupted by military expenses yet still doubtful about its defence capability against Israel, and (4) Iraq, dependent militarily, but bitter and hotly pursuing available alternatives to its Moscow link. In short, the West has much more to lose.

An extreme version of the 'welcoming an Iranian victory' view is held by some Likud Party members in Israel and for shorthand purposes could be called the General Ariel Sharon view. Herein the Arab states are seen as artificial creations of European colonialism comprised of ethnic and religious groups whose loyalties are not to the state. Israel's strategy, therefore, is to destroy these states and replace them with small balkanised entities so preoccupied with mutual enmities that Israel could dominate the area with ease. Lebanon as a test of this strategy is hardly a success story, but Jordan, Syria, and Iraq are all candidate victims. Therefore, in this Sharon view, an Iranian victory might well dismember Iraq into three separate states – Kurdish, Sunni, and Shiah – and would therefore be in Israel's interest.

The legion of flaws in this brutally primitive analysis transcends the scope of our discussion, but clearly the widespread impetus such a victory might give to radical Islamic fundamentalism would further dampen prospects for eventual peace negotiations between Israel and its neighbours. Though the Sharon school would not object to this the probable upsurge of fundamentalist-inspired anti-Israeli feeling and activity by Arabs in the occupied territories and Israel proper would be a disaster for Israel. While there are tactical advantages to some Israeli-Iranian cooperation the prospect of the balkanised region dominated by Israel hardly accords with Khomeini's vision of one dominant Islamic state. The two visions are contradictory and destroy the credibility of any implied Israeli-Iranian condominium to redraw the map of the Middle East.

The threat from an Iranian collapse

Before treating the more likely threats from Iran – those consequent to a dramatic Iranian breakthough in Iraq – a less likely Iranian threat needs mention, namely, an Iranian defeat. This would not be the kind of Iraqi military triumph that was feared early during the war, leaving Iraq with an intimidating posture in the Gulf and much of the

Arab world. Rather, Iran's strategy of attrition might backfire and some combination of economic and leadership fracture bring down the Tehran government. As ethnic groups in Iran tried to capitalise on the confusion and as struggles occurred between factions of the military and militia groups the dangers would be obvious for the Gulf. Might the Soviets intervene? Might prolonged civil war ensue, with leftist factions supported by Moscow? Although presumably a remote possibility, such a development is a reminder that US interests will be served best by a soft landing for this war. Iran could become a threat in collapse *or* triumph.

A triumphant Iran

Obviously an Iran in triumph is the focus of our concern. The concern centres on the added impetus victory would give to Tehran's ideological and military expansionism. 'Worst case' projections seem to predominate. A senior Jordanian official recently was reported saying that an Iraqi military defeat would take us back to Ottoman times where ten thousand Iranian troops could sweep through the Gulf conquering regimes. A Middle East specialist returned from a tour of the Gulf in February 1987 with vivid words of doom.[5] An Iraqi defeat would leave Iran free to overwhelm the Gulf states, and achieve control over 'half the globe's oil reserves, which would mean for Western consumers a tripling of the oil price, to $50 a barrel'. Beyond the Gulf Tehran would also provide 'money, leadership, and dynamism' to fundamentalists throughout the Middle East, using local militias instead of Iran's forces to turn the region into a 'satellite bloc' devoid of any American influence.

In a far more probing review another analyst finds that a decisive Iranian victory would open the way for a Middle East '. . . polarized between two hostile regional superpowers – Israel in the west and Iran in the east – with dangerous and unpredictable consequences'.[6]

The authors' purpose, in fairness, is partly to awaken what they see as a complacent Washington. Calculated exaggeration undoubtedly plays a role. But variations of these views are widespread. Distortion arises not because the views are entirely off base, but because significant distinctions are overlooked.

Iranian power and important distinctions

First, most of us would agree that nations in the immediate aftermath of revolution behave differently than nations whose revolutions have mellowed somewhat. The same is true of nations at war rather than at peace. Despite all that has been written about young Iranians' attraction for martyrdom the war is ghastly and devastating for the populace. For purposes of comparison US deaths in Vietnam over seven years of war instead of 55 000 would need to have numbered 1 250 000 or 2 500 000 (depending on whether low 250 000 or high 500 000 estimates of Iranian deaths are used) in order to approach Iran's experience.[7] Like all nations at war, particularly when the war spans over seven years, the leadership will resort to extreme actions anywhere in order to help the battlefield effort. This is plain to us in, say, judging the actions of the allies in the two great wars. Granting the differences of Iran's revolutionary philosophy, is it wise to assume that Tehran's association with terrorism, for instance, necessarily will remain characteristic of Iran's post-war behaviour? Iran sees itself battling an Iraq supported by the wealthy nations of the Arab world, by Egypt, by Jordan, and by France. Both superpowers tilt toward Iraq, despite Moscow's intermittent charm campaigns in Iran. Tehran can physically threaten its Gulf neighbours in return, but elsewhere is limited to terrorism and subversion in the guise of revolutionary Islamic activism. Iraq can financially and logicistically survive by its enhanced oil pipeline export capability and by other support from Gulf and other neighbours. Iran's constraints in thwarting this survivability are many. Yet Iraq's air power is theoretically capable of strangling Iran's exports and essential imports. This asymmetry helps explain, though by no means justifies, Iranian behaviour.

Second, is there sufficient distinction made between actions taken by fundamentalists outside Iran at their own initiative as opposed to actions, say in Lebanon, actually managed and financed by the Iranian government? Islamic fundamentalism's ancient roots are spread widely. The crude imagery of Iran's revolution 'defeating' America and of the Shiah in southern Lebanon 'defeating' and expelling Israel have been a powerful stimulus, particularly among the Arab masses of the Middle East for obvious reasons. But does this power mean an Iranian ability to manipulate fundamentalist cadres in Arab countries throughout the region? Lebanon is unique. There is no effective central government. The Shiah militias are heavily armed and their goals overlap with an array of other groups' ambitions quite apart from the precepts of Islamic fundamentalism. The Shiah are probably now Lebanon's largest religious group. Neighbouring Syria to date abets Iranian efforts in Lebanon which have assumed steadily greater potency as the Lebanese economy collapsed and the supply of outside funds and weapons competed against diminished internal resources. Iranian supported Shiah could therefore gain disproportionately against Shiah groups dependent on traditional avenues of support. Similar conditions are not found elsewhere in the Middle East.

Third, the US should not accept at face value all allegations about Iranian-linked terrorist and other subversive acts in the Middle East. For countries with strong fundamentalist movements a far better face may be put on, say, arrests following a student riot if foreign involvement is alleged. This political device, common for centuries, flourishes widely today in most political cultures. Repression can be justified and the fundamentalists' extra-territorial loyalty attacked rather than their ideas *per se*.

Fourth, there are important distinctions between Iran's military power in the immediate Gulf region versus the rest of the Middle East. And in the Gulf context there is a requirement to distinguish, (1) between Tehran's ability to influence events by the threat or actuality of stand-off military action such as missile, mining, or air attack as opposed to, (2) the threat of Iranian expeditionary military actions such as amphibious or paratroop landings across the Gulf or moving forces overland into Kuwait and/or Saudi Arabia. The comparison of Iran with Israel as a regional superpower is doubly flawed. Israel is a superpower in strictly military terms only. Iran, with aspirations for economic and ideological superpowerdom, on the other hand, is decades if not generations away from military capability of the same order as Israel's. But Iran possesses the population and resources for an eventual regional role of a different order than Israel's.

Iran's military capability

These distinctions suggest two questions. Is Iran militarily capable of expeditionary action to conquer the Arab side of the Gulf, assuming an end to the war that eliminates Iraq as an obstacle? Second, how charismatic is the Iranian revolution to the Arabs of the Gulf and to what extent would an Iranian victory stimulate Iran-style revolutions in the GCC countries? On the military question there is need to quarrel with the concept implied in many analyses that somehow during these seven-plus years of war Iranian power has grown. While it is true that the war has enabled the mullahs to hold the country together, to postpone difficult decisions, and to entrench themselves, it is also true that Iran has been bled nearly white by revolution and war. This has evolved in loss of skilled manpower (through emigration and combat) and disruption of the economy as a whole. Infrastructure damage alone will take at least a decade to repair by conservative estimates. Although Iran is free of Iraq's huge debt burden, its infrastructure has suffered greater damage.

The deficiencies in Iran's military capability are as obvious. Iran has resourcefully cannibalised its huge inventory of American equipment, has scraped the world arms market for critical spares, and acquired some new items from Western Europe, North Korea, China and the USSR. This has enabled it to acquire skills in infantry management to keep pressure on Iraq. But the once gigantic Iranian inventory of surface to air missiles, fighter/bombers, tanks, helicopters, and naval vessels reportedly has been reduced to handfuls that are operational. The combination of this inventory deficiency, logistics confusion, and extreme vulnerability to air attack does not suggest ready capability for expeditions into the Arabian peninsula. Weapons and organisation aside, such basics as reliable fuel supplies for vehicles at times are absent. Iraqi air attacks have severely damaged Iranian refining capability and many of the tankers bringing refined petroleum products through the Gulf to Iran. Petrol rationing began in Iran last October.[8] Oil income has been halved.

All of this suggests a post-war Iran severely weakened. And even assuming the unlikely scenario of a collapsed Iraq, the GCC states under Saudi leadership possess sizeable air defence and offensive capability, however much in need of better coordination and standardisation. While the GCC defence system is largely untested, Saudi F–15 fighter bombers bolstered by AWACS brought down an intruding Iranian fighter in June 1984. While the more fundamental restraints for Iran lie in other factors, there are serious obstacles to the kind of sweeping Iranian panzer-type conquest of the Arab Gulf often projected. Mass infantry attacks are one thing. Reconstruction of Iran's professional defence forces and support base to anything approaching its pre-revolutionary level would require massive absorption of new equipment and training over many years. Would the US or Europe or the USSR provide this to a militant Iran? Would

Turkey and Egypt remain passive as Iran built its expeditionary capability? Apart from these questions it seems clear that any Tehran government will confront staggering post-war economic and social challenges bound to limit the scope for conventional military adventure.

Ideological and military expansion

Before mentioning some even more fundamental restraints there is the second question – how charismatic is Iran's revolutionary message in the Gulf? Could handfuls of Iranian-trained Kuwaitis, Bahrainis, Abu Dhabians, or Saudis combine with Iranian-supplied weapons and other support to stimulate the overthrow of governments? Could post-war Iranian propaganda prove so compelling, and Iranian physical power so towering, that the GCC leaders would simply buckle to Tehran's dictates? The answers to these questions must be based on impressionistic rather than scholarly data.

But past assessments in most cases have underestimated the Gulf countries. Nasserism was to sweep away all Arab monarchies. Egyptian forces in North Yemen during the 1960s were to topple the Saudi kingdom. In 1970 many saw the British military departure from the Gulf bringing widespread collapse for the sheikhdoms as ancient rivalries and border disputes surfaced. The Dhofar rebellion of the 1970s coupled with Marxist subversion from the People's Democratic Republic of Yemen (PDRY) would dethrone Sultan Qabus of Oman. The PDRY would then pick off the Saudi kingdom. The sudden outpouring of money from the oil boom was to have entirely swept away the traditional societies of the Gulf. Kuwait's large Palestinian population often has implied their imminent seizure of power just as the Shiah communities in Saudi Arabia's eastern province and in several of the smaller Gulf states were to have been so captivated by Khomeini as to spark major rebellions.

Iran's revolution provoked similar predictions about all the Gulf states, particularly those with substantial Shiah populations. As Khomeini built his power from exile in Iraq and then returned from Paris there was high excitement throughout the Gulf which combined attraction with elements of awe and fear as he returned home triumphant. Tapes of his speeches were everywhere, along with his portrait. But as the excesses of the revolution became known and as the Iranian economy ran down, much of the attraction of the revolution dissipated. Similarly, early sympathy for Iran as the invaded state began to dissolve once Iraqi troops withdrew from Iranian territory in 1982. Iran is now viewed as the aggressor who is prolonging a war which endangers the lifeline flow of commerce in the Gulf. While Khomeini's personal charisma may remain a factor in the Gulf states, there is little evidence that Iran as a revolutionary state holds wide appeal even among the Shiah. Post-revolution Iran is seen as a large and important trading partner by the smaller Gulf states, as a balance against Saudi power (and in the past against Iraq), and also, like the Pahlavi state, as an occasional font of strident and bullying rhetoric. Post-war Iran may not appear all that different from Pahlavi Iran – large, rhetorically and at times physically aggressive, but not in a position to dominate the region.

Threat to the Gulf apart from the wider middle east

In short, there is no evidence that Khomeini has made ideological headway in the Gulf region itself. Iran is too close and the regime's problems too visible. Resistance to Iranian hegemony comes naturally from historical memory. Rule by mullahs, including many unsavoury actions taken in the name of the revolution, and returning women to their veils apparently holds limited appeal to the relatively cosmopolitian Gulf trading communities. There are of course great variations among states and communitues in the Gulf; some of the Shiah in Bahrain or the UAE would undoubtedly disagree with this analysis. But most Gulf states' populations are mixed Arab, Iranian, and Baluchi, implying a diversity of views. The revolution's stimulus to radical fundamentalism in Indonesia, Pakistan, Egypt, Tunisia, Jordan, the West Bank of Lebanon is another question. Perhaps because the revolution has not captured the imagination of Iran's neighbours – excepting some Afghan rebel groups – and because so much of the Arab world has resolutely continued to support Iraq, Iran has worked to fire Shiah extremism in places like Lebanon and Tunis. Fundamentalist origins and movements long predating the Khomeini revolution are important throughout the Muslim world. Their problematic relationship to Iran understandably creates confusion in analysis.

IRAN: RESTRAINTS AND STRATEGIC WEAKNESSES

No doubt Iran is in many ways a regional colossus. This is rightfully recognised, but often without looking beneath the surface of land mass, population, and oil wealth.

There are strategic weaknesses in Iran's posture apart from its present military and economic over-extension. While simple and obvious they are frequently overlooked. Iran, as the only Shiah state and the only Persian state, is one of a kind. Persians and the Arabs are ancient enemies. Tehran's isolation in the war has been only slightly relieved because of Syria's enmity toward Iraq; Syria's support has in part also been purchased with preferential oil deals. The Gulf Arabs could readily outbid Iran. Libya and the PDRY have been preoccupied with their own internal and external conflicts. Iran, then, is somewhat of an island, with shifting and unstable alliances. Its geography and manpower resources are partly compensating factors, but Iran in a practical sense is ill-equipped for a continuing campaign to unseat the governments of the Arab (and most of the Islamic) world. Marxist PDRY, anti-fundamentalist, Ba'athist Syria, and Libya – current 'allies' – all know that in time they would be added to Tehran's hit list. By the end of 1987 the PDRY's foreign minister, in apparent acknowledgement of this reality, stated, 'We will back Kuwait in defending its lands and independence against any external assault'.[9]

Iran's relationships with its neighbours are universally uneasy and require careful tending. No neighbour provides a solid wall against which the Iranian back might rest while dealing with enemies. The USSR's physical and political intrusions into Iran historically are well documented. Moscow permits clandestine anti-Khomeini radio broadcasts in the name of the Iranian communist (Tudeh) party and openly propagandises the Iranian province of Azerbaijan in favour of Soviet Azerbaijan and a level of cultural autonomy supposedly unavailable to the Azerbaijanis in Iran.[10] When Iran unilaterally renounced those clauses of the Soviet–Iran treaty of 1921 permitting Soviet military intervention if Soviet security were threatened from Iran, Moscow refused to accept the move and insisted on keeping its right of intervention.[11] An even more obvious source of tension is the Soviet occupation of Afghanistan with its strong religious implications, the financial burden of a million or more Afghan refugees, and the issue of Iranian military supplies for the rebels. The result is a complex game of pressures and counter-pressures dominated by

Soviet support for Iraq versus Iranian support for several Afghan rebel groups. Moscow and Tehran at the same time advertise their partially renewed economic relationship in the context of 'normalcy'.

The 1972 Treaty of Friendship and Cooperation between the USSR and Iraq also adds limits, however uncertain, on Iran's freedom of action in Iraq. Renewal of the treaty was celebrated in Baghdad on 9 April 1987 coicident with the visit of Petr Demichev, CPSU Central Committee Politburo candidate member and First Deputy Chairman of the Supreme Soviet Presidium.[12] While the treaty is vague about obligations in the absence of peace, it raises the question how much Iranian military force in Iraq the Soviets will tolerate before reacting. Moscow has many options for pressuring Iran, short of actual military intervention. These range from military pressures on Iran's northern provinces to providing 'volunteers' for Iraqi forces. Or may the Soviets already have warned Iran not to move closer to Basra? Alternatively, Moscow might well be happy to see Saddam Hussein overthrown, but the risks of becoming an accomplice with Iran, and the uncertainties of the succession would be formidable.

Soviet signals in the Gulf

The Soviets have responded eagerly to overtures from various GCC states that are motivated strongly by fear of Iran. Both Oman and the UAE have opened diplomatic relations with Moscow and the Soviets have exchanged numerous high level delegations with Kuwait for over a year. Oil and other issues are an element as well as security considerations, of course. Not only war and revolution have brought the Soviets more into Gulf affairs, but the oil price collapse in addition. In response to Saudi oil minister Hisham Nazer's visit to Moscow in January 1987 Soviet official statements have sought to demonstrate a cooperative attitude toward OPEC's oil export cut-back efforts.[13] As early as June 1986 high level USSR–Kuwait discussions focused on possibilities for Kuwaiti investment projects in the USSR and the press referred to plans for major cooperation between the two countries such as financing oil, gas, industrial, and construction projects in the Arab world and constructing oil and petrochemical facilities in the USSR.[14] Whether significant tangible results will follow this publicity is uncertain. One sign – the chairman of Kuwait Foreign Trading Contracting and Investment Co. announced on 15 February 1987 the signing of a medium term $150 million syndicated loan for the Bank for Foreign Trade of the USSR.[15]

The Soviets by these and other steps continue demonstrating strong interest in a country the Tehran regime excoriates for its support of Baghdad. Even more plain was the Soviet offer to provide Soviet tankers for Kuwait's oil export or possibly to provide naval escort for Kuwaiti tankers. The Soviets also signed a new merchant shipping agreement with Iraq in March 1987 for 'expansion and promotion' of maritime navigation, merchant shipping and training for Iraqis. On 25 March Soviet Ambassador to Kuwait, Ernest Zverev pledged 'support for the freedom of shipping in the Strait of Hormuz and in the . . . Gulf'.[16] As in most Gulf security matters the Soviet degree of commitment to Iraq or Kuwait is ambiguous. Tehran none the less must reckon carefully regarding the superpower on its northern border. This seems to be the case. Tehran's domestic radio in late April noted bitterly that Soviet Deputy Foreign Minister Petrovskiy's visit to Basra, Kuwait and Abu Dhabi and the content of his speeches reflected growing Soviet departure from its neutral stance in the war, opening the way for an increased US role in the Gulf.[17] Iran got the point particularly in Petrovskiy's Basra visit, with Tehran's domestic radio noting angrily, 'the Russians have adopted a hostile policy with regard to the Islamic Republic . . . with the . . . Basra inspection and, finally the USSR's involvement in the US plan of leasing ships to Kuwait, [amounting to] some sort of declaration of war against the Islamic Republic of Iran'.[18] Since the US reflagging effort the Soviets have rushed forward with economic missions to Tehran and grandiose plans have been announced for industrial projects, shipping and new pipeline links between the USSR and Iran. While the Soviets have demonstrated an ability to deal with both sides in the war – a capacity denied the US – their already poor reputation for reliability as a partner in the Middle East has declined even further. The GCC states and Iraq reacted bitterly to Soviet blockage of UN Security Council Resolution 598 toward an arms embargo against Iran in late 1987. The Arab summit meeting in Amman during November appeared to focus this reaction with sufficient force to cause a Soviet flip-flop of sorts in which part of Moscow's newly minted goodwill in Iran will be sacrificed to recoup lost ground in the Arab world.

These steady expressions for support for Kuwait and against Iran's threats to close the Gulf have not been a superpower monopoly. Admiral Branko Mamula, Yugoslavia's Defence Minister visited

Kuwait in March 1987, 'to discuss military cooperation and the situation in the Gulf region'.[19] A month earlier Rumanian First Deputy Minister of National Defence General Victor Stanculescu made a five day official visit to Kuwait, 'to discuss military cooperation'.[20] Representing a more traditional friendship British Minister of State for Defence Procurement Lord Trefgarne also visited in March.[21] None of this suggested the imminent dispatch of an international armada and brigade to Kuwait. In all cases the visitors were seeking arms sales, investments, and loans as well as expressing broader political messages to Iran. But Kuwait is supported by a very large and powerful cross-section of the international community and the cost to Iran of violating Kuwaiti sovereignty cannot be dismissed lightly. The risks from Iranian-supported terrorism or sabotage continue as do the dangers to the vulnerable Kuwait infrastructure from missile attack launched from the Faw peninsula. But as attacks increase Iran must weigh the advantages gained against the proportionately mounting anti-Iranian hostility of the Arab world.

Turkey and the Gulf

While Iran and Turkey have had good post-Second World War relations and remain major trading partners, the revolution's proselytising outreach has complicated Turkish control of its own fundamentalist movements. Historically, moreover, there is a long traditon of Turkish-Iranian hostility. A reversion to this hostility would be a financial blow for Iran that further constricted its world supply and trading access. Even the existing transit arrangements between Ankara and Tehran have been troubled; in October 1986, 2000 Turkish trucks were forced to transfer their loads to Iranian vehicles at the border before the shipment could proceed into Iran.[22] Iraqi-Turkish ties, on the other hand, have become much closer during the war as Iraq's oil pipeline through Turkey to the Mediterranean has been significantly enlarged. A second, parallel, line begun in 1984 is virtually complete, adding at least a half million barrels per day to Iraqi export capacity. According to Iraq's oil minister, Isam al-Chalaby, oil exports by the end of May 1987 had reached more than two million barrels per day for the first time since the war began in 1980.[23] Recent Turkish military incursions into northern Iraq, with Iraqi permission, have not only been to help protect the pipelines from Kurdish sabotage (no doubt encouraged by Tehran), but to retaliate for attacks against Turkish authority by Turkish Kurds who represent almost a quarter of Turkey's population. Threats have been exchanged, particularly after Iran fired several missiles into the Kirkuk area in the summer of 1986. Turkey has issued warnings to Iran and a leading Tehran daily, *Ettelaat*, recently accused the Turks of placing forces, 'so that it may enter the northern parts of Iraq should Iranian forces advance inside Iraqi territory'.[24] Turkey, Iraq, Iran, and the USSR are *all* vulnerable on the complex Kurdish issue. Turkey, however, has a strong interest in Iraq's territorial integrity as a consequence. Turkey has sharply increased its military presence in the east over past months, amounting to 60 per cent of its ground forces by some estimates.[25]

Turkey's ample motives for expanded relations in the Gulf were demonstrated in early March 1987 when Turkey and Kuwait initialled an agreement for the 'protection of investments and encouraging mutual investments . . . the first drawn with an Arab country . . . and to become a model for the Gulf countries'. According to the *Ankara Anatolia* of 3 March, Turkey is preparing similar agreements with the UAE and Saudi Arabia which, 'will facilitate the flow of capital to Turkey'.[26]

Ankara also has signalled its specific interest in GCC security. In mid-February the Turkish Minister of National Defence Zeki Yavuzturk made a five-day visit to Kuwait with a high ranking military delegation. 'Avenues of military cooperation and exchange of expertise' were discussed.[27] Against the backdrop of Ottoman history the visit, while no doubt mainly symbolic, is a plain message to Tehran. Once again, another ambiguous yet tangible obstacle became posed against freewheeling Iranian ambitions, this time by Turkish interests.

Pakistan, Egypt and Jordan

Pakistan, in contrast to Turkey, has long had a large security role in the Arab Gulf states, Saudi Arabia and Oman particularly. Estimates of actual forces and seconded officers vary, but the numbers certainly exceed ten thousand. This positions Pakistan against Iranian military expansion much as the existence of a large Pakistani Shiah population already influenced by its own fundamentalists makes Islamabad wary of Tehran's proselytising. Tehran and Islamabad of course both support the Afghan rebels, but the mullah's efforts to convert rebel factions conflicts with Pakistan's goals. But until Soviet forces are removed from Afghanistan (if indeed they are to be) along with whatever remnant regime might temporarily survive their departure, Iran's government will have strong reasons to cooperate with Pakistan. The reported withdrawal of Pakistani units from Saudi Arabia during late 1987 signalled Saudi sensitivity to potential Shiah leanings by the Pakistanis following the Mecca riots rather than an inclination in Islamabad to placate Tehran.

Egypt, in contrast, is sufficiently remote both literally and figuratively for Iran to rail freely about its ties with the US, its peace treaty with Israel, its secularism, and its support for Iraq. One consequence of the war, however, has been Egypt's gradual return, in substance if not form, to the Arab fold. As war pressures have mounted on the GCC states they have enhanced their political as well as financial relationships with Cairo. The Amman summit in November 1987 was the turning point of this process wherein most of the GCC states resumed relations with Cairo. Visits to the Gulf by President Mubarak and Egypt's defence minister followed, together with substantial discussion in the Cairo and Gulf presses about possibilities for Egyptian military cooperation with the GCC. Stories were leaked in Cairo about contingency plans for intervention in Kuwait by Egyptian forces. The weight of Egyptian military and cultural power in the Middle East becomes more evident as the natural balance against Iran with each sign of increasing threat from Tehran. While Egypt certainly would commit actual forces to Iraq only under the most extreme circumstances, the large number of Egyptian workers (estimates vary from half a million to well over a million) in Iraq alone creates an Egyptian security interest in Iraq. In a sense, Egypt already supports the Iraqi war effort by freeing so many Iraqi workers for military duty. This is beyond the actual military equipment supplied by Egypt. While Egyptian inhibitions against direct military involvement in Iraq are powerful and compounded by memories of the Yemen disaster as well as the now more vocal role of Egyptian fundamentalism, Cairo depends vitally on Arab Gulf financial support. For these reasons the dispatch of Egyptian 'volunteers' for rear guard duties might be considered by Egypt, or, perhaps more likely, participation in an Arab force designed at least symbolically to bolster Kuwaiti defences. By mid-May 1987 Egypt, like Tunisia, had broken diplomatic relations with Iran, blaming Iranian involvement with Egyptian radical fundamentalists. On 20 May, Jim Muir reported in *The Christian Science Monitor* from Nicosia that 'well placed sources say Egypt has given Iraq assurances that its armed forces will intervene if necessary to hold the line in the Basra sector'. While it is difficult to weigh the impact on Tehran of these earlier events as well as the far more explicit later Egyptian-Gulf signals of military cooperation, some among Iran's leadership could not help but fear the implications of a war increasingly cast as Arab against Persian.

Jordan's capacity to intervene is limited by the small size of its forces which are more than pinned down by Syria. None the less, Jordan's well trained units have been active in advising Iraq, and Jordan, like Pakistan, has a long standing security relationship with the Arab Gulf countries – in training and actual command roles. While Jordan already is fully committed as an Iraqi ally, an overplayed Iranian hand might well cause Syria to desert Iran and join Jordan in defence of the Arab countries of the Gulf. Given sufficient Iranian provocation – such as the occupation of substantial parts of southern Iraq – Saudi Arabia and Kuwait might both eliminate their financial subsidies to impoverished Syria, while simultaneously dangling the promise of greatly increased future subsidies and free oil that would sharply outbid Iran. The 'reconciliation' of Syrian President Assad and Saddam Hussein at the Amman summit meeting, however cosmetic, could not have pleased Iran.

Arab sensitivity to foreign occupation of land is in the forefront of Middle East politics, whether by Israel or, potentially, by Iran. Even Algeria, long allied with Iran on oil pricing issues – preferring higher prices because of smaller reserves than most of the GCC states – has made clear its objection to any permanent occupation of Iraqi territory by Iran. The complex oil pricing issue during the current phase of overproduction and price weakness constitutes a potent source of potential Arab pressure and restraint on Iran. This became evident during the December 1987 Vienna meeting of OPEC with Iran blustering that it would double oil production in the absence of the kind of substantial price increase required for its war effort. The reality, however, is that Iran is having difficulty maintaining its already reduced production because of Iraqi-inflicted damage. Coupled with Iran's reduced market – because of US and some European refusal to buy – and the obvious GCC ability to keep prices low, Iran confronts the possibility of a gradually diminished ability to finance its war effort.

Iran then, overall, faces a quite different Arab world alignment today than before the war. Iraq, whose pre-war bluster and puffery caused apprehension in the Arab world, added to this apprehension by its initial occupation of Iranian territory. Today, despite the uncertain survivability of Saddam Hussein, Iraq has a degree of infrastructure integration and political support with the GCC, Jordan, and Turkey scarcely imaginable in 1980. While Iran has become increasingly isolated, Iraq has broadened its international relationships, particularly as Iran's refusal to negotiate and occupation of Iraqi territory has undercut Tehran's bargaining position as the injured party.

All of this may increase Iranian determination to press on for a 'total victory' in order to preclude a post-war situation with Iraq well accepted and supported in GCC circles. This 'total victory', however, remains illusive. Whether Iran could follow a battlefield victory in one of more sectors with political success is open to question. While the removal of Saddam Hussein by his own military might provide Tehran with the convincing stuff of 'victory' for internal purposes, there is no reason to expect the state of Iraq and the overall Arab will to collapse as a result.

A double edge to the proselytising sword?

Finally, mention should be made of a further restraint on the mullah's ability to sweep the Islamic world with its revolution. Granted that the revolution appeals to both some Sunni and Shiah Muslims, the latter are most likely to be linked directly to Iranian support whether purely inspirational, or physical in terms of training, funds, or weapons. The Shiah are an Islamic minority in most countries. Should a backlash develop against the fundamentalists, the Shiah may take the brunt of reprisals. Memory of bloody Shiah–Sunni riots on the Indian subcontinent is a reminder of the potential for further destruction within this schism. The war itself can be seen as a Shiah battle against Sunni Iraq despite the importance of Iraq's Shiah population. The Persian versus Arab caste of the war poses its own set of risks for Iran. Evidence of Shiah involvement with sabotage in Kuwait has already damaged the community's status there. The mullahs can only rely so much on religious zeal to overcome nationalism and ethnic identity as they fight to spread their doctrine. Religious zeal itself, moreover, might damage Iranian interests in the Arab world even while quickening the pace of Islamic resurgence.

Iran's national needs can only be subordinated so far to the revolution's militant international Islamic evangelism.

US RESPONSE

The US position in the Gulf is heavily burdened by Middle East policy reverses during the post-Camp David era – over West Bank settlements, Lebanon, and a series of missteps that have sharply weakened the US position both as a guarantor of Saudi (and by extension, GCC) security and as a somewhat evenhanded broker between Israel and the Arabs. The recent arms sales to Iran have further weakened US credibility. Yet one often hears that we are not involved in a popularity contest and that 'they need us more than we need them' – modern versions of the old 'they can't drink their oil; they have to sell it to us' refrain. True only to a point. The Arab leaders of the Gulf, though 'rulers', operate by consensus. When the USA is seen to be following Israeli policy as in Lebanon or in selling arms to Iran or in denying sales of weapons systems to the GCC states, the liability side of the ledger of the US relationship rises; the legitimacy of an Arab leader is weakened by association. The negative symbolism is specifically potent in the Gulf where tribal traditions remain strong. The ultimate guarantor of the GCC states' military security, the USA, is seen precisely damaging the defence capability of the Arab leaders whose chief responsibility as the guardians of their people is on trial while war rages across the Gulf. This situation has added credibility and force to the Ayatollah Khomeini's external progaganda which portrays the US as treacherously engaged against Islamic interests everywhere.

None the less, the US role in the Gulf remains important, however much weakened. Immediate challenges include the post-Iran arms sales damage repair, renewed efforts to bolster GCC security, the containment of Iran and support of Iraq without major departure from our tilted neutrality.

The required reassurances to the GCC in the wake of the Iran scandal have been taken. High level US emissaries have gone to the Gulf, including the Chairman of the Joint Chiefs of Staff, Admiral William Crowe. Diplomatic reassurances and re-tightening of Operation Staunch against arms sales to Iran are underway along with the highly publicised White House staff changes. New arms sales have been proposed for Saudi Arabia and Bahrain and most important,

US escort of Kuwaiti tankers has given tangible evidence of Washington's seriousness. In the absence of such tangible evidence, no amount of demonstrations could have salvaged a credible Gulf role for the US.

Other US efforts show good intentions but also inability. Secretary of State Shultz has asked China not to sell more arms to Iran. Congressional reaction to the arms sales proposals in the Gulf will determine whether US credibility as an offset to Soviet and/or Iranian expansion in the Gulf will improve or further deteriorate.

US military credibility

The political handicaps mentioned above have reduced the ability of the GCC countries to cooperate with the USA in their own defence. US preparedness for military intervention in the Gulf has none the less improved dramatically since 1980, a fact evident to Iran, of course, and to the Soviets. This deterrence factor is an important reality in Gulf politics despite the towering ambivalence about possible US intervention. The list of US capability improvements is impressively long and begins with greatly enhanced facilities and reaction times. Dual use facilities in the Azores, Morocco, Diego Garcia have been upgraded substantially. Regional access facilities in Kenya, Somalia, Djibouti, Oman, and Pakistan – air fields as well as port facilities – have been upgraded as a cost of billions. In contingencies acceptable to the host country US forces could use these as staging points to the Gulf. Combat support equipment is prepositioned ashore or afloat in cargo vessels sufficient to support a significant US force. For example, the total ammunition aboard pre-positioned ships in the region would require more than 6100 C–141 cargo aircraft sorties to airlift from the US east coast to the Middle East.[28] Fast cargo shipping capability has sharply reduced sealift reaction times for critical elements to support initial forces. The development of off-loading equipment for austere ports has increased delivery flexibility.[29]

Extensive training exercises for US forces applicable to Gulf and other Middle East scenarios have occurred in US desert areas and in Southwest Asia and North Africa. New generation water purification and distribution equipment, new communications capability, and a wide range of other modifications have significantly upgraded the US ability to respond. Sealift capability has more than tripled since 1981.

Overall readiness of US forces has also improved markedly.

Many problems remain, but today we are fully capable of quick military reaction to support a threatened GCC state – initially with small combat units, but followed by major forces if necessary. Graduated military responses are now available that were hardly thought of in 1980. The US now has sufficient prepositioned equipment available to avoid much of the crippling time lag problem evident in 1980. A 16 500 man marine brigade, for instance, could be moved to the Gulf region by air (or by a combination of air and sealift), and quickly joined with its support equipment. Formidable problems remain, however, particularly in multi-crisis conditions where several global emergencies might compete for the use of the same US combat unit.

Contingencies

If the preceding analysis of the Iranian threat is accurate no commitment of US ground forces is likely to be required, other than as an 'over-the-horizon' presence. US response, beyond this, will likely continue to involve naval escort, mine clearing or symbolic boosting of the GCC's own small rapid deployment force. This could involve the airlift of emergency supplies to Dhahran as GCC units moved into Kuwait, or up the scale to stationing F–15 squadrons with aerial refuelling tankers in Dhahran or Oman. The US might also assist in the transport of Egyptian and Jordanian forces into the Gulf. US aircraft carrier launched strikes at Iranian targets are a theoretical option, as is naval bombardment. But the adverse political consequences of such actions in all but the most extreme circumstances, make them highly remote and undesirable options.

Speculation about a situation as fluid as the Gulf's is of very limited use. These sketchy and incomplete comments about options are intended to parallel the assessment of Iran's military limitations. They are further intended to indicate how easily any US military action in the Gulf that is not keyed to the right kind of invitation could upset the entire political applecart that is the basis of our vital interest there. Once the situation in the Gulf has deteriorated to the extent that the insertion of division level US forces is required it would probably be too late. Successful outcomes involving US military assets in the Gulf will be those where the victories or strengths revealed are the GCC's and Iraq's, not the US's.

The goal of stability

Neither the USA nor the USSR can impose stability in the Gulf. Eventual equilibrium will be achieved only when Iran and its Arab neighbours can agree on reasonable terms. The least helpful step by the US at this stage would be to move from a naval escort role to direct military intervention against Iranian forces. US pressure against Iran to prevent expansion of the war, either across the Gulf or further into Iraq itself, must be confined to defence of GCC shipping or territory. US messages to Iran should be conveyed through diplomatic channels, avoiding gratuitous or provocative public challenges. Iran's leaders remain in power despite the disastrous war and economic dislocation partly through the imagery of Iranian-inspired Islamic resistance against the Soviets in Afghanistan and against the US and its friends in the Gulf. We need to avoid the tragic irony of US threats and provocations that bolster the national and international prestige of the Khomeini regime.

Dialogue with Tehran should be maintained through official channels on relatively technical matters to do with Iranian claims. Washington has absolutely no cause to woo Tehran, a government where seriously divided factions are jockeying for the post-war, post-Khomeini transition. Nothing would be more foolish than US efforts to influence this factional struggle, in the process likely sealing the doom of whichever faction we favoured. If the Soviets are to make greater headway in Iran it will not be because of US refusal to court Tehran. Iran's national power becomes optimised when its diplomacy is able to play Moscow against Washington. Deprived of that opportunity plus vital US military and other equipment the Iranians have a more urgent policy requirement for reconciliation than does the US. In turn, a wise US policy will burn as few remaining bridges to Iran as possible, keeping in mind among many other factors the eventuality of a new Iraqi leadership with resurrected designs on the moderate Arab states.

Where the US does require activism for the sake of its Gulf policy is in the congressional affairs and public opinion arena, (1) to permit arms sales proposals for GCC countries, and, (2) to articulate consistent support for GCC security without locking into a confrontational approach toward Iran. During the first weeks of the war the US promised to, 'respond to requests for assistance from nonbelligerent friends in the Gulf region'.[30] The Statement was consistent with US policy in the region since the Second World War. Kuwait has become the test case of this policy, albeit in complex circumstances. The US technically is neutral in the war and supports freedom of navigation through the Gulf. But the US has not protested Iraqi attacks on ships entering or leaving Iranian ports, attacks far more numerous than those inflicted by Iran. Public confusion has resulted because US policy spokesmen have not clearly identified the Iranian attacks occurring for the most part in international waters against non-belligerent as opposed to the Iraqi policy of generally striking ships in Iranian waters directly serving a belligerent power.

Beyond these factors, undoubtedly labelled technicalities by some, there are further fundamentals at issue. Since early in the war Iraq has agreed to negotiate a peaceful settlement. Iran still refuses. Iran's claim that Iraq started the war assumes the status of a technicality rather than of moral high ground in view of the long series of Iranian physical and ideological post-revolution aggressions against Iraq prior to Iraq's actual invasion of Khuzistan province. This happened while the US was preoccupied with the Tehran hostage crisis. Iran threatens to close the Gulf. Iran openly expresses its intention to change the governments of the region to its own radical Islamic liking. Iranian pressure on Kuwait translates into the use of force to halt GCC support for Iraq. Without GCC support Iraq would collapse. Without firm support from the GCC and the West, Kuwait's political structure would collapse, endangering political structures in all GCC states. The industrialised world cannot tolerate such a course of events induced by Iranian military pressure. The eventually supportive European reaction to US reflagging and escort naval operations reflected a realisation of this fact.

Nor can long-range US interests in any way be associated with efforts to crush Iran or join a campaign to reverse the Iranian revolution. Carrots must accompany the sticks. The US should remain the consistent and steadfast prop to GCC security rather than be manoeuvred into a political and military lead position out ahead of the GCC in direct confrontation with Iran. This has proved tricky in military as well as political terms, but at least throughout 1987 the US met with success.

The lessons of the Iran-contra scandal must be drawn upon to stress once more that Washington requires its own Middle East and Gulf policy directed toward the US national interest. Israel's interests and policies must be kept distinct. Policy-makers must realise that the present government of Israel views the prospect of a post-war Iraq more closely linked to the GCC and the US with alarm in political/

psychological terms. In the long run perhaps the greatest boost to US policy in the Gulf would lie in the United States ability to convince Israel and its more zealous US supporters that Israel has a strategic interest in US ability to maintain good realtions with the GCC and Iraq. Many Israelis support this concept as do many pro-Israeli activists in the US. To move this understanding to the political level in either country is the problem, particularly during election years.

If the war ends with both Iran and Iraq territorially whole and functioning independently, a surge of arms modernisation activity sadly can be expected in both countries. US policy may confront even more difficult challenges then. Iraq will urgently require the very best in air defence to offset strategic vulnerabilities and Iran's manpower advantages. Iran will want to rebuild its elaborate air defence system, its navy, and its inventory of high performance aircraft and missiles. Both may want portions of their more sophisticated power, port, oil, and other damaged facilities rebuilt by US companies. Political inhibitions against normalisation will abound. Congress and to an extent even the GCC states will be wary of too much Iraqi military power. Almost any likely ruling coalition in Tehran will not easily shift from the revolution's gospel anti-Americanism. This is notwith-standing (1) that much of Iran's industry and infrastructure, putting aside its largely US military inventory, is of US origin, and (2) the strong feelings of goodwill toward Americans on the part of many Iranians. None the less, it is difficult in the longer perspective to imagine a definitive break between Tehran and Washington, particu-larly in view of Iran's strategic requirements. If Iraq, on the other hand, can be encouraged further in its direction of cooperation with Jordan, Turkey, Egypt and the GCC states there should be less post-war Iranian temptation to mount military and subversive press-ure against an isolated Baghdad. The US has a natural role in that scenario best played in the context of gradual *rapprochement* rather than confrontation with Tehran.

CONCLUSION

Unique circumstances complicate the American view of the Gulf. A profusion of grey areas and a very long war substitute for the quick, militarily decisive Middle East wars between the clearly defined good guy and bad guy to which we are accustomed. Also complicating in this long test for US policy are the many exaggerations and distortions in American perceptions of Iran. The image of Iran has become overblown, in part because Iran's image of its own power and importance has been overblown both before and after the revolution. We are well aware that the transition from the Shah to Khomeini represented *dis*continuity in the extreme. Awareness of certain continuities, however, would help balance the perspective. The Shah, particularly in the latter stages of his reign, sought enormous international expansion of Iran's temporal power through military and financial clout. Khomeini and some of his followers seek expansion and power in the spiritual realm throughout Islam as well as by subversive and military means against Iraq and the GCC states. Nationalism, anathema for Khomeini yet extolled by the Shah, arises more and more as the war drags on and Iran's isolation increases. For neither the Shah nor Khomeini was the expansionist international goal realistic. This policy element has brought tragic hardship for the Iranian people. The continuity of contempt for the Arab regimes of the Gulf is plain. For the Shah it was the 'medieval' neighbouring regimes about to topple that could be bluffed. For Khomeini it is the 'corrupt and godless' GCC regimes that must be overthrown and bound to Iran's obscure brand of revolutionary fundamentalism.

This Iranian preoccupation with an expanded international role reflects an uneasiness with Iran's geopolitical position. The uneasiness seems to derive from dreams of a much larger ancient empire that contrast with the modern realities described above as strategic limitations. Fear of hostile encirclement and foreign meddling encourage defensive and then aggressive reaction. For Americans, in any event, the lesson lies in recognising that the USA's uncritical backing of the Shah helped create some of the exaggerations of his world view. In this, it was not helpful to a friend. What an irony, then, were it inadvertently to help the hostile Khomeini regime by indulging in a similar lapse of critical analysis.

We need to weigh Iranian rhetoric, and while acknowledging Iran's considerable capacities, avoid exaggerations. The general rise of fundamentalism throughout much of Islam has roots predating the Khomeini revolution. The revolution may inspire, but it does not lead or direct with a few exceptions. Iran's military power and the capabilities of its leadership must be kept in perspective. Particularly, we need to avoid accepting the popular media portrayal of the wily and clever clerics moving from triumph to triumph by running rings around all physical and political barriers posed by other nations. Despite fervent dedication and many tactical successes the Khomeini leadership's lack of strategic vision is demonstrated amply by the shambles of their economy, their lost generations of youth, and the disparity between the rhetorical goals and the actuality of their military capability. Their stimulation of the riots in Mecca, threats against Kuwait and other GCC states, and refusal to negotiate an end to hostilities with Iraq has alarmed and united the Arab world to an extent unknown for decades. They have induced a degree of Soviet-US dialogue on the Gulf bordering at times on cooperation. This and the greatly expanded US, Western European, and even Soviet naval presence has constricted Tehran's ability to manoeuvre the GCC intimidation, to transport and sell oil, and to obtain critical supplies on the world market.

Iran is not alone in manifesting pre- and post-revolution continuities. The American view that the Shah would 'invite the Soviets in' if his every wish were not satisfied has transferred in different form to the Khomeini regime. Neither the USSR nor Iran are in a position to move to an exclusive relationship. The revolution and the war have brought at least as many problems as benefits for the Soviets.

All these factors point to the requirement for a steady and quiet US determination and policy consistency which will reduce Iran's capabilities for bluff. Measured US physical as well as rhetorical responses are essential. Descriptions of Iran as a barbaric country by US leaders would usefully be replaced by reference to Iran's criminal leadership which is misrepresenting a great civilisation and people. The point is as much salving Iranian sensitivities as it is calming the American political climate this election year (1988) to avoid drawing US Gulf policy any further into the fray. Inflamed rhetoric about terrorism and barbarism can only help generate a climate conducive to opportunistic exploitation by politicians. This could occur either as a demand that the US leave the Gulf altogether or that it takes foolish military action against Iran. Certainly *one* factor tempting Tehran to stall in ending the war may be the hope of manoeuvring the war and US Gulf policy into becoming an important election issue wherein a new US administration might deliver a triumph for the revolution.

The US must be at least as patient as Iran. Despite declining oil revenues, increased Arab and other solidarity with Kuwait and Iraq, operation staunch and even an eventual UN embargo, Iran is not likely to bend quickly. The US public opinion problem arises because while these actions, together with the US and European naval presence, do not produce quick results they are none the less effective and necessary as part of a long-term strategy.

Unless US naval presence can be drawn down gradually in response to valid political and military reasons two risks that it must live with will likely increase. First, congressional and other demands for the US to leave the Gulf will increase. Second, for the sake of increased cost effectiveness and safety there may be requests to the GCC for military facilities that represent unassailable military logic, but which would undercut (if implemented) the political stability of the very nations the United States are trying to bolster. We will have to accept this inherent tension between military and political logic in the Gulf as a constant.

This delicate, adroit, and yet steady use of US military and diplomatic power implied is a tall order, particularly during an election year. So is the need to outgrow old images about Iran. Paramount here is a nostalgia for the Shah's era which generates the false belief that successful relations with Iran can only recur under a comparably pro-Western leadership.

Notes

1.   Said, Edward in 'The MESA Debate: The Scholars, the Media and the Middle East', *Journal of Palestinian Studies*, Winter 1987, p. 89.
2.   Eisenhower to Anderson, 30 July 1957. Dwight D. Eisenhower Library, Abelene, Kansas,. Quoted from Burton I. Kaufman, 'Mideast Multinational Oil, U.S. Foreign Policy, and Antitrust: The 1950s' *Journal of American History*, vol. 63, March 1977.
3.   See *Oil and Gas Journal* for figures; various issues but particularly December 1984 and 1985.
4.   Reisman, Michael, 'U.S. Gain From an Iranian Victory', *Wall Street Journal*, 19 February 1987.
5.   Viorst, Milton, 'Iran's Threat to the US', *Wall Street Journal*, 24 February 1987; for a more thorough discussion by the same author see, 'Iraq at War', *Foreign Affairs*, Winter 1986/87.
6.   Sick, Gary, 'Iran's Quest for Superpower Status', *Foreign Affairs*, Spring 1987.
7.   *Washington Times*, 14 and 31 March 1986 and *Insight*, pp. 28–30 estimates Iranian battle fatalities at least at 250 000. Drew Middleton in the *New York Times*, 23 September 1985 estimates between 420 000 and 580 000.
8.   For data on Iran's economy see the *Iran Country Report*, no. 4, 1986. Economist Intelligence Unit, London.
9.   *Foreign Broadcasting Information Service* (*FBIS*)–NES, KUNA, 17 December 1987.
10. 'Soviet Steps Up Propaganda in Azerbaijan', Radio Free Europe/ Radio Liberty, Soviet East European Reports, 10 October 1985.

11. Goldman, Stuart D., *Soviet Policy Toward Iran and the Strategic Balance in Southwest Asia*, Congressional Research Service, Library of Congress, October 1986.

12. Ginsburgs, George and Slusser, Robert M., *A Calendar of Soviet Treaties 1958–1973* (The Netherlands and Rockville, MD: Sijthoff & Nordhoff, Alpen aan den Rijn, 1981).

13. *New York Times*, 23 January 1987.

14. *FBIS*, KUNA, 21 June 1986; *FBIS*, *Arab Times* and *Al-Siyasah*, 18 June 1986.

15. *FBIS*, KUNA, 17 February 1987.

16. *FBIS*, 25 March, KUNA, 24 March 1987.

17. *FBIS*, 29 April, Tehran Domestic Service in Persian, 25 April 1987.

18. *FBIS*, 12 May, Tehran Domestic Service in Persian, 11 May 1987.

19. *FBIS*, 25 March, KUNA, 22 March 1987.

20. *FBIS*, 27 February, KUNA, 26 February 1987.

21. *FBIS*, 19 March, KUNA, 19 March 1987.

22. Economist Intelligence Unit, *Iran Country Report*, no. 1, 1987.

23. *The New York Times*, 2 June 1987.

24. *The New York Times*, 16 March 1987.

25. Gray, Simon, 'Turkish Kurdistan – the Forgotten Quarter', *Middle East International*, 20 March 1987, no. 296.

26. *FBIS*, 5 March 1987.

27. *FBIS*, 18 February 1987.

28. Crist, General George B., Commander-in-Chief, US Central Command, Statement Before the Senate Armed Services Committee, 11 March 1986.

29. Weinberger, Caspar, *Annual Report to Congress, FY 1987* and Organization of the Joint Chiefs of Staff, *United States Military Posture, FY 1987*.

30. *The New York Times*, 8 October 1980. From a speech by Deputy Secretary of State Warren Christopher one week after US AWACS aircraft were stationed in Saudi Arabia. He added that the US was willing to supply similar help to other non-belligerent Gulf nations.

7 Soviet Interests in the Gulf
Mark N. Katz

The Soviets initially saw the Iranian revolution of 1979 as an event that greatly enhanced their security interests in the Gulf region. This was because the fall of the Shah was accompanied by the end of the strong Iranian-American alliance that flourished during his reign. Bitterly anti-American, the government of Ayatollah Khomeini immediately moved to end military cooperation with the United States. The seizure of the American embassy in Tehran by fundamentalist students acting with the approval of the government served to further embitter Iranian-American relations. Because the Khomeini regime ascribed nearly all the ills of Iranian society to American machinations (a point of view Moscow encouraged), the Soviets looked forward to establishing a *de facto* alliance with Tehran on the basis of a common anti-American foreign policy.

At the same time, the internal situation in Iran appeared highly unstable in 1979. In the aftermath of the fall of the Shah, other groups besides the Islamic fundamentalists also became more powerful. These included the Tudeh (communist party) which the Shah had suppressed and others such as the leftist mujahideen. Many in the Soviet Union seemed hopeful that as the revolution developed, the fundamentalists would become weaker and the leftists stronger. There was even the possibility that the revolution would take on a Marxist character.

Yet even without a Marxist revolution, the fact that Iranian foreign policy had suddenly changed from being strongly pro-American to virulently anti-American promised certain rewards to the USSR. First and foremost, the end of American influence in Iran offered the prospect for increased Soviet influence there. Second, because Iran was the strongest state in the Gulf, the USSR would now have an important ally in attempting to reduce Western influence throughout the entire region.

Nearly a decade later, Soviet optimism about the Iranian revolution has markedly declined. The Islamic fundamentalist regime of Ayatollah Khomeini has proven to be remarkably durable. He was strong enough to crush the Tudeh, leftist mujahideen, and other opposition groups that wanted to transform the revolution onto a more leftist, pro-Soviet path. Perhaps even more disturbing for the Soviets, Khomeini's anti-American foreign policy has not led him to pursue a significantly pro-Soviet foreign policy. Instead of allying with Moscow to rid the region of American influence, Tehran has sought to undertake this task on its own while at the same time competing with the USSR for influence both in the Gulf and in the Middle East and South Asia as a whole. Far from serving as a blessing to Soviet foreign policy interests, the Iranian revolution has in many ways come to be a threat to them.

Just what are Soviet interests in the Gulf region? How does Iran threaten them? How has the USSR attempted to counter this Iranian threat? It is these questions that this chapter will seek to answer after first examining the historical background of Soviet-Iranian relations.

HISTORICAL BACKGROUND

Moscow's efforts to gain influence in Iran are not new to the Soviet era. During the nineteenth century, much of Russian expansion into Central Asia took place at Iran's expense. During the 1890s, the Russians actively challenged the British for influence in the region. They sent naval vessels to the Gulf, tried to ally with the Saudis, subsidised a steamship line from Odessa to the Gulf, and like Germany, had plans to build a railroad through the Middle East with a terminus at Kuwait. In 1907, though, this competition ended when Britain and Russia agreed to divide Iran into a Russian sphere in the north and a British one in the south, leaving only a weakened independent government in the centre.[1]

The new Soviet government renounced this agreement, but soon became interested in Iran itself. In 1921, a Soviet-Iranian treaty was signed giving the Russians the right to send troops into Iran if forces threatening the USSR entered Iran's territory. In the negotiations conducted between Nazi and Soviet officials in 1940, the Germans recognised the area 'in the general direction of the Persian Gulf . . . as the centre of the aspirations of the Soviet Union', though precisely what this meant was not specified. After Hitler's invasion of the Soviet Union, the USSR and Britain again divided Iran in 1941 in order to oust the pro-German Shah and provide a secure land route for the supply of Western arms to the Soviets.[2]

At the end of the Second World War, Stalin did not want to leave Iran, but under American pressure he did so in 1946, and two 'autonomous' Marxist republics in Azerbaizhan and Kurdistan collapsed. Soviet support to the Tudeh continued, but after the 1953 US-backed coup against the liberal Prime Minister Mossadegh, Iran became pro-Western. Iran joined the Baghdad Pact in 1955 and signed a security agreement with the United States in 1959; the Soviets objected to both actions. But when the Kennedy Administration cut back on military aid to Iran, the Shah decided to improve relations with Moscow. Soviet-Iranian ties were good until 1972 when the Soviet-Iraqi treaty of friendship and cooperation was signed.[3]

Even though the Shah developed closer military relations with the United States during his remaining years in power, it was still Soviet policy to maintain friendly relations with him. The USSR did not announce its support for his overthrow until that event was imminent. Moscow then welcomed the coming to power of Khomeini and applauded his anti-American policy. But by 1980 it was evident that the Tehran government was not pro-Soviet, since the ayatollahs had condemned the USSR as the other 'great satan' and denounced the Soviet invasion of Afghanistan. Moscow, however, hoped that its relations with Iran might improve on the basis of a common anti-American foreign policy and that more pro-Soviet elements such as the Tudeh or the mujahideen would gain influence or even power.[4]

Soviet efforts to befriend the new regime were seriously embarrassed, however, by the Iraqi invasion of Iran on 22 September 1980. The official Soviet position on the war was then and continues to be one of neutrality, urging both sides to end the conflict peacefully. At the beginning of the war, though, Moscow took measures that helped Iran and not Iraq. By late 1980 or early 1981, the USSR had ceased direct arms shipments to Iraq and had reportedly begun limited military assistance to Iran. Indirect Soviet arms shipments to Iraq, however, reportedly occurred during these years.[5]

When in 1982 Khomeini's forces not only pushed the Iraqis off Iranian territory but also advanced into Iraq itself, the Soviets reversed their policy. Moscow had not only failed to establish close ties with Tehran, but the USSR's allies in Iraq now had to defend their own territory. While Saddam Hussein might not have been Moscow's ideal ally (he had brutally suppressed the Iraqi Communist Party), the Soviets realised that they would lose what influence they had in Iraq if a government beholden to Tehran overthrew him. Thus, the Soviets resumed direct arms shipments to Baghdad soon after Iranian forces crossed over into Iraq.[6]

Since 1982, Iranian attacks against Iraq have made slow but steady progress against Baghdad's forces. The Iranians captured the Fao Peninsula, completely cutting Iraq off from the Gulf. Tehran's forces have moved closer and closer to Basra in the south. Some analysts fear that if Basra falls to the Iranians, the Ba'ath regime will collapse. The Iraqis have launched several counter-attacks. Some of these have succeeded in halting or slowing down Iranian advances, but not in driving the Ayatollah's forces back altogether. Saddam Hussein has repeatedly offered to settle the conflict peacefully, but the Ayatollah insists that one condition be met for the war to end: Saddam Hussein must be replaced. Not surprisingly, Saddam Hussein has been unwilling to leave office even if this would mean an end to the war.[7]

In early 1987, Moscow accepted a Kuwaiti request to charter three Soviet oil tankers which the Soviet Navy would escort in the Gulf in order to protect them against Iranian attack. This was followed by a Kuwaiti-American agreement whereby Washington reflagged and provided a US Navy escort to eleven Kuwaiti oil tankers. The Iranians were unhappy with both superpowers for doing this since Kuwait has used some of its oil export revenue to finance the Iraqi war effort. The Soviets, however, kept their arrangement with Kuwait in perspective. Moscow did not compete with Washington to be the superpower with the most naval vessels protecting the most tankers in the Gulf. The Kremlin realised that a rapid Soviet naval build-up in the Gulf would lead to an equal or greater American naval build-up. Even more important, the Soviets did not want to improve relations with the GCC at the expense of their long-standing goal of improving ties with revolutionary Iran.

In May 1987, a speedboat reportedly operated by the Revolutionary Guards attacked a Soviet freighter. The Soviets, however, did not retaliate but instead played down the incident. Soviet media mentioned the attack, but insisted that no one was injured and little damage was done.[8] Nor did Moscow raise a fuss when another Soviet vessel struck a mine also in May.[9]

Soviet minimisation of the risks of conflict with Iran as well as restraint after these two incidents stands in stark contrast to American behaviour toward Iran. When one of the reflagged Kuwaiti tankers struck a mine, the US Government moved greater force to the region. Provocative Iranian actions were met with increased American force levels as well as open discussion by US officials about how the US might retaliate against Iran in different situations.

As the war of nerves between Washington and Tehran escalated during the summer of 1987, the Soviet Navy maintained a low profile in the Gulf. Suddenly, in early August 1987, Moscow and Tehran announced a major economic cooperation accord. The Soviets agreed to build a pipeline to carry Iranian oil to the Black Sea. An additional connection between the Soviet and Iranian railway systems was also planned.[10] Despite the fact that Soviet-Iranian relations improved during 1987, Moscow has been unable to persuade Tehran to agree to a ceasefire. So far, these improved relations have not led to increased Soviet influence in Iran.

SOVIET INTERESTS IN THE GULF REGION

Are Soviet intentions toward the Gulf region basically offensive or defensive? Many in the West have feared that Soviet intentions are offensive. Now as well as a century ago, there has been concern that Russia seeks to gain a warm water port on the Gulf or the Indian Ocean to which they would have overland access through Iran. Since the 1917 revolution, the fear has arisen that the USSR seeks to promote Marxism revolution in this region, as well as many others. Finally, many fear that the Soviets wish to gain control of this region in particular because of the enormous oil reserves the Gulf possesses. Controlling this region could provide the Soviet Union with the oil it might not be able to produce itself in the future. In addition, by controlling the Gulf, the USSR could limit or cut off the region's oil supplies to the West. Unless additional oil supplies were found rapidly, this could cripple the economies of Western Europe and Japan which are so heavily dependent on Gulf oil.[11]

Others, including the Soviets themselves, claim that Soviet intentions toward the Gulf region are completely defensive. They say that the Soviet Union does not have expansionist aims at all. Moscow is interested in the security of a region located directly on its southern border, especially since the other superpower is so active there even though the Gulf is several thousand miles from its shores. They point out that the USSR has enormous oil and natural gas reserves. It is the West which is deficient in these resources and thus it is the West that seeks to control the Gulf's oil. As for promoting Marxist revolution, the Soviets solemnly state that the USSR is opposed to the export of revolution; where it does occur, it is an indigenous phenomenon. They would also point out Moscow's efforts to establish normal relations with the conservative Gulf Cooperation Council states as evidence that the Soviet Union desires peaceful coexistence with states possessing social systems different from the USSR's. The Soviets also point to their long-standing peace proposals for the Iran–Iraq war as evidence of their peaceful, defensive intentions in the region.[12]

In reality, Soviet policy toward the Gulf contains both offensive and defensive elements. The USSR may want a warm water port on the Gulf or Indian Ocean, but it is not prepared to incur the possible costs in terms of war with Iran and possibly others attempting to obtain this goal. Of course, if Iran ever experienced a pro-Soviet Marxist-Leninist revolution (or even *coup d'état*), these costs would be greatly reduced. Under what conditions Soviet intentions are offensive or defensive could be debated at length. What I will do here instead is attempt to identify what are Soviet interests – which may have both offensive and defensive aspects – in the Gulf region.

One of the most important interests that the USSR has in the region is the preservation of a peaceful, Moscow-controlled Soviet Central Asia. Many analysts have pointed out that Islamic fundamentalism in Iran could conceivably spread to Soviet Central Asia. The Soviet government has a strong interest in preventing this. The preservation of a tranquil Soviet Central Asia is clearly a defensive goal for Moscow.

Another interest the USSR has in the region is the pacification of Afghanistan where a strong anti-Soviet insurgency has continued to rage after the Soviet military intervention of 1979. The Soviets may consider the defence of a Marxist-Leninist regime to be a defensive interest. The states of the region as well as the West consider this an offensive Soviet interest instead since Afghanistan was the first direct Soviet invasion of a country outside the Warsaw Pact. To the extent that Iran supports various mujahideen groups inside Afghanistan, it hinders the USSR from pacifying the country.

A third Soviet goal in the Gulf is both to prevent from growing and reduce where possible American influence in the region. The reduction of American influence is an offensive goal while preventing its growth is a defensive one. The Soviets were pleased when America lost influence in Iran when the Shah was overthrown. They have no desire to see Washington ever regain influence in Tehran.

The Soviets also have a strong interest in maintaining in power governments in the region which are friendly toward Moscow. In addition to leftist regimes allied to Moscow in Afghanistan, Syria, and South Yemen, the Soviet Union has had a long friendship with the Ba'ath regime in Iraq. Iran's efforts to defeat or overthrow this government clearly threatens Soviet interests in Iraq. Keeping friends in power is a defensive goal for the USSR.

A fifth goal that the USSR has in this region is to keep the Arab world united in its opposition to Israel and any Arab state such as Egypt which agrees to participate in a Camp David style peace effort. So long as Arab governments and nations see Israel as their main enemy, they will oppose American aid to Israel. The Soviets also hope that this will provide them with a greater opportunity to ally with Arab governments opposed to American foreign policy. To the extent that the Arabs see Iran and not Israel as their main enemy, this may lead them to seek greater American assistance.[13]

In addition, Moscow has a strong interest in seeing that Islamic fundamentalism does not become a strong rival with Marxism-Leninism as an ideology for those who seek radical political change in the Gulf and Middle East as a whole. The Soviets, of course, welcome any change in which a pro-American government is replaced by an anti-American one. Moscow would prefer, though, that radical anti-American regimes not be anti-Soviet as well.

A seventh Soviet interest in the region is to establish good relations with the conservative governments of the Gulf Cooperation Council (Saudi Arabia, Kuwait, Bahrain, Qatar, Oman, and the United Arab Emirates). From 1963 to 1985, the USSR had diplomatic relations with only one GCC state – Kuwait. The others were all anti-Soviet and cooperated militarily with America and Britain. In 1985, however, Moscow succeeded in establishing relations with both Oman and the UAE. Soviet contact with Saudi Arabia has also increased. Improving Soviet relations with these states is an offensive interest, but the offensive is only a diplomatic one.

The Soviets may have other, more long-term goals in the region as well, such as the promotion of Marxist revolution, acquisition of a warm water port, and control of the region's oil resources. These, of course, are all offensive goals, but the USSR does not appear to be in a position to achieve these in the foreseeable future. Great changes favouring the Soviet Union – especially in Iran – would have to occur first. What is striking about this list of immediate Soviet interests in the Gulf is that they are mainly defensive. Even where Soviet goals are offensive (i.e., keeping the Arab world united on seeing Israel as the main enemy and seeing that Islamic fundamentalism does not become a strong rival with Marxism-Leninism in the region), Moscow has found that it must act defensively to preserve the potency of these offensive strategies.

IRANIAN THREATS TO SOVIET INTERESTS

Not all Soviet interests and goals in the Gulf region are under serious threat, and not all of those that are can be said to be seriously threatened by Iran. Nevertheless, Iran is the primary threat to several of Moscow's interests and goals in the region.

As Moscow's control of Soviet Central Asia is not being challenged significantly, Iran is really not threatening this most vital Soviet interest in the region. The Soviets would have serious problems if pro-Islamic fundamentalism ever did infect Central Asia. At present, however, those seeking to incite Islamic insurgency in Soviet Central Asia face huge obstacles: the Soviet-Iranian border is probably not porous enough to allow Tehran to arm potential rebel groups, and such groups would find it extremely difficult to obtain arms in the USSR. So far, the Ayatollah Khomeini has done very little to spread Islamic revolution across Iran's northern border; he may well fear how the Soviets might retaliate against him if he did. Soviet Central Asia is not yet ripe for Islamic insurgency. Moscow defeated the rebellions that occurred there in the 1920s and 1930s. The standard of living in Central Asia is higher than in Iran, as Moscow regularly points out to the citizens of the region. Moscow has formidable armed forces to deal with any rebellion, or even dissent, that might occur. The nationalist and religious sentiment of Central Asia should not be underestimated, but at present Tehran has little to gain and much to lose by attempting to foster Islamic revolution there.

In Afghanistan, the mujahideen have thwarted Moscow's efforts to pacify the country, making it impossible for the Marxist-Leninist regime to survive without the presence of Soviet troops. Iran gives some military assistance to certain mujahideen groups. It also allows some to use Iranian territory as sanctuary. Iranian assistance, though, is not the main source of external aid to the mujahideen, which also comes from the United States, China, Saudi Arabia, Egypt, and Pakistan. Iranian aid appears to be limited primarily to Shiah groups; the majority of Afghans are Sunni. At present, Iranian involvement in Afghanistan poses a lesser threat to Soviet goals than the main mujahideen groups and their external backers, especially the US and Pakistan. In fact, to the extent that the groups Iran supports have differences with the others, Iranian aid to them supports internecine conflict among the Afghans which benefits the USSR.

Because Tehran's attention is focused on the Iran–Iraq war, Iranian involvement in Afghanistan may be less than what it could be. Depending on how the Iran–Iraq war came to an end, Tehran might (or might not) decide to focus its attention on helping Islamic fundamentalists in Afghanistan. The Iranians would clearly not want to become so involved that they risked direct Soviet retaliation. But Tehran could increase its involvement in Afghanistan to the extent that Pakistan has. Until the Iran–Iraq war ends, however, Tehran is unlikely to direct more of its resources to opposing Soviet interests in Afghanistan than it does now.

Iran poses a much greater threat to the preservation of a regime friendly to the USSR in Iraq. There have been differences between Moscow and Baghdad over several foreign policy issues, including the Soviet intervention in Afghanistan, Soviet aid to the Marxist Ethiopian government fighting against Eritrean rebels, and close Soviet relations with Iraq's rival, Syria. The USSR and Iraq are united, though, in their opposition to Israel, the American-sponsored Camp David peace process, and to an Arab-Israeli settlement that does not grant independence to the Palestinians. The USSR and Iraq signed a twenty-year treaty of friendship and cooperation in 1972. Before Iran sealed off Iraq's access to the Gulf, Soviet naval vessels occasionally made use of Iraqi ports. While not a Marxist regime, the Iraqi Ba'ath regime was strongly leftist. Before the outbreak of the war, Iraqi foreign policy had served Soviet foreign policy interests by working so strenuously to limit American influence in the Middle East. Since the war began, though, Iraq has expanded its ties to the West and has moderated its position on Israel. Baghdad has done this in order to receive weapons and other assistance from the West while continuing to rely on the USSR.[14]

If Iran defeated Iraq or if a pro-Khomeini regime replaced Saddam Hussein, Soviet influence in Iraq would decline dramatically. So far, Saddam Hussein has managed to avoid being defeated or overthrown, but has been unable to expel Iranian forces from Iraq or persuade Tehran to end the war peacefully. With its greater manpower reserves and willingness to accept much higher casualties than Iraq, the possibility that Iran will prevail in this war looms larger. And while a Khomeinite Iraq might be anti-American, it would probably be anti-Soviet like Iran. At the very least, the Soviet-Iraqi military relationship would probably be reduced or come to an end.

At worst, Iran and Iraq together might work to overthrow other pro-Soviet regimes such as Syria. Yet while Tehran currently poses a serious threat to the pro-Soviet regime in Baghdad, it poses only a marginal or non-existent threat to pro-Soviet regimes elsewhere in the region.

It is possible, of course, that Saddam Hussein will remain in power and that the USSR will continue to have strong relations with Iraq. The continuation of the Iran–Iraq war with Iraq on the defensive, however, has already harmed another Soviet interest: the reduction of American influence in the region. The fear of an Iranian victory has induced the conservative Gulf Cooperation Council states to increase their military cooperation with the United States. Iraq itself has improved its relations with Washington since the war began. Diplomatic ties which had been broken in 1967 were restored in 1984. The United States has also provided Iraq with various forms of assistance, including intelligence data, but not weapons. The growing threat of an Iranian victory over Iran, then, has led several Arab states to seek a greater American presence in the region to protect or assist them. This is a development that Soviet foreign policy had hoped to prevent.

While the growth of American influence in the Arab world is undesirable from Moscow's point of view, the resurgence of American influence in Iran would be even more so. From the Soviet perspective, the one great achievement of the Iranian revolution was the ending of the Iranian-American alliance that had existed under the Shah. The Soviets were jolted by the recent revelations that the Reagan Administration had been secretly shipping arms to Khomeini in an effort to improve relations with Iran. They were undoubtedly gratified that the effort failed, but must fear that a future American attempt to befriend Iran might succeed, especially in the post-Khomeini era. Soviet foreign policy has a very strong interest in preventing this from taking place. Thus, the Soviets have attempted to take advantage of deteriorating Iranian-American relations in 1987 to improve their own ties to Tehran. Yet while the Soviets may not have gained much influence in Iran yet, they undoubtedly hope that their friendly policy toward Tehran combined with the continuation of Iranian-American hostility will improve their ability as well as further reduce American opportunities to gain influence there in the future.

The continuation of the Iran–Iraq war also threatens the Soviet goal of keeping the Arab world focused on Israel as its main enemy.

This is important because when the Arabs focus on Israel, they also tend to oppose the American policy of aiding Israel – which is what the Soviets want. When they regard Iran as the primary threat, though, they tend to see America as a potential protector – which is what the Soviets do not want. But this competition between Israel and Iran as the main enemy of the Arab world has implications beyond America's influence in the Middle East. So long as the Arabs regarded the Arab-Israeli dispute as the main conflict in the Middle East, then the Soviets hoped to rally the entire Arab and Moslem world in opposition to both Israel and America. Even those conservative governments that wanted to cooperate with the United States were constrained for fear that they would be overthrown as a result of being identified with Israel and America by radical governments and their own people.

Until the Arabs became increasingly fearful of Tehran winning the Iran–Iraq war, this situation afforded the Soviets the possibility of allying with the entire Arab and Muslim world. In practice, of course, this has not worked out as well as the Soviets had hoped, but the fact that the USSR backed the Arab side in the Arab-Israeli conflict while America did not greatly help Moscow in its efforts to gain influence in the region.

The Iran–Iraq war has also divided the Arab world as a whole. Like the USSR, most Arab states support Iraq. Two Arab states, however, support Iran: Syria and Libya (South Yemen used to favour Iran, but now is more neutral). These states, of course, are allies of the Soviet Union. Especially at a time when it is widely believed in the Arab world that Israel is supporting Iran, the fact that two of Moscow's Arab allies are sending Soviet weapons to Iran contributes to intra-Arab rivalry and does not help the USSR keep the Arab world focused on the Arab-Israeli conflict.

When the Iranian revolution took place, many Soviet scholars expected that the forces of Islamic fundamentalism would soon yield to 'progressive', socialist-oriented forces. Marxist-Leninist notions of history did not anticipate that a modernising, capitalist oriented monarchy would succumb to religious zealots instead of the vanguard of workers and peasants. But Islamic revolution has proven strong enough to defeat its pro-Soviet rivals and survive in Iran. Like the Bolsheviks before him, Khomeini wishes to see the benefits of his revolution spread to nations beyond his borders, at least in the Middle East. Despite differences between Arabs and Iranians, there are large Shiah populations in several Arab countries who could well be resentful of Sunni domination and receptive to Khomeini's message. There are substantial Shiah populations in Iraq, Kuwait, the eastern province of Saudi Arabia, Bahrain, and Lebanon. But even where Shiah fundamentalism has little strength, Sunni fundamentalist groups have gained strength, as in Syria, Egypt, Tunisia, and elsewhere. Indeed, in many countries, Islamic groups have replaced leftist ones as the main opposition force. Moscow may be pleased if Islamic opposition groups can overthrow pro-Western regimes, but may gain little if the new leaders are as anti-Soviet as they are anti-American. In addition to opposing pro-Western governments, Islamic opposition groups may oppose pro-Soviet governments too, which is not in Soviet interests at all. At present, though, it is unclear how strong Islamic fundamentalists in Arab countries are now or may become in the future, and thus their threat to Soviet interests is uncertain.

One Soviet goal which Iranian actions have actually helped Moscow achieve is the improvement of Soviet relations with the conservative Gulf Cooperation Council states. For while all these states have felt so threatened by Iran that they have increased their military cooperation with the West, they have also increased their contacts with the USSR for the same reason. The GCC states hope that by improving their relations with Moscow, Iran would have an additional disincentive to harm them. More important, broadening ties with Moscow has helped the GCC states obtain greater American involvement in the region. The American naval escort of reflagged Kuwaiti tankers as well as the build-up of the US Navy presence in the Gulf generally occurred only after Kuwait chartered three Soviet oil tankers in early 1987. The GCC states have found a greater Soviet presence in the Gulf useful in terms of its relations both with Iran and the United States. These conservative monarchies, however, do not want the Soviet military presence in the region to grow too strong; they still fear that Moscow would work to overthrow them if it had the opportunity. Thus, while the Iranian threat to the GCC has helped the USSR improve its ties with these states, there are severe limits to which these conservative governments are willing to become involved with Moscow.

What emerges from this analysis is that Iran poses a serious threat to several Soviet interests in the Gulf and Middle East. This threat to Soviet interests will be even greater if Iran defeat Iraq.

COUNTERING THE IRANIAN THREAT TO SOVIET INTERESTS

Moscow's response to the Iranian threat to its interests has been to take actions directly opposing Iran while at the same time working to improve relations with Tehran. The primary Soviet policy opposing Iran has been to heavily arm Baghdad ever since Iranian troops pushed into Iraq in 1982. The purpose of this policy is obvious: through arming Iraq, the USSR seeks to preserve in power a radical regime friendly toward the USSR and halt the expansion of Iranian-backed Islamic fundamentalism which threatens to become a more powerful revolutionary ideology than Marxism-Leninism in the region.

Because the USSR has such a strong interest in seeing that Iran does not prevail in this war, it is not surprising that Moscow has continued to support Baghdad. The Kremlin, however, has also taken steps that help Iran. Although the Soviets have apparently not sent arms directly to Tehran since 1982 (and perhaps earlier), Soviet weapons have continued to reach Tehran via Syria, Libya, North Korea, and Czechoslovakia. Moscow does not control Syria or Libya, but it also does not appear to have made a serious effort to stop them from re-transferring Soviet weapons to Iran. It may be that the Kremlin does not wish to risk harming its relations with these two radical states by making an issue of this matter. However, it may also be that the Soviets tacitly approve of this trade. This certainly must be the case with Czechoslovakia and probably North Korea too.[15]

During the summer of 1987, the United States had launched a major campaign to isolate Iran internationally for continuing the war. Washington succeeded in its efforts to have a United Nations Security Council resolution passed (with Soviet approval) calling for both sides in the conflict to accept a ceasefire. As expected, Iraq accepted but Iran did not. The US then proposed a Security Council resolution calling for an arms embargo against Iran until it accepted a ceasefire. The Soviets, however, made it clear that they would not vote in favour of such a resolution for the time being.[16]

At first glance, it appears irrational for the Soviets to undertake such actions. By helping Iran either directly or through its allies, Moscow not only hurts its relations with Baghdad, but also appears to be undermining a regime which it has such a strong interest in protecting. Yet Moscow does have good reason to build and maintain good relations with Tehran even though Iran is threatening Soviet interests.

As mentioned before, the Soviets considered the overthrow of the Shah to be a great foreign policy victory because it resulted in the expulsion of American influence from a country directly bordering the USSR. The seizure of the US embassy in Tehran and the holding of American diplomats as hostages for over a year served to make any *rapprochement* between Washington and the new Iranian leaders extremely difficult. The Soviets, however, are very concerned that Iran did not return to being an ally of America or its friends.

The Soviets are keenly aware that Khomeini will not live forever and that a new leadership will succeed him. Like the Iraqis, the Soviets may hope that a new Iranian leader would bring the war to an end. But even if this is not the case, Moscow has no guarantee that the new Iranian leadership would share Khomeini's extreme hostility toward the United States. Like previous Iranian governments, a post-Khomeini leadership might see Russia as much more threatening than America. Through having friendly contacts with high-level Iranian officials now, the Soviets hope to persuade them that the USSR is not a threat to Iran and that there is no reason for the new leaders – whoever they may be – to ally with America against the USSR. Indeed, the Soviets hope that any new Iranian leadership would remain anti-American. Preferably with the war ended in a stalemate, the Soviets could seek to ally with this new leadership on the basis of a common anti-American foreign policy, just as the Soviets hoped when Khomeini first came to power.

The Soviets may find that once the war ends, they do not have any strong allies in Iran at all, especially if the Tudeh and mujahideen remain weak. Their contacts with current Iranian officials may not serve them well in the future if these people are ousted. However, as weak as these contacts may be, they give the Soviets hope that they can influence the succession more effectively than the Americans.

By backing both sides to a certain extent in the Iran–Iraq war, Moscow hopes to be in a position to take advantage of potential opportunities as well as minimise America's ability to restore its influence in Iran. The greatest opportunity for the Soviets would be if Khomeini suddenly died and through a subsequent succession struggle Moscow were able to gain predominant influence in Iran. Even if this completely alienated the Iraqis, Iraq is not in a position to spurn the Soviets: even with the war ended, tension between Iran and Iraq is likely to remain and Baghdad may not dare to expel the Soviets the way Egypt and Somalia did. So long as the war continues, Iraq has even less incentive to expel the Soviets: such a move would be suicidal.

The Soviets hope that this 'double-track' policy will allow them to defend their existing interests while at the same time putting them in a position to exploit new opportunities in the region. Helping both sides militarily may indeed benefit Moscow in the short-run. Despite the fact that each receives arms from other sources, neither Baghdad nor Tehran want to alienate Moscow to the extent that Moscow cuts off its arms supply and greatly expands military support to the other side. But while Moscow may hope that this policy leads to Soviet influence in both Iran and Iraq over the long-run, there is also a great risk that Soviet arms will keep Iran defeat Iraq and the USSR will end up with no influence in either nation. A victorious Iran may then be an even greater challenge to Soviet interests in the Gulf, Middle East, and South Asia. Yet by not helping Iran at all and only helping Iraq, the Soviets run the risk that a post-Khomeini Iran will seek closer relations with America and the West.

CONCLUSION

The Iranian threat to Soviet interests in the Gulf as well as the Middle East and South Asia is great and would be greater still if Iran defeated Iraq. One of the biggest challenges that Iran poses for Soviet foreign policy is that the Iranian threat to Soviet interests is largely separate from the American threat to them. Successful Iranian foreign policy may lead to the decline of American influence in the region. This decline of American influence, however, does not necessarily mean that Soviet influence will gain; Iranian influence may instead. What is especially worrisome to Moscow is that a victorious Iran may ultimately prove more harmful to Soviet interests in the region than America ever was.

Notes

1.   For a fascinating reprint of a 1912 account of these events, see W. Morgan Shuster, *The Strangling of Persia* (Washington, DC: Mage Publishers, 1987).

2. See George Lenczowski, *Russia and the West in Iran, 1918–1948: A Study of Big Power Rivalry* (Ithaca, NY: Cornell University Press, 1949).

3. Aryeh Y. Yodfat, *The Soviet Union and the Arabian Peninsula* (London: Croom Helm; New York, NY: St Martin's Press, 1983), pp. 22–3.

4. Ibid., pp. 67–71, 75–86.

5. Ibid., pp. 120–8.

6. Zalmay Khalilzad, 'Islamic Iran: Soviet Dilemma', *Problems of Communism*, January–February 1984, pp. 1–20.

7. On Iraq, see Christine Moss Helms, *Iraq: Eastern Flank of the Arab World* (Washington, DC: The Brookings Institution, 1984), and Frederick W. Axelgard (ed.), *Iraq in Transition: A Political, Economic, and Strategic Perspective* (Boulder, CO: Westview Press; London: Mansell Publishing, 1986).

8. Bernard E. Trainor, 'Soviet Ship Attacked by Iran in Gulf, US Says', *The New York Times*, 9 May 1987, and *Trud*, 12 May 1987, p. 3 as translated in *FBIS Daily Report: Soviet Union* (hereinafter referred to as *FBIS: SU*) 14 May 1987, pp. H1–2.

9. Moscow TASS in English, 17 May 1987 in *FBIS: SU*, 18 May 1987, p. H1.

10. Philip Taubman, 'Iran and Soviet Draft Big Projects, Including Pipelines and Railroad', *The New York Times*, 15 August 1987.

11. This speculation was fuelled by a Central Intelligence Agency report released in 1977; see CIA *Prospects for Soviet Oil Production*, ER 77–10270 (April 1977).

12. For representative Soviet statements on these issues, see Moscow in Farsi to Iran, 23 March 1985 in *FBIS: SU*, 25 March 1985, pp. H5–6; and Moscow in Farsi to Iran, 13 September 1986 in *FBIS: SU*, 15 September 1986, pp. H3–4.

13. For a typical Soviet statement exhorting Iran and Iraq to end their war so that the entire Arab and Moslem world can unite in the struggle against Israel, see Moscow TASS in English, 14 November 1986 in *FBIS: SU*, 17 November 1986, pp. A8–9.

    The Soviets emphasise this point because they do not want other Arab states to regard Iran as so threatening that they are prepared to come to a peace agreement with Israel that does not establish an independent Palestinian state as Egypt did. The Soviets must have been sorely disappointed at the result of the 1987 Arab summit in Amman which focused primarily on the Iranian danger and opened the way for most Arab states to restore diplomatic ties with Egypt which were broken after it signed the Camp David accords.

14. Mark N. Katz, 'Iraq and the Superpowers', in Axelgard, *Iraq in Transition*, note 7, pp. 85–96.

15. On arms transfers by Moscow's allies to Iran, see David K. Shipler, 'Level of World Arms Sales to Iran Regarded as Largely Unchanged', *The New York Times*, 11 April 1987, and US Department of State, 'US Policy in the Persian Gulf', Special Report No. 166, July 1987, p. 5. Some sources claim that the USSR is itself transferring arms to

Iran; Safa Haeri, 'Tehran to Receive Soviet Weapons', *The Independent* (London), 24 October 1987.

16.   'Gorbachev's Gulf, Too', *The Economist*, 24 October 1987, pp. 13–15.

Epilogue
M. E. Ahrari

The analysis in this chapter will revolve around the four future-oriented questions raised in the introduction to this study. Briefly stated, these questions are concerned with: first, the nature and the dynamics of the power game in the Gulf from the perspectives of the Gulf states; second, the stakes for the superpowers; third, the underlying patterns of conflict and cooperation among the Gulf states that might emerge in the aftermath of the Iran–Iraq war; and fourth, policy options that are likely to be adopted by both superpowers to sustain strategic dominance in the Gulf, and the way such policies would affect the nature of security issues and stability in the Gulf.

THE NATURE OF THE POWER GAME IN THE GULF IN THE 1980s AND BEYOND

The behaviour of the Islamic Republic of Iran remains as the focus of strategic concerns of the Arab states of the Gulf and both super-powers in the 1980s and beyond. Since the 1970s, Iran has emerged as a major force in the region, and it promises to play a similar role in the foreseeable future. What is disconcerting from the perspective of all these actors is the modality of this role.

Imperial Iran promoted the strategic interests of the United States, while it remained a source of consternation to the Arab states, especially to Saudi Arabia and Iraq, who were also nurturing hegemonic ambitions. But as long as the United States remained content with the hegemonic tendencies of imperial Iran, the Arab states did not have other options to fall back on. The Soviet Union, the other superpower, was geographically too close for forging military affiliations. Moreover, it had a profound imperialistic history whereby it permanently absorbed Muslim areas of Central Asia. The communist nature of the Soviet government has also remained an anathema to the Muslim states. Even though Ba'athist Iraq, which emphasised secular Pan-Arabism, became a Soviet ally in the early 1970s, its leaders have manifested a strong tendency of suppressing the communist party in their country.

Saudi Arabia, the guardian of Islamic shrines and the other major Arab actor of the Gulf, could not get close to the Soviet Union. Aside from political reasons for keeping their distance, the Saudis were also quite sensitive to the symbolic effects of their close ties with the USSR on the Muslim world at large. From the perspective of their strategic interests, however, the Saudis were waiting for an environment that was to be more conducive to their dominant role in the Gulf.

As Ahrari points out in Chapter 3, by becoming a stabilising force within the framework of OPEC in the 1970s, yet going to the extent of adopting a radical measure of the nature of an oil embargo on the US, Saudi Arabia emerged as one of the major actors in the Middle East. The wherewithal of political leadership had to be properly utilised in order for the Saudis to be recognised as a military leader in the Gulf. The petrodollars were there to build a sophisticated military infrastructure, but the small population of Saudi Arabia remained an obstacle. A major obstacle with which Saudi Arabia could not come to grips was how to alter the American contentment with the Iranian leadership role in the Gulf.

The Iranian revolution provided that long-awaited opening. The anti-American nature of the Khomeini regime made Iran and the US drift apart. From the American perspective, the vacuum created by the demise of the pro-Western Shah had to be filled by another actor. Saudi Arabia was the only major pro-American state of the Gulf.

The exportability of the Islamic revolution became the basis for cooperation among the Arab states of the Gulf. The United States was also equally concerned about the destabilising potential of the exportability principle. Under the leadership of Saudi Arabia, and with a green light from the US, the GCC was established.

The creation of the GCC provided the much-sought framework of military leadership for the Saudis. Even though the present military capability of this organisation is rather modest, the GCC is important for the Saudis for two reasons. First, given the weakened posture of the power projection of Iran, Saudi Arabia is only interested in building on the defensive nature of this alliance in order to buy time in the wake of an Iranian attack. The United States is already on record for its willingness to intervene under such a happenstance. Second, with the passage of time, Saudi Arabia may be able to strengthen the offensive capabilities of this organisation for flexing its muscle under future military exigencies in the Gulf.

It should be emphasised, however, that the creation of the GCC has not lowered tensions in the Gulf. As Hunter quite correctly points out, since Iran believes that part of the US strategy is to eliminate the Islamic regime, it considers the GCC as an instrument of American policy, a threat to its security, and a vehicle for the expansion of Saudi influence. Presently, Iraq views the GCC as a weapon that may be used defensively against Iran in the short run. The fact that Iraq is not now a member of the GCC is not an issue. In the future, especially after the end of the Iran–Iraq war, the Iraqi membership is likely to become a source of tension among the Arab states. If Iraq is allowed to join the organisation, the Iranian threat-perception *vis-à-vis* this grouping is also likely to heighten precipitously.

The economic and military aspects of regional leadership between Iran and Saudi Arabia remain quite unsettled and unsettling. Within OPEC Saudi Arabia is definitely a leader, if not because of the sheer size of its proven oil reserves, then because of the sustained nature of its constructive leadership. In the 1970s, under a sellers' market, Saudi Arabia remained a stabilising force on the pricing issue. In a buyers' market of the 1980s, that country has been spearheading OPEC's quest for price stability. The Iranian role within OPEC during the days of the Shah remained a bit involved. Iran was a constructive force in negotiating price increases during the Tehran negotiations. On the issue of linking the erosive effects of inflation to the price increases of crude oil, however, the Shah indulged in grandstanding, while the burden of conducting serious negotiations largely fell on the shoulders of Saudi Arabia's oil minister Sheikh Zaki Yamani. Iran remained one of the leading proponents of unrealistic price escalations in the 1970s and 1980s and played a divisive role within OPEC. In the 1990s, that country is likely to continue this role.

On the military aspect of leadership of the Gulf, the pendulum of advantage continues to swing in favour of Iran. That country, despite the fact that its military infrastructure is in shambles, is a natural leader of the Gulf because of its size, strategic location, and more important, as a matter of the historical self-perception of its leaders. The fact that Iran is interested in minimising, if not eliminating, the sphere of influence of the United States only heightens the tensions in the region. The mantle of leadership in the Gulf is not for the United States to give to an actor of its choice. If Saudi Arabia wants it, it has to earn it by demonstrating a willingness to protect its own interests and those of the neighbouring states, even by taking military action against Iran if necessary.

At least in the foreseeable future, oil-related economic payoffs might remain the basis of cooperation among oil states of the region, especially if the oil prices were to firm up. After all, oil states of different political leanings cooperated on the issue of pricing throughout the 1970s. In the 1980s, despite fighting a war, both Iran and Iraq opted against abandoning their respective membership because the other party remained in OPEC. Both these countries are also being represented in OPEC's endeavours to workout production-programming arrangments at present with a number of non-OPEC countries.

WHAT IS AT STAKE FOR THE SUPERPOWERS?

Both the United States and the USSR might live with a more conventional Iran even if it were to remain an Islamic Republic. A necessary condition for this conventionality has to be that Iran must considerably lower, if not neutralise, its threat potential by earnestly renouncing the exportability principle. Both superpowers are equally concerned about this principle for different reasons. The United States wants to defend the pro-Western status quo; and the Soviet Union would like to insulate its own Muslim areas from the potentially destabilising effects of Islamic internationalism propounded by Khomeini.

Political realities of the Gulf in the 1980s and beyond promise to affect the United States and the Soviet Union quite differently. Despite its enhanced naval presence, the United States might not be able to make long-range strategic gains. The chief reason for that is the Arab feelings concerning American-Israeli ties. There has been a profound belief in the Arab world at large that the unquestioned American support of Israel is the chief reason underlying the sustained refusal of the Jewish state to initiate negotiations aimed at its withdrawal from the occupied West Bank and the Gaza Strip. The Camp David agreement, the crown jewel of diplomatic achievements of the Carter Administration, became a euphemism in the Middle East for Egyptian sell-out. Even if Sadat did not intend to work out a separate peace with Israel when he visited Jerusalem in 1977, about the only meaningful outcome of the Camp David agreement for Egypt was Israeli withdrawal from the Sinai desert as the price for a peace accord and recognition from the most powerful Arab state.

From the American perspective, the Camp David agreement was a piecemeal negotiating approach to the enormously intractable and obdurate Arab-Israeli conflict. For Arabs, that was an American ploy to deepen political cleavages among already divided Arab countries. No matter how noble American intentions might have been in finding a solution to the Palestinian question, the fact remained that no progress was made on this issue since the signing of the peace treaty between Egypt and Israel. And this fact convinced Arab leaders of all political leaning that, by serving as a mediator between Egypt and Israel, the United States was chiefly interested in legitimising the status of Israel in the Middle East and its occupation of Arab territory.

Iran under the Shah was not overtly concerned about the strong historical ties between the United States and Israel. In fact, he himself established diplomatic relations with the Jewish state and, in a Machiavellian fashion, remained primarily motivated to acquire the American military wherewithal for the fulfilment of his objectives of regional dominance. Iran under Khomeini, though no less Machiavellian in pursuing its objectives of regional dominance, has been effectively focusing on the American-Israeli ties to condemn the pro-US nature of the Gulf monarchies. Because American ties with Israel are unpopular in the Gulf (as well as in the rest of the Arab world), the states of the Arabian Peninsula cannot afford to establish strong military ties with the US. That is precisely why they continued to insist on an over-the-horizon American presence. Even if they were to allow the United States to use their naval and air facilities under heightened threats from the Islamic Republic of Iran, such a use is destined to be of a temporary nature. Once the threat-potential either dissipates or is considerably lowered, they are likely to insist on reverting back to the over-the-horizon American presence lest they are criticised by Iran as friends of the chief supporter of 'Zionist expansionists'.

Given the nature of the anti-American environment in the Gulf, and given the fact that no significant movement is likely to be made in initiating negotiations on the Arab-Israeli questions in the remainder of the 1980s, the United States does not have any alternative but to follow a course suggested by Noyes: burning as few bridges to Iran as possible, promoting arms sales proposals for GCC states, and articulating consistent support for GCC security without locking into a confrontational approach toward Iran.

For the Soviet Union, the strategic realities in the Gulf are somewhat promising. The 'new political thinking' of Gorbachev has emphasised the establishment of friendly ties with capitalist-oriented countries in the Third World. There has been a renewed focus on the economic restructuring of the Soviet society, the ultimate purpose of which is to provide that country with respite to refurbish its domestic economy and enhance competitiveness against the United States in military as well as in non-military sectors.

For the Middle East as a whole, the new political thinking includes the following: (a) establishment of diplomatic ties with moderate Arab states; (b) willingness to withdraw from Afghanistan without necessarily abandoning the puppet regime in Kabul; (c) continued search for a political solution to the Iran–Iraq war while directly and indirectly supplying arms to Iraq and Iran, respectively; (d) attempted mediation between competing factions of the Palestinian Liberation Organisation (PLO); (e) continued discussion with Israel with a view to establishing diplomatic ties in the near future; (f) soothing of Kuwaiti fear by leasing three tankers and avoiding antagonising Iran by maintaining a low naval profile in the Gulf.

Of the variables mentioned above, the ones that are likely to provide the USSR significant diplomatic leverage in the Gulf are its willingness to withdraw from Afghanistan, its continued arms supply to Iran and Iraq, and the leasing of tankers to Kuwait. The Soviet commitment to the resolution of the Palestinian question has been a long-standing one. So, the uprising in the occupied territory since December of 1987 was quite beneficial to the Soviet strategic objectives. The escalation of violence in Israel has only underscored the Arab perception of injustice in the occupied territory and the perceived American support for it. In this sense, as Katz points out, the Soviets envisioned rallying the entire Arab world in opposition to Israel and the United States. But the outbreak of limited naval skirmishes between Iran and the United States in October 1987 and in April 1988, to the dismay of the Soviet Union, also underscored the importance of the United States for the moderate Arabs.

It is interesting to note that while the long-standing American support for Israel has been proving to be quite detrimental to the strategic interests of the United States, an equally prolonged Soviet support for the resolution of the Arab-Israeli conflict has not enabled the USSR to be perceived as a friend of the Arabs. The communist nature of the Soviet government, the atheistic nature of Marxism, and most important, the absorption of a large portion of Muslim population in the Soviet empire has, perhaps, permanently damaged the image of the Soviet Union in the Arab world. Most recently, the Soviet involvement in South Yemen, the only Marxist Arab state, brought home the subjugating nature of communist control for the people of the Arabian Peninsula. Then, in 1979 came the Soviet invasion of Afghanistan. If the Soviet declarations about their willingness to withdraw from Afghanistan are correct, then the new political thinking of Gorbachev might be given considerable credibility in the Gulf as well as in the Middle East.

What is beneficial from the perspective of the Soviet Union is that despite negative Arab perceptions concerning their hegemonic tendencies, it might be asked to help individual Arab states of the Gulf in the form of arms sales and naval presence under crisis conditions. But once the crisis dissipates that Arab state is likely to reconsider the scope and nature of its relationship with the Soviet Union. Kuwait has already established a precedence in this regard.

In the foreseeable future, neither superpower has a substantial advantage over the other in the Gulf. The United States remains too constrained by its historical ties with Israel to be taken seriously as a friend by the Arab states. The Soviet Union is most likely to be kept at bay, as noted above, but asked for help when necessary. These countries used to operate on the principle of 'friend of my enemy is my enemy'. Now, they seem to be operating on the principle of 'friend of my enemy is not exactly my friend or foe but I would use him whenever necessary'.

REGIONAL PATTERNS OF CONFLICT AND COOPERATION IN THE AFTERMATH OF THE IRAN–IRAQ WAR

The settlement of the Iran–Iraq war, perhaps, is the most important variable in determining the dynamics of the Gulf politics in the 1980s and beyond. This protracted war has to come to an end. Neither Iran nor Iraq has the capability or resources to continue it indefinitely. Given this reality, one can think along three possible scenarios and their implications for the Gulf: Iranian victory, Iraqi victory, or a negotiated settlement to this conflict. A potential Iranian victory is likely to heighten the fear of Iran among the Gulf states. it is a mistake to think that Iran, under such a scenario, is going to be highly unreasonable with the Arab states. Even if there is no intervention from either superpower to forestall an Iranian victory, the United States is not likely to accept a subjugation of the Arab states of the

Peninsula by Iran. This might be a decisive variable moderating the behaviour of a victor Iran. A likely outcome is a *rapprochement* between Iran and the Arab states of the Gulf. What Iran is likely to do is to insist that the Arab states adopt more of a neutral stance *vis-à-vis* both superpowers, especially the United States. If Iran were to renounce the exportability principle and lower its related threat potential, the Gulf states are not likely to object too strongly to the Iranian insistence on their neutrality *vis-à-vis* the US. A possible intervention of the Soviet Union to forestall the military defeat of Iraq under this scenario cannot be totally ruled out, the foreign policy-related new political thinking of Gorbachev notwithstanding.

A potential Iraqi victory, the second scenario, is likely to resuscitate the security-related fears of the states of the Arabian Peninsula, and, equally important, Iran. Iraq under this scenario, also cannot afford to be highly unreasonable toward any actors in the Gulf. The United States is not likely to allow a military domination of Iran by Iraq. A potential Iraqi victory might lead to two developments with mixed results for the strategic interests of both superpowers. First, a possible Iraqi victory is bound to trigger the now dormant Saudi-Iraqi rivalry to dominate the Gulf region. Initially, such a rivalry has to be settled on the issue of Iraqi membership of the GCC. Saudi Arabia, as one of the founding members of this organisation, is not likely to accept Iraqi leadership by giving up its own. Even the possibility of accepting Iraq as an equal is not going to be without considerable acrimony and tensions within the GCC. Second, a possible Iraqi victory is likely to serve as a jolt to Islamic resurgence, both in the Gulf and in the Middle East. But Islamic resurgence is not likely to disappear from the political scene in the Arab world. Even a temporary setback to Islamic resurgence is a welcome option for both superpowers because, aside from viewing it as a major threat to their respective strategic interests in the Middle East, neither superpowers really understood it, nor did they manifest a willingness to live with it.

A political solution to the war between Iraq and Iran, the third scenario, might enable the states of the Arabian Peninsula to play somewhat of a major role in the negotiating process itself. But the deeply-rooted suspicions of a possible 'ganging up' of Arab states on the part of Iran, as alluded to by Hunter, might turn out to be one of the major obstacles to the negotiating role of Arab states.

Purely from the perspective of acceptability to all parties, a political solution to this war appears most feasible, its sustained rejection by Iran notwithstanding. It is not entirely infeasible that

Iran is likely to abandon its insistence on one or more of the frequently mentioned conditions, such as the removal of Saddam Hussein, the branding of Iraq as an aggressor, and the Iraqi payment of reparations to Iran. The Iranian foreign policy behaviour under Khomeini has demonstrated that it is quite capable of exercising pragmatism when it suits its interests (Ahrari labels this behaviour as 'selective pragmatism' in Chapter 3).

Of the abovementioned war-related Iranian demands, the issue of reparations is the easiest one to settle. The Gulf states are quite flexible about it. The removal of Saddam Hussein is likely to become irrelevant with the passage of Khomeini from the political scene, or if the tide of war is to turn decisively against Iran. The American naval action in the Gulf of April of 1988 might have been aimed at materialising that reality (i.e., providing Iraq an upperhand), the official American reiterations to the contrary notwithstanding. It might not have been a sheer coincidence that Iraq was also able to drive Iran out of the Faw Peninsula at the same time.

POLICY OPTIONS FOR THE SUPERPOWERS

What are the superpowers likely to do in the Gulf in the remainder of the 1980s and beyond? The American naval action of April 1988 against Iran involves that superpower in a deadly game in the Gulf. Obviously, since the United States has decisive naval and air advantages over Iran, limited naval actions or even air strikes against various economic or military targets in Iran might be viewed as 'bringing Iran to its knees' without absorbing much loss of life. But the political implications of poisoning the air and refreshing the wounds cannot be ignored. A superpower might be well-advised to indulge itself in such a deadly game only if ample forethought is given to its related implications. Given the seat-of-the-pants nature of the conduct of foreign policy of the Reagan Administration toward the Middle East, it is most likely that the naval action of April 1988 was not an outcome of much deliberation about its long-range effects on the US strategic interests in the Gulf. The Iranian behaviour in the Gulf (in the aftermath of American military operations in October 1987 and April 1988) has proven that limited actions of that nature do not create a restraining effect. These naval actions, as Rose points out, are perceived by many in Iran as direct US involvement in the war on Iraq's behalf.

As long as a political solution does not emerge, the war should be allowed to take its own course. As noted above, the ability of either warring party to conduct this war is not unlimited. By avoiding military actions in the future, no matter how 'measured', the United States might improve its chances of playing a major role in creating a political *rapprochement* between Iran and the Arabs. The complex realities of the Gulf are such that the United States has to play a major role, if not for other reasons, purely to insure that the Soviet influence in the Gulf is not enhanced at the expense of American interests.

What the superpowers are likely to do is to safeguard their strategic concerns in the Gulf. To begin with, it should be noted that the risk of military involvement has risen for both superpowers since the summer of 1987. The United States has raised the level of its naval presence as an outcome of the Kuwaiti manoeuvres of asking both superpowers to protect its tankers and thereby minimising the exposure of its coasts to potential Iranian attack. The Reagan Administration understood the risks, but chose to accept the Kuwaiti request of reflagging only when it became clear that the Soviet Union would be in the Gulf. In this sense, the American presence in the Gulf is a reaction to Kuwaiti manoeuvres. The importance of this development should be fully appreciated. If this Kuwaiti action were to establish a pattern in the future, either superpower would be forced to expose its military vessels and personnel to heightened risks because the other is invited. Once present, neither superpower might control the extent of its involvement in the fast-paced developments in the Gulf, thereby further heightening the turbulent nature of politics in that region.

There does not seem to be much immediate threat to the supply of oil or to the continued opening of the international waterway in the Gulf. The Iran–Iraq war has endangered it but, given that most of its oil is transported through the Gulf, Iran is not a major threat to a potential closure of the Gulf. Iraqi attacks may trigger a chain reaction leading to its closure.

The Iranian threat to the political status quo in the Gulf appears more serious than it really is. As Peterson points out, the Gulf states have outlived and outlasted the myopic expectations and spurious forecasts of a number of experts. The storm created by the Iranian revolution appears to be settling. Once this revolution is institutionalised, Arabs and Iranians may be able to reach a *rapprochement*. The reaching of such *rapprochement* is no guarantee that the politics of the Gulf is likely to become conventional and serene. Only the level of turbulence may be lowered. It is possible that we are entering an era when the superpowers have to learn to live with dominant regional actors. The Gulf is a good case in point. The Iranian dominance was a *sine qua non* to the US as long as it protected and even promoted Western interests. The Iranian predilection for regional dominance is also prevalent under Khomeini; only its interests are different. What the United States appears to be doing is trying to bring back the 'old days' by continuing to rely on a major regional actor to protect and promote Western interests *a la* the Shah. This time that actor happens to be Saudi Arabia.

It is possible that no country in that region can play such a role any longer. The reality of Gulf politics points out that the days of dominance by any superpower in that region may be gone forever. What might emerge in the Gulf is a condominium of power between Iran, Saudi Arabia, and, possibly, Iraq. Iran is likely to be number one among equals under such an arrangement. Both superpowers are likely to play the role of mediators and ultimate guarantors of the interests of their respective allies. Before such a condominium is in place, a *rapprochement* has to be reached between the Arab states and Iran on the one hand, and between Iran and both superpowers on the other. This *rapprochement* has to take into consideration the further expanded Saudi leadership role in the 1990s, which promises to be expanded in the 1990s. As an ally of Iraq, the USSR would prefer that an equally serious consideration be given to the role of the rulers in Baghdad by all parties.

The Iran–Iraq war ended in July 1988, and the Soviet Union continued its promised withdrawal from Afghanistan during the production phase of this book. While it is too early to write conclusive analysis of the nature of security and stability in the Gulf in the wake of these developments (especially the former), the significance of these events warrants some observations.

It should be noted that the end of this war was brought about as a result of a combination of events discussed in scenarios two and three. In all likelihood, the chances for the outbreak of hostilities between Iran and Iraq in the near future are minimal. Iran did not lose this war because of the superior performance of the Iraqi armed forces in battle fields, even though that state had a definite qualitative edge over Iran. The GCC states, especially Saudi Arabia and Kuwait, had poured in a considerable amount of their economic and *matériel* support for Iraq.

The debate over the causes underlying the Iranian acceptance of a ceasefire is likely to continue. What is important for the purpose of analysis here is an acknowledgement of certain factors which contributed to Iranian defeat. First and foremost is the presence of the American navy, which not only engaged the rag-tag Iranian navy in limited actions in 1987 and 1988 but also inflicted heavy damages. Even though the United States maintained an official policy of neutrality regarding this war, American actions belied that stated position. The United States reportedly continued to supply satellite intelligence information to Iraq on the Iranian troop deployments, thus providing a decisive edge to Iraq concerning the potential Iranian military manoeuvres. When the Iran–Contra fiasco became public and the Reagan Administration came under heavy criticism for supplying arms to Iran in exchange for Americans held as hostages in Lebanon, the United States not only immediately ceased arms supply to the Islamic Republic, but launched a worldwide campaign to close all avenues of such supplies. The continued pounding that the Iranian cities received from Iraq in the wake of the so-called war of cities and the sustained Iraqi use of chemical weapons, destroyed the fighting zeal of the Iranian armed forces and shattered the morale of Iranians in general. When an Iranian civilian airliner was shot down by the USS *Vincence* in July of 1988, Iran did not receive the kind of support such a tragedy usually invokes from the international community. The cumulative effect of these variables led to the Iranian decision to stop the war.

The end of the war was a definite victory for the confrontation posture of the GCC. After all, it was the invitation of Kuwait that legitimised not only the highly visible US naval presence in the Gulf, but the American decision to engage the Iranian navy. The American involvement in the Gulf itself was a clear-cut evidence of the earnestness attached to the security of the Gulf by that superpower. The naval engagements were a modified application of the Reagan doctrine, which was originally aimed at the Soviet occupation troops in Afghanistan and the Soviet-backed Sandanista regime in Nicaragua.

Through limited air and naval actions, the United States manifested its willingness to flex its muscle to shore-up the political status quo in the Gulf. There was considerable ill-will within the domestic American political arena emanating from the Iran hostage crisis of 1980. If the Reagan Administration could 'punish' Iran only by absorbing minimal human and *matériel* losses, no systematic protest was going to be developed back home. Thus, the decision to engage Iran in the Gulf definitely enhanced the American clout *vis-à-vis* the peninsular Arab states since it played a crucial role in the cessation of the Iran–Iraq war. The conclusion of this war also enhanced the clout of the GCC and Saudi Arabia. Since Iran was forced to accept the ceasefire, Iraq perceives itself as a 'winner' of this war. Iran's own perception appears to be that it has only lost a battle.

What are the implications of the end of this war for the Gulf states and for the superpowers? First, Saudi Arabia is likely to expand the scope of its leadership by concentrating on building the offensive capabilities of the GCC. The clashes between the Iranian pilgrims and Saudi security forces in July of 1987, which resulted in 402 reported deaths, initiated a series of actions that made it clear to Iran that the Saudis are willing to hit hard if pushed further by Iran. King Fahd of Saudi Arabia announced that his country would not hesitate to use the Chinese-built CSS–2s intermediate range (1600 miles) missiles against Iran. These missiles, which were originally designed to carry nuclear war-heads, were threatening the balance of power in the Middle East. King Fahd's statement was intended to serve as a warning to Iran not to use the Silkworm missiles which that country had also purchased from the PRC.[1] In April of 1988, Saudi Arabia broke diplomatic ties with Iran and also signed an $8 billion arms purchase deal with Great Britain. In view of these actions, Iran might be forced to seriously reconsider any menacing future actions toward the peninsular states.

Second, even though the end of war appears to have signalled a taming of the Iranian revolution, that country, by no means, has abandoned its leadership aspirations in the Gulf. In the near future, Iran is not likely to reiterate its exportability principle, however. The Iranian leaders would concentrate most of their energy on rebuilding the economic and military infrastructures of their country. At the same time, they would continue to keep a wary eye on the GCC. If the past Saudi behaviour is a good indicator of their future actions, they are likely to concentrate on stabilising the Gulf by continuing a two-pronged policy of strengthening the security arm of the GCC and soothing Iranian fears *vis-à-vis* the military objectives of that organisation.

Third, the continued Saudi refusal to allow Iraq to join the GCC would be a litmus test of their earnestness about alleviating Iranian fears. Besides, it also behooves Saudi Arabia to keep Iraq out.

Especially since Iraq regards itself a victor of its war with Iran, it might want to cash in on this 'victory' by challenging the Saudi dominance of that organisation, once it is allowed to join. The potential resuscitation of Saudi-Iraqi rivalry discussed in the second scenario might become a reality of the 1990s.

Fourth, the end of war has increased the American clout in the Gulf. Even though the Soviet Union has not made similar gains, its very presence in the Gulf signals that the Gulf monarchies are in the process of reexamining their conventional perceptions of a menacing Soviet Union. While the Soviet withdrawal from Afghanistan underscores the new political thinking under Gorbachev, the USSR's presence in South Yemen and Ethiopia still serves as an uneasy reminder of the potential military actions related to such a presence.

Finally, the cessation of war does not seem to have made any affect on the chances of dominance of the Gulf politics by either superpower in the 1990s. In fact, now more than ever before, the end of war appears to have increased the significance of the condominiums of power between regional powers in the Gulf. The superpowers are likely to serve as facilitators of such an agreement (or agreements) and, once it is reached, they are likely to serve as its guarantors. In its roles as facilitator and guarantor of condominiums of power between Iran, Saudi Arabia, and Iraq, the United States seems to have enhanced its strategic advantages in the near future. The Soviet Union under Gorbachev is not only not far behind, but promises to nullify American advantages in the not too distant future, by emphasising the non-military aspects of the superpower competition in the Gulf and elsewhere.

Note

1.   Jim, Mann, 'US Caught Napping by Sino-Saudi Missile Deal', *Los Angeles Times*, 4 May 1988.

Bibliography

ABDULGHANI, JASIM, *Iraq and Iran: The Years of Crisis* (Baltimore: Johns Hopkins, 1984).

ADAMIYAT, FEREYDOUN, *Andisheh-e-Taraghi va Hokoumat Ghanoun* (The Idea of Progress and the Rule of Law) (Tehran: Intesharat Kharazami, 1973).

ADAMIYAT, FEREYDOUN, *Bahrain Islands: A Legal and Diplomatic Study of the British-Iranian Controversy* (New York, NY: Praeger, 1955).

AHRARI, M. E., *OPEC – The Failing Giant* (Lexington, KY: The University Press of Kentucky, 1986).

ALEXANDER, YONAH and ALLEN NANES, *The United States And Iran: A Documentary History* (Tempe, AZ: Aletheia Books).

AL FARSY, FOUAD, *Saudi Arabia: A Case Study In Development* (New York, NY: Methuen, 1986).

ALGAR, HAMID (translator), *Islam and Revolution: Writings and Declaration of Imam Khomeini* (Berkeley: Mizan Press, 1981).

AL MOOSA, ABDULRASOOL A., 'Stability of the Foreign Labour Force in Kuwait', *Arab Gulf Journal*, no. 1, April 1986, pp. 53–6.

AL-SABAH, Y. S. F., *The Oil Economy Of Kuwait* (London: Routledge & Kegan Paul, 1981).

ANTHONY, JOHN D., *U.S.-Arab Relations: The Iran–Iraq War and the Gulf Cooperation Council* (Washington, DC: National Arab Council).

ARMACOST, MICHAEL H., 'U.S. Policy in the Persian Gulf and Kuwaiti Reflagging', *Department of State Bulletin*, August 1987.

AXELGARD, FREDERICK W., (ed.), *Iraq in Transition: Strategic Perspective* (Boulder, CO: Westview Press, 1986).

ATKINS, MURIEL, 'Soviet Relations with the Islamic Republic', *SAIS Review*, Winter/Spring 1983, pp. 183–94.

BAKHASH, SHAUL, *Reign of The Ayatollahs: Iran and The Islamic Revolution* (New York, NY: Basic, 1986).

BAYAT, ASSEF, *Workers And Revolution In Iran* (London: Zed, 1986).

BERTRAM, CHRISTOPHER, *Prospects of Soviet Power in the 1980s* (London: International Institute of Strategic Studies, 1979).

BIDWELL, ROBIN (ed.), *Affairs of Kuwait 1896–1905* (London: Frank Cass, 1971).

BIDWELL, ROBIN, *The Two Yemens* (Boulder, CO: Westview Press, 1983).

BILL, JAMES A., *The Eagle and the Lion: America and Iran* (New Haven, CT: Yale University Press, 1988).

BILL, JAMES A., 'Resurgent Islam in the Persian Gulf', *Foreign Affairs*, no. 1, Fall 1984, pp. 108–27.

BURRELL, R. M., and A. J. COTTRELL, *Iran, Afghanistan and Pakistan:*

Tensions and Dilemmas (Washington, DC: The Center for Strategic and International Studies, 1974).

BURROWES, ROBERT D., *The Yemen Arab Republic: The Politics of Development, 1962–1986* (Boulder, CO: Westview Press, 1987).

CATTRELL and DOUGHERTY, *Iran's Quest For Security: U.S. Arms Transfers And The Nuclear Options* (Unipub., 1977).

CHRISTOPHER, WARREN, *et al.*, *American Hostages in Iran: The Conduct of a Crisis* (New Haven, CT: Yale University Press, 1985).

CHOUCRI, NAZLI, *International Politics of Energy Interdependence: The Case of Petroleum* (Lexington, MA: D. C. Heath, 1976).

CHUBIN, SHAHRAM, *Soviet Policy Toward Iran and the Gulf*, Adelphi Paper, no. 157 (London: The International Institute for Strategic Studies, 1980).

CORDESMAN, ANTHONY H., *The Gulf and the Search for Strategic Stability* (Boulder, CO: Westview Press, 1984).

CORDESMAN, ANTHONY H., *U.S.-Arab Relations: The Iran–Iraq War and U.S.–Iraq Relations: An Iraqi Perspective*, no. 11 (National Arab Council).

COTTAM, RICHARD, 'Goodbye to America's Shah', *Foreign Policy*, Spring 1979, no. 34, pp. 3–14.

COTTRELL, ALVIN J., 'The Political–Military Balance in the Persian Gulf Region', in JOSEPH S. SZYLIOWICZ and BARD E. O'NEILL (eds), *The Energy Crisis and U.S. Foreign Policy* (New York, NY: Praeger, 1975).

COTTRELL, ALVIN J. and JAMES E. DOUGHERTY, *Iran's Quest For National Security: U.S. Arms Transfers and the Nuclear Options* (Landham, MD: Unipub., 1977).

DARIOUS, ROBERT G., JOHN W. AMOS III, and RALPH H. MANGUS (eds), *Gulf Security into the 1980s: Perceptual and Strategic Dimensions* (Stanford, CA: Hoover Institution Press, 1984).

EDELMAN, MURRAY, *The Symbolic Uses of Politics* (Urbana, IL: University of Illinois Press, 1964).

EL AZHARY, M. S. (Ed.), *The Iran–Iraq War: Historical, Economic, and Political Analysis* (New York, NY: St Martin's Press, 1984).

EL MALLAKH, RAGAEI, *The Economic Development Of The Yemen Arab Republic* (London: Croom Helm, 1986).

ELWELL-SUTTON, LAURENCE P., *Persian Oil: A Study in Power Politics* (CT: Hyperion, 1976).

ESPOSITO, JOHN L., 'Islam in the Politics of the Middle East', *Current History*, no. 508, pp. 53–7.

The Europa Yearbook 1987 (London: Europa Publications, 1987).

FENELON, KEVIN G., *The United Arab Emirates: An Economic Social Survey* (Ann Arbor, MI, Books Demand UMI).

FRANKLIN, ROB., 'Migrant Labor and the Politics of Development in Bahrain', *MERIP Reports*, no. 4, 4 May 1985, pp. 7–13.

FUKUYAMA, FRANCIS, 'Patterns of Soviet Third World Policy', *Problems of Communism*, September–October 1987, no. 36, pp. 1–13.

FUKUYAMA, FRANCIS, *Soviet Civil-Military Relations and the Power* (Santa Monica, CA: The Rand Corporation, 1987).

GINSBURGS, GEORGE and ROBERT M. SUSSLER, *A Calendar of Soviet Treaties 1958–1973* (The Hague: Sijthoff and Nordhoff, 1981).

GOLDMAN, STUART D., *Soviet Policy Toward Iran and the Strategic Balance in Southwest Asia*, Congressional Research Service of the Library of Congress (Washington, DC: Government Printing Office, October 1986).

GRAYSON, BENSON L., *United States–Iranian Relations* (Landham, MD: University Press of America, 1981).

HAIM, SYLVIA (ed.), Arab Nationalism in a Wider World (New York, NY: American Association for Peace in the Middle East, 1971).

HAMEED, MAZHER A., *Arabia Imperilled: The Security Imperatives of the Arab Gulf States* (Washington, DC: Middle Assessments Groups, 1986).

HELMES, CHRISTINE MOSS, *Iraq: Eastern Flank of the Arab World* (Washington, DC: The Brookings Institution, 1984).

HELMES, CHRISTINE M., *The Cohesion of Saudi Arabia: Evolution of Political Identity* (Ann Arbor, MI: Books Demand UMI, 1984).

HIRST, DAVID, *Oil and Public Opinion in the Middle East* (London: Faber & Faber, 1966).

HOFFMAN, STANLEY, 'Obstinate or Obsolete?': The Fate of Nation-state and the Case of Western Europe', *Daedalus*, Summer, no. 95, pp. 862–915.

HOUGH, JERRY E., *The Struggle for the Third World: Soviet Debates and American Options* (Washington, DC: The Brookings Institution, 1986).

HUDSON, MICHAEL C., 'United States Policy in the Middle East: Opportunities and Dangers', *Current History*, no. 526, February 1988, pp. 49–52.

HUNTER, ROBERT E., 'The Reagan Administration in the Middle East', *Current History*, no. 517, February 1987, pp. 49–52.

HUNTER, SHIRIN T. and ROBERT E. HUNTER, 'The Post-Camp David Arab World', in ROBERT O. FREEDMAN, *The Middle East Since Camp David* (Boulder, CO: Westview Press, 1985).

HUNTER, SHIRIN, T., 'After the Ayatullah', *Foreign Policy*, no. 66, Spring 1987, pp. 77–97.

HUNTER, SHIRIN, T., *The Politics of Islamic Revivalism* (Bloomington, IN: Indiana University Press, 1988).

HUNTINGTON, SAMUEL, 'Patterns of Intervention', *The National Interest*, Spring 1987.

HUSSEIN, SADDAM, *Social and Foreign Affairs* (London: Croom Helm, 1979).

Iran Country Report, no. 4 (London: Economic Intelligence Unit, 1986).

'Iran's Use of International Terrorism', *Department of State Bulletin*, January 1988.

ISMAIL, J. S., *Kuwait: Social Change in Historical Perspective* (New York, NY: Syracuse University Press, 1982).

ISMAIL, J. S. and T. Y. ISMAIL, 'Social Change in Islamic Society: The Political Thought of Ayatollah Khomeini', *Social Problems*, no. 5, June 1980, pp. 601–19.

ISMAEL, TAREQ Y., *Iraq and Iran: Roots of Conflict* (New York, NY: Syracuse University Press, 1982).

ISSS, *The Military Balance, 1985–1986* (London: International Institute for Strategic Studies, 1985).

KASHANI, JAMAL, *Iran's Men of Destiny* (New York, NY: Vantage, 1985).

KATZ, MARK N., 'Soviet Policy in the Gulf States', *Current History*, no. 498, January 1985, pp. 25–8.

KAUFMAN, BURTON I., 'Mideast Multinational Oil, U.S. Foreign Policy, and Anti-trust: The 1950s', *Journal of American History*, no. 4, March 1977, pp. 937–59.

KEOHANE, ROBERT O., *After Hegemony: Cooperation and Discord in the World Political Economy* (Princeton: Princeton University Press, 1984).

KHALILZAD, ZALMAY, 'Islamic Iran: Soviet Dilemmas', *Problems of Communism*, no. 33, January–February 1984, pp. 1–20.

KHOMEINI, AYATOLLAH ROUHOLLAH, *Islamic Government* (New York, NY: Manor Books, 1979).

KOSTINER, JOSEPH, *The Struggle For South Yemen* (New York, NY: St Martin's Press, 1984).

LENCZOWSKI, GEORGE, *Russia and the West in Iran, 1918–1948: A Case Study of Big Power Rivalry* (Ithaca: Cornell University Press, 1949).

LONGUENESSE, ELISABETH, 'Migration sa et Societe Dans les Pays du Golfe', *Maghreb-Machrek*, no. 112, April–June, 1986, pp. 8–21.

LOONEY, ROBERT E., *Economic Origins of the Iranian Revolution* (Boulder, CO: Pergamon, 1982).

MANSURA, ABDUL KASIM, 'The Military Balance in the Persian Gulf: Who will Guard the Gulf States from their Guardians?', *Armed Forces Journal International*, no. 3, November 1988, November 1980, pp. 44–86.

MARTIN, LENORE G., *The Unstable Gulf: Threats from Within* (Lexington, MA: D. C. Heath, 1984).

McMATHIAS, CHARLES, 'Dateline Middle East: The Dangers of Disengagement', *Foreign Policy*, no. 63, Summer 1986, pp. 169–82.

McNAUGHER, THOMAS, L., *Arms and Oil: US Military Strategy and the Persian Gulf* (Washington, DC: The Brookings Institution, 1985).

MOSSAVAR-RAHMANE, BIJAN, *Energy Policy in Iran: Domestic Choices and International Implications* (Boulder, CO: Pergamon, 1981).

MURAVCHIK, JOSHUA, 'Is Israel Good for America?', *National Review*, no. 5, March 1986, pp. 36–46.

MURPHY, RICHARD W., 'Arms Sales Policies Toward the Middle East', *Department of State Bulletin*, June 1986.

NAFF, THOMAS, *Gulf Security and the Iran–Iraq War* (Washington, DC: Government Printing Office, 1985).

NAFI, ZUHAIR A., *Economic and Social Development in Qatar* (London: Frances Pinter, 1983).

NAKLEH, EMILE A., *The Persian Gulf and the American Policy* (New York, NY: Praeger, 1982).

OWEN, ROGER, 'Migrant Workers in the Gulf', *Middle East Review*, no. 3, September 1985, pp. 24–7.

PAHLEVI, M. REZA, *Mission for My Country* (London: Hutchinson, 1961).

PAPP, DANIEL S., *Soviet Policies Toward the Developing World During the 1980s: The Dilemmas of Power and Presence* (Maxwell Airforce Base, AL: Air University Press, 1986).

PERRARA, JUDITH, 'Together Against the Red Peril: Iran and Saudi Arabia Rivals for Superpower Role', *The Middle East*, no. 43, May 1978.

PETERSON, J. E., *The Arab Gulf States: Steps Toward Political Participation* (New York, NY: Praeger, 1988).

PETERSON, J. E., *Defending Arabia* (London: Croom Helm, 1986).

PETERSON, J. E., *Yemen: The Search for a Modern State* (Baltimore, MA: The Johns Hopkins University Press, 1982).

PHILLIPSON, EUGENE, *The Arming of Saudi Arabia: The United States' Role in the Middle East and the World Oil Crisis* (Washington, DC: Institute Economics and Finance, 1985).

QUANDT, WILLIAM, *Saudi Arabia in the 1980s: Foreign Policy, Security, and Oil* (Washington, DC: The Brookings Institution, 1981).

RAMAZANI, ROUHOLLAH K., *The Persian Gulf: Iran's Role* (Charlottesville, VA: The University of Virginia Press, 1973).

RAMAZANI, R. K., *Revolutionary Iran: Challenges and Responses in the Middle East* (Baltimore, MA: The Johns Hopkins University Press, 1986).

RAMAZANI, R. K., *The United States and Iran: The Patterns of Influence* (New York, NY: Praeger, 1982).

RASHID, NASSER I. and I. SHAHEEN, ESBER, *King Fahd and Saudi Arabia's Great Evolution* (Washington, DC: International Institute of Technology, 1987).

REZUN, MIRON, *The Soviet Union and Iran* (San Diega, CA: Westview, 1988).

RUBIN, BARRY, *Paved with Good Intentions: The American Experience in Iran* (New York, NY: Penguin, 1981).

RUBINSTEIN, ALVIN Z. (ed.), *The Great Power Game: Rivalry in the Persian Gulf* (New York, NY: Praeger, 1983).

SAID, EDWARD, 'The MESA Debate: the Scholars, the Media and the Middle East', *Journal of Palestinian Studies*, Winter 1987.

SELCOMBE, IAN J., 'Economic Recession and International Labour Migration in the Arab Gulf', *Arab Gulf Journal*, no. 1, April 1986, pp. 43–52.

SAPIR, EDWARD, 'Symbolism', *Encyclopedia of Social Sciences* (New York, NY: 1934).

SHUSTER, W. MORGAN, *The Strangling of Persia* (Washington, DC: Mage Publishers, 1987).

SICK, GARY, *All Fall Down: American's Tragic Encounter with Iran* (New York, NY: Random House, 1986).

SICK, GARY, 'Iran's Quest for Superpower Status', *Foreign Affairs*, Spring 1987, no. 4, pp. 697–715.

'Soviet Steps Up Propaganda in Azerbaijan', Radio Free Europe/Radio

Liberty, Soviet East European Reports, 10 October 1985.

STEMPEL, JOHN D., *Inside the Iranian Revolution* (Bloomington, IA: Indiana University Press, 1981).

SNIDER, RICHARD III and J. E. PETERSON (eds), *Crosscurrents in the Gulf: Arab, Regional, and Global Interests* (London: Routledge, 1988).

SULLIVAN, WILLIAM H., *Mission to Iran* (New York, NY: Norton, 1981).

TAHIR-KHELI, *The Iran–Iraq War: Old Conflicts, New Weapons* (New York, NY: Praeger, 1983).

TOWER, JOHN, EDMUND MUSKIE, and BRENT SCROWCROFT. *Tower Commission Report* (New York, NY: Bantam Books, 1987).

US CONGRESS, *Economic Consequences of the Revolution in Iran*, A Compendium of papers submitted to the Joint Economic Committee, 96th Congress, 1st Session (Washington, DC: Government Printing Office, 1979).

US CONGRESS, House of Representatives, Committee on Foreign Affairs, *US Security Interests in the Gulf*, Report of a Staff Study Mission to the Persian Gulf, Middle East, and the Horn of Africa (Washington, DC: Government Printing Office, 1981).

US CONGRESS, House of Representatives, Foreign Affairs Committee, *Economic and Security Assistance in Asia and the Pacific*, pp. 236–65, 98th Congress, 1st Session (Washington, DC: Government Printing Office, 1983).

US CONGRESS, House of Representatives, Foreign Affairs Committee, *Foreign Assistance Legislation for Fiscal Year 1984–1985, Economic and Military Aid Programs in Europe and the Middle East*, pp. 150–205 and 594–607), 98th Congress, 1st Session (Washington, DC: Government Printing Office, 1983).

US CONGRESS, House of Representatives, Foreign Affairs Committee, *Soviet Role in Asia*, 98th Congress, 1st Session (Washington, DC: Government Printing Office, 1983).

US CONGRESS, House of Representatives, Foreign Affairs Committee, *Foreign Assistance for Fiscal Year 1985* (part 3), pp. 221–53 and 513–73, 98th Congress, 2nd Session (Washington, DC: Government Printing Office, 1984).

US CONGRESS, *The Soviet Union and the Third World 1980–85: An Imperial Burden or Political Asset?*, Report prepared by the Congressional Research Service of the Library of Congress (Washington, DC: Government Printing Office, 1985).

US CONGRESS, House of Representatives, Subcommittee on Europe and the Middle East of the Foreign Affairs Committee, Hearings, *Islamic Fundamentalism and Islamic Radicalism*, 99th Congress, 1st Session (Washington, DC: Government Printing Office, 1987).

US CONGRESS, House of Representatives, Foreign Affairs Committee, *Developments in the Middle East*, July 1985, pp. 1–87, 99th Congress, 1st Session (Washington, DC: Government Printing Office, 1985).

US CONGRESS, House of Representatives, Foreign Affairs Committee, *Foreign Assistance Legislation for Fiscal Year 1986–1987*, pp. 254–328 and 673–84, 99th Congress, 1st Session (Washington, DC: Government Printing Office, 1985).

US CONGRESS, House of Representatives, Foreign Affairs Committee, *Overview of the Situation in the Persian Gulf*, 100th Congress, 1st Session (Washington, DC: Government Printing Office, 1987).

US CONGRESS, House of Representatives, Merchant Marines and Fisheries Committee, *Kuwaiti Tankers*, 100th Congress, 1st Session (Washington, DC: Government Printing Office, 1988).

US CONGRESS, Senate, Appropriations Committee, Report, *US Presence in the Persian Gulf: Cost and Policy Implications*, 100th Congress, 1st Session (Washington, DC: Government Printing Office, 1988).

VIORST, Milton, 'Iraq at War', *Foreign Affairs*, no. 2, Winter 1986–7, pp. 349–65.

WEAD, R. DOUGLAS, *The Iran Crisis* (South Plainfield, NJ: Croom Helm, 1983).

YODFAT, ARYEH Y., *The Soviet Union and the Arabian Peninsula* (London: Croom Helm 1983).

Index